THE JAPANESE DISCOVERY
OF EUROPE, 1720-1830

An Early Use of a European Invention

THE JAPANESE DISCOVERY OF EUROPE, 1720-1830

Revised Edition

DONALD KEENE

Stanford University Press   Stanford, California   1969

This is a revised and expanded edition
of *The Japanese Discovery of Europe: Honda
Toshiaki and Other Discoverers, 1720–1798*
(London, 1952). The Introduction, Chapters
6 and 7, and most of the illustrations are new.

Preface

Japan is today such an important industrial power, so prominent
a participant in all fields of scientific and cultural endeavors, that
it is hard to realize that a little over a century ago the country was
isolated from the rest of the world and scarcely aware of the West.
Yet even in those days—and much earlier—a few Japanese were
making enormous efforts to learn everything they could about
the outside world, to discover Europe. To read the works of these
men or their biographies is to make the sudden emergence of Japan from the obscurity of the past considerably less of a mystery.

A dozen or more figures associated with the *rangaku*, or "Dutch
studies," movement of the eighteenth and early nineteenth centuries command our attention. Any one of them might be used as
the pivotal figure in an account of the movement, depending on
the interests of the writer. I have chosen Honda Toshiaki (1744–
1821) as my central figure. A page from any one of his writings
suffices to show that with him one has entered a new age, that of
modern Japan. One finds in his books a new spirit, restless, curious, and receptive. There is in him the wonder at new discoveries,
the delight in widening horizons. Honda took a kind of pleasure
even in revealing that Japan, after all, was only a small island in
a large world. To the Japanese who had thought of Chinese civili-

zation as being of immemorial antiquity, he declared that Egypt's was thousands of years older and far superior. The world, he discovered, was full of wonderful things, and he insisted that Japan take advantage of them. Honda looked at Japan as he thought a Westerner might, and he saw things that had to be changed, terrible drains on the country's moral and physical strength. Within him sprang the conviction that Japan must become one of the great nations of the world.

I have presented in this book an account of the growth and uses of Western learning in Japan from 1720 to 1830. These are the dates of the beginning of official interest in Western learning and of the expulsion of Siebold from the country, the first stage of a crisis that could be resolved only by the opening of the country to the West. The century and more included by the two dates was a most important period in Japanese history, when intellectuals, rebelling at the isolation of their country, desperately sought knowledge from abroad. The amazing energy and enthusiasm of men like Honda Toshiaki made possible the spectacular changes in Japan, which are all too often credited to the arrival of Commodore Perry.

In describing the activities of the Dutch, the source of Japanese information about the West in the eighteenth century, I realize that I may seem at times unnecessarily harsh. I am well aware that similarly unattractive portraits might be drawn of other Western merchants in the East. It is nonetheless difficult at times to restrain a feeling of indignation that the Dutch merchants did so little to make Japan known to the West. But, as they might well have answered, it was their example that inspired Honda Toshiaki and many other progressive men to a vision of a new Japan, and for this the nation was ever to be in their debt.

An earlier version of this book was issued in 1952. I am glad to have had the opportunity to correct my errors and to incorporate here the fruits of recent research by scholars in Japan and the West. I have included in this edition material from my article "Hirata Atsutane and Western Learning," published in *T'oung Pao*, Vol. XLII, and have added an entirely new chapter describing some of the men of the generation after Honda Toshiaki. I have retained the geographical spellings of my earlier edition, even though in a few instances (Sakhalin for Saghalien, Iturup for Etorofu, etc.) the preferences of cartographers have apparently changed. Most of the illustrations are new; I am indebted to Mr. Sayaka Iwata of Chūō Kōron Sha for help in obtaining the photographs.

I cannot refrain from expressing my grief that my mother, to whom this book was dedicated, and my friend William Dickins, who drew the map for it, have both died since the first edition appeared. It is to their memory that I dedicate the present edition.

Karuizawa   D. K.
1968

Contents

Descriptive List of Illustrations

the solar calendar. This was on January 1, 1795, or the eleventh day of the eleventh intercalary month of the sixth year of Kansei. The host was Ōtsuki Gentaku, and the party was held at his school, the Shirandō in Edo. The guests ate Dutch food with knives and forks, and drank Dutch liquor. The man sitting on the chair in Western clothes is presumably a Japanese, no Dutchmen having been in Edo at the time. He has been identified by some as Kōdayū, but more probably Kōdayū is the man writing Russian letters with a quill pen. Perhaps the "Dutchman" is Ōtsuki himself. Directly below his pipe is Morishima Chūryō, and to Morishima's left is Katsuragawa Hoshū, his brother. The painting on the wall is of Hippocrates, a popular subject with admirers of Western medicine. Dutch New Year parties continued to be held until 1837. (Waseda University.)

THE JAPANESE DISCOVERY
OF EUROPE, 1720-1830

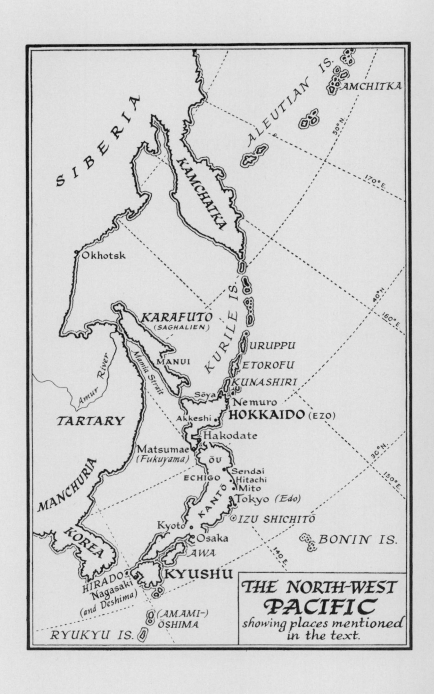

SIBERIA

KAMCHATKA

ALEUTIAN IS.

AMCHITKA

50° N.

170° E.

Okhotsk

KARAFUTO
(SAGHALIEN)

KURILE IS.

160° E.

40° N.

Amur River

Mamia Strait

TARTARY

MANUI

URUPPU

ETOROFU

KUNASHIRI

Sōya

Nemuro

Akkeshi

HOKKAIDO (EZO)

Hakodate

30° N.

150° E.

MANCHURIA

Matsumae
(Fukuyama)

ŌU

ECHIGO

Sendai
Hitachi
Mito
Tokyo (Edo)

KANTŌ

KOREA

Kyoto

Osaka

IZU SHICHITŌ

BONIN IS.

AWA

140° E.

HIRADO
Nagasaki
(and Deshima)

KYUSHU

(AMAMI-)
ŌSHIMA

RYUKYU IS.

THE NORTH-WEST
PACIFIC
showing places mentioned
in the text.

1. The Dutch in Japan

At the end of the eighteenth century, when a few Japanese began with immense effort the serious study of the civilization of Europe, the center of their interest was the tiny island of Deshima in Nagasaki harbor. There, in the rather mean buildings of a trading station, lived a dozen or so Dutchmen, the sole Europeans permitted to enter the Japanese islands.

The nation had not always been thus isolated from the West. During the little less than a century between the discovery of Japan by the Portuguese in 1542 and their expulsion in 1639, the Japanese had had considerable opportunity to examine Western ways, and some of them had even made journeys to Europe and America. But although the government was aware of the advantages of trade with the foreigners, the ever-growing menace of Christianity (introduced as early as 1549 by St. Francis Xavier) led to the enactment of a series of laws that culminated in the expulsion of all Europeans but the Dutch.

It was not the theological aspects of Christianity, or more particularly of Catholicism, that had so disturbed the Japanese government, but the fear that native converts to the religion might have conflicting political loyalties, and might even facilitate the invasion of the islands by a European power. The example of the

Philippines, conquered by the Spaniards on the heels of missionary activity, served as a warning to the Japanese, and the successive revelation of supposed plots to endanger Japanese sovereignty caused the government to banish first the Spaniards and then the Portuguese. Of the other nations that had traded with Japan, England had left voluntarily, finding the business unprofitable. The Dutch, with a superior flair for trade perhaps, remained.

Although the Japanese government was absolutely determined to erase every trace of Christianity within the realm, there had been adequate proof of the innocuousness of the Dutch variety of the religion. In 1637–38, when tens of thousands of Japanese Christian converts banded together on the peninsula of Shimabara in a desperate last stand, the Dutch had obligingly lent artillery support to the government forces. They were not greatly concerned at having to play a part in the destruction of the Christian religion in Japan, for they were friends neither of Catholicism nor of the Portuguese, their deadly rivals in the East and the people most likely to benefit commercially from Christian successes in Japan. The support that the Dutch lent helped to persuade the Japanese that they had come exclusively for trade, and though there was nothing in the world for which the Japanese military leaders officially had greater contempt than commerce, they preferred to deal with docile Dutch merchants rather than with proud and unruly Portuguese soldiers.

In 1641 the Japanese government ordered the Dutch to move their trading station, or factory, as it was called, from Hirado at the western end of Kyushu to the island of Deshima.¹ At first the Dutch welcomed the change to the more convenient harbor of Nagasaki, and they may even have felt as they took over the buildings erected originally for the Portuguese that the act was symbolic of the passing of supremacy in the Orient from Portugal to Holland. The Dutch, indeed, were rising to the height of their glory, and their successes were due as much to the efforts of their merchants as to the prestige of Dutch arms.

Vondel, the greatest of Dutch poets, in an ode written on the

occasion of Marie de Médicis' visit in 1639 to the Amsterdam East
India House, described the achievements of the Dutch traders:

> 'Twas not enough they'd won the field in Netherlands;
> They sailed the earth to distant and exotic lands,
> As far as shines the sun, resolved the sun would see
> Their mighty deeds. Our Holland serves as granary
> For all the Indies grow. The North has filled its ships
> With Eastern crops. The Winter Prince who warms his lips
> With pepper, guards in these domains the boast
> Of all that heav'nly fires of summer cook and roast.
> Arabia of incense burners gives the best.
> The commerce with the Persians ever keeps abreast;
> They trade their silks and all their cotton ware.
> Great Java shares with us her treasures fair,
> And China, porcelain. We Amsterdammers journey
> Where Ganges casts its waters down into the sea:
> Wherever profit leads us, to every sea and shore,
> For love of gain the wide world's harbors we explore.[2]

It was the "love of gain," the motive of all Holland's far-flung
ventures, that enabled the Dutch merchants in Japan to endure
the repeated humiliations to which they were subjected. Already
in their Hirado days they had humbled themselves to save their
necks and their business: a newly erected warehouse was torn
down to appease an official who had noticed the Christian date on
the cornerstone. But if they had any illusions that Deshima would
be better than Hirado, the Dutch were soon made aware of the
manner of living that they would be expected to follow. They
were prisoners, free only to walk up and down the two streets of
their tiny isle, watched, guarded, and spied on. Once a year, in the
spring, the factory director and a few of his assistants journeyed to
Edo (now Tokyo) in order to offer presents to the shogun and thus
demonstrate their fealty. Accounts of the embassies in the years
1691 and 1692 have been preserved in the *History of Japan* by
Engelbert Kaempfer, a German physician serving with the factory
during those years. Kaempfer related,

having waited here upwards of an hour, and the Emperor having in the
mean while seated himself in the hall of audience, Sino Cami and the
two Commissioners came in and conducted our Resident into the Em-

peror's presence, leaving us behind. As soon as he came thither, they cry'd
aloud Hollanda Captain, which was the signal for him to draw near, and
make his obeisances. Accordingly he crawl'd on his hands and knees, to
a place shew'd him, between the presents rang'd in due order on one side,
and the place, where the Emperor sat, on the other, and then kneeling,
he bow'd his forehead quite down to the ground, and so crawl'd back-
wards like a crab, without uttering one single word.[3]

The shogun (whom Kaempfer called "the Emperor"), not content with these formalities alone, summoned the Dutch embassy
for a second interview, during which he had the foreigners interrogated on a great variety of subjects. Then, to end the entertain-
ment properly,

he order'd us to take off our Cappa, or Cloak, being our Garment of
Ceremony, then to stand upright, that he might have a full view of us;
again to walk, to stand still, to compliment each other, to dance, to jump,
to play the drunkard, to speak broken Japanese, to read Dutch, to paint,
to sing, to put our cloaks on and off. Mean while we obey'd the Emperor's
commands in the best manner we could, I join'd to my dance a love-song
in High German. In this manner, and with innumerable such other apish
tricks, we must suffer ourselves to contribute to the Emperor's and the
Court's diversion.[4]

It was not only in Japan, of course, that the Dutch were willing
to submit to such indignities in the hope of profit: in China they
did not hesitate to kowtow three times and then nine times before
the emperor when their trade mission visited Peking in 1685.[5] The
view of the Dutch merchants was that anything which would benefit the Company must be done. To justify their acts of submission
they could point to the fact that mighty princes of Japan pros-
trated themselves before the shogun, and that monarchs of distant
nations paid reverent homage to the Chinese emperor. It must be
noted, however, that representatives of other European nations
were not always willing to demean themselves (as they thought) in
this manner. A Russian envoy to the Court of Peking, for example,
once refused to kowtow to the emperor because he "only knelt to
God." The Chinese court was offended, and the mission accordingly suffered.[6]

The treatment of the Dutch by the Japanese grew somewhat
more lenient as the years passed and as the fear of Christianity

gradually subsided, but as late as 1804 Captain Adam Krusenstern, who had brought a Russian envoy to Nagasaki, was unable
to find words to express how shameful and barbarous the conduct
of the Dutch appeared to him and "how much it is to be regretted
that an enlightened European nation, owing its political existence
to a love of freedom, and which has acquired celebrity by great
actions, should so far debase itself from a desire of gain as to attend
with submission and devotion to the hateful commands of a set of
slaves." At an order from the interpreter, "Mr. Factory-Director,
make your compliment to the High Official!," the Dutchman was
required to incline his body until it formed nearly a right angle,
and was forced to remain in this position with his arms extended
until the official at length gave him permission to stand in his
natural posture. After one brief and unsuccessful attempt to induce
the Russians to bow in a similar manner, the Japanese gave no
more trouble on that score.* But, as the Dutch may well have
argued, the Russians went home empty-handed.

The glory of Holland, of which Vondel had sung, was already
much faded by Kaempfer's time. The people that had risen to
greatness by driving the Spaniards from their country had so given
themselves to the commercial spirit that "when Louis XIV was actually advancing in the conquest of their country with the most
rapid success, he was regularly supplied with gunpowder and ammunition by this nation of merchants."[7] In the eighteenth century,
conditions in Holland grew steadily worse. The fleets that had

* A. I. Krusenstern, *Voyage Round the World* (London, 1813), I, 257–62. It
should be noted, however, that this ungainly "compliment" was far less humiliating than the bow on hands and knees exacted of Japanese subjects, or of the
Dutch in Kaempfer's day. The director at the time, Hendrik Doeff, was extremely sensitive to Krusenstern's criticism, and devoted much of his *Remem-
brances of Japan* (*Herinneringen uit Japan*, Haarlem, 1833) to a defense of his
compliance with Japanese custom: "Krusenstern . . . finds it intolerable that the
Hollanders comply with the customs and etiquette of the Japanese, and considers it self-abasement. I for my part cannot understand wherein the alleged
abasement lies. The compliments we observe with respect to the Japanese are
the same that they themselves show each other; no greater expression of respect
is required of us toward their rulers than of the Japanese themselves. . . . Besides, one cannot expect that a nation to which one comes in order to seek the
friendship of the same should conform to the customs of the visitors." See pp.
90–91.

swept up the Medway and Thames in 1666 and had tolerated no
rivals in the seven seas could no longer afford adequate protection
to Dutch merchant shipping. There was constant quarreling
among the men in high position, and "there were in every city
men, who wished more for the plunder than the prosperity of
their country."[8]

The decline in the fortunes of the Dutch nation was paralleled
by that of its East India Company. All the sins of the home government were reproduced in the Company, and to them were added
the variations and enlargements made possible by the atmosphere
of the colonies. The corruption and greed of the officials has been
described by one eminent Dutch scholar as "putting in the shade
the worst that has been attributed to oriental peoples."[9] In Japan,
where strict regulations curbed the élan of the Dutch merchants,
there was nevertheless considerable smuggling. Indeed, as the
eighteenth century advanced and there was less and less profit to
be derived from the legitimate trade at Deshima, the chief excuse
for maintaining the factory was the private smuggling in which
the Dutch engaged.

Few skilled or learned men entered the service of the Company
in the eighteenth century. The "surgeons" were usually no more
than barbers' apprentices, and the chief qualification of a director
was apt to be his family relationship to other directors.[10] In Batavia, the overseas headquarters of the East India Company, one
governor founded a Latin school in an attempt to bring some culture to his organization, but the school was short-lived. The dregs
of the Dutch nation, for that was what most of the Company's men
represented, could not have been expected to respond to such efforts. Their sole purpose was to make money, and to this end they
devoted themselves with unbounded energy and complete ruth-
lessness. Even when measured by the eighteenth-century yardstick
of economic exploitation, the activities of the Dutch company in
the Indies cannot fail to horrify us. In 1740 occurred the massacre
of 10,000 Chinese in Batavia, a senseless and barbarous step by the
Company. Many Dutchmen in Holland were profoundly shocked

when they heard this news, and one of them wrote a long poem in which he described the brutality of his compatriots abroad.*

From such misfortunes Japan was spared by the severe treatment she afforded the Dutch. Insolent and overbearing in Batavia, where they held military power, the Dutch were servility itself on Deshima. Already in the eighteenth century they had gained notoriety in Europe for their behavior in Japan. It was commonly believed, although it does not appear to have been true, that the Dutch were made to trample on pictures of the Virgin and Child to prove their indifference to the Christian religion. Swift in *Gulliver's Travels* did much to give this story currency, but the Deshima businessmen were sometimes criticized even by Dutch writers for their lack of religious principles. In the play *Agon, Sultan of Bantam* (1769), for instance, an Indonesian princess is made to reply to the boastful remarks of a Dutchman with the words

> Th'enslavement of a Race may be by Fate compelled,
> But ere the Dutch arrived the East had not beheld
> Free Men who in Japan themselves do base Slaves make,
> And but for Gain their God on Deshima forsake.[11]

The Dutchmen on Deshima were typical of the Company. Not many more than a half dozen of those who visited Japan during the two hundred and fifty years of the factory's existence could be described as cultured men. Most of them were completely uninterested in Japan, and regarded it as a great imposition if they were required to attend a local festival, or indeed to do anything that kept them away from their accounts. The pages of the factory

---

* W. van Haren, "Gedicht op den moord gepleegd aan de Chineesen te Batavia," quoted in E. Du Perron, *De Muze van Jan Companjie* (Bandoeng, 1948), p. 164. The poem contains such lines as this description of the murder of a Chinese family. The father begs his Dutch assailants to spare his child's life, if not his wife's or his own:

> For an answer he feels the steel slash his vitals,
> And sees while still dying his dearest ones perish.
> They seize the poor child by his tender and chubby legs
> And swing him thrice through smoke and flames,
> And dare to crush him thus, still moaning, against the wall,
> So that brains and blood stain the executioner's face.

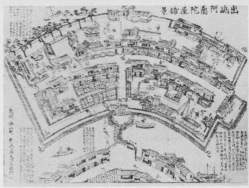

1. Dutch Factory on Deshima
   in Nagasaki Harbor

journals kept by the successive directors form a dreary succession of business calculations, with seldom a word to suggest that the Dutch were living in what was one of the most fascinating countries in the world. The Swedish scientist C. P. Thunberg, who served as surgeon of the Dutch factory in 1775–76, declared that a European who was condemned to pass the rest of his life on Deshima would be buried alive. There was not the slightest intellectual stimulation to relieve the dull monotony of the days.

Here, just as in Batavia, we pay a visit every evening to the chief, after having walked several times up and down the two streets. These evening visits generally last from six o'clock to ten, and sometimes eleven or twelve at night, and constitute a very disagreeable way of life, fit only for such as have no other way of spending their time than droning over a pipe of tobacco.[12]

There were, it is true, numerous obstacles placed by the Japanese in the way of Dutchmen who sought to learn more about the country in which they were living, but such men as Kaempfer and Thunberg, who really wished to spend their time more profitably than "droning over a pipe of tobacco," overcame official opposition to their projects.* From the rest, little or nothing reached Europe to enlighten an exploration-mad society. As Krusenstern complained of Holland, "Europe owes nothing to this nation with respect to a knowledge of the Japanese empire. . . . I cannot help attributing this reserve of the Dutch to a ridiculous, mean, and at all events a very useless policy, contrary to the spirit of a philosophical age, and unbecoming a republican government."[13]

But even when the point is reached at which the nullity, if not the viciousness, of most of the representatives of the East India Company becomes perfectly apparent, one cannot but remark that the Japanese were fortunate to have the Dutch, of all the Europeans, as their mediators with the West. The fact that the Japanese

* Isaac Titsingh (factory director twice between 1779 and 1783) declared that it was want of initiative that kept the directors from learning about Japan, not lack of opportunity. But the Company replied to his suggestions for the selection of directors that it was "a general rule in these parts to sacrifice to Mercury, but never to Pallas." See C. R. Boxer, *The Mandarin at Chinsura* (Amsterdam, 1949), p. 4.

were spared the outrages inflicted on the native populations of the
Indies was in large part due to the skill with which they handled
the Dutch, but had the factory at Deshima been English or Russian, the Japanese would probably have been forced, to the detriment of their country, to yield greater concessions than the Dutch
enjoyed. On the other hand, had a weak nation like Spain or Portugal been the channel of information, the Japanese would have
been able to learn very little about modern advances in science.
Holland, in spite of her decline in grandeur, possessed in Leiden
an important center of medical research, where students from all
parts of Europe gathered to work under the celebrated Boerhaave
and others. Some of the achievements of Dutch science were transmitted directly to the Japanese by the factory doctors, and much
was also learned from books as Japanese came gradually to read
Dutch.

Even apart from those fields in which the Dutch maintained
their old eminence, they knew much they could teach the Japanese.
It did not matter to the Japanese, for example, that the eighteenth-
century Dutch painters were not as good as Rembrandt or Ver-
meer; the techniques of perspective and shading, which even the
most mediocre of Dutch painters could handle, were in themselves
profound discoveries to the Japanese. Hundred-year-old Dutch
books on astronomy or navigation were as exciting to such men as
Honda Toshiaki as if they had just been written. Even the ignorant, money-minded merchants on Deshima knew a thousand
things with which no one else in Japan was familiar.

The great problem lay in establishing communication between
the Dutch and their would-be Japanese students. The earliest dealings with the Dutch had been conducted in Portuguese, the then
lingua franca of the Orient, but as that language lost its importance there were fewer Dutchmen who could use it easily, and the
Japanese realized that they would have to talk to the Dutch in
their own language. The study of Dutch began in Nagasaki during
the second half of the seventeenth century, and by 1670 there were
interpreters who could not only speak but read the language.[14]
This is not to say that Portuguese was at once entirely abandoned;

there continued to be Portuguese interpreters into the eighteenth century, as well as experts in Chinese (of several dialects), Korean, Ryukyu, Siamese, and the languages of other countries with which Japan permitted herself to have commercial relations.

The Nagasaki interpreters were government officials who enjoyed hereditary positions. Their abilities, of course, varied from man to man, but on the whole their achievements were not impressive. We possess a kind of report card for the 1693 interpreters: "Barely knows any Dutch at all"; "Because he is either stupid or lazy, he knows only the slightest amount of Dutch in spite of the fact that he has been studying for years"; "He, like his father, has a reputation for being an interpreter of Portuguese, but he has not the slightest comprehension of the language."[15]

These were not very good marks for the aspiring interpreters to receive from their Dutch teachers. To aid these frail vessels in the comprehension of their communications, the Dutch for a time sent Chinese translations along with the originals. These can scarcely have been of much help to the Japanese, however, for they are in such bad Chinese that they are virtually unintelligible unless one already knows what the Dutch text means.

In their defense, it must be said that the problems confronting the interpreters were enormous. They had no dictionaries save rough-and-ready lists of words and phrases, no grammars, and no competent teachers. As one of the interpreters put it to a prospective student of Dutch, it was easy enough to learn the Dutch word for wine, and one might in time learn to say "I drink wine," but it was extremely difficult to acquire such phrases as "I enjoy drinking wine," let alone more subtle expressions.[16] It was a matter not only of learning a language with a totally dissimilar grammatical structure, but also of attempting to pronounce complicated series of consonants and vowels with the simple open Japanese syllables. And it was just as hard for Japanese then as now to distinguish between "l" and "r."*

---

* Narabayashi Jūbei, an outstanding interpreter of Dutch, described the difficulty of distinguishing between *lijk*, a corpse, and *rijk*, rich. See Tachihara Jingorō (Suiken), *Narabayashi Zatsuwa* in *Kaihyō Sōsho* (Kyoto, 1928), II, 28.

Although interest in the West among Japanese scholars (as opposed to the interpreters) did not die out entirely after the "Christian century," it became increasingly difficult to obtain any information. The government, it is true, was furnished each year
with a report on happenings (*fūsetsugaki*) by the Dutch factory
director on his annual visit to Edo, but only those high in the
administration had access to it. From time to time the Dutch also
presented the court in Edo with maps and illustrated books. These
were accepted along with the more usual offerings of cotton cloth
and strong liquors, and were then carefully stored away. In 1717 a
factory director was asked, to his surprise, to translate the title of a
zoology book presented by the embassy of 1663. The same book,
still looking quite new, reappeared in 1741, and questions were
again asked about its contents.

The Japanese attitude toward Western books continued to be
influenced by the fear and hatred of Christianity, even when that
religion no longer presented any threat to the security of the
country. It was fear of Christianity that dictated the policy of banning books written in Chinese by the Jesuit priests and converts in
Peking, regardless of whether or not the works had to do with religious matters. In 1630 a decree was issued forbidding the importation of thirty-two religious and scientific works by Matteo Ricci
and other Jesuit scholars. Copies already in Japan were confiscated
and either burned or secretly stored by the government. Included
among these books were translations of Euclid's *Elements* and
Cicero's *On Friendship,* as well as geographies and astronomical
treatises.[17]

The period of greatest severity in the censorship of Chinese
books began in 1685 when a zealous official in Nagasaki discovered
a book relating to Christianity aboard a Chinese ship. Rewarded
for his diligence by being made censor of all books imported from
China, he went to great lengths to prove that his position was not
a sinecure. His office either destroyed or sent back to China with
the offending passages blotted out any work that mentioned Christianity in whatever context. When censorable books were discovered aboard a Chinese vessel, the captain and crew were cut off

from contact with other ships, the cargo could not be unloaded, and the chief officers of the ship were generally forbidden to return to Japanese waters. But however careful a Chinese captain might be to see that no objectionable literature was aboard his ship, he could not have been expected to know, for example, that the Japanese censor would take umbrage at a novel because it contained the words "Lord of Heaven" (*tenju*), a term commonly used by Christians for God, when the words did not actually have that meaning in the book.[18] To such lengths was the anti-Christian censorship carried.

The banning of Chinese books on European religion and science had the effect of cutting off Japanese scholars almost entirely from the achievements of the West. A few copies of the forbidden books were hidden in private libraries, and some even circulated in manuscript, but such works were prized for their bibliophilic value rather than for their contents. It was not felt necessary to prohibit the importation of books in European languages, since no one in Japan except possibly a few interpreters could read them. Occasionally some Chinese translation of a Western scientific work was tacitly permitted into the country on account of its manifest practical value, but the number of such books was trifling.

It was not until 1720 that any general relaxation of the restrictions occurred. In that year the shogun decreed that previously banned books which did not actually expound Christian doctrine might circulate in Japan. This shogun, Tokugawa Yoshimune, was greatly interested in the sciences, particularly mathematics and astronomy, and his decree is traditionally associated with his desire to obtain an improved calendar. In Japan, as elsewhere in the orbit of Chinese civilization, the calendar held a position of utmost importance in the administration of the state. It was the obligation of the ruler "to give the time to the people": that is, to promulgate a calendar that was in keeping with the observable motions of the planets and stars, and thus to ensure that rites took place at the proper time. In addition, the calendar served as an almanac for the nation, with information on the correct days to plant crops, lucky days for beginning enterprises, etc. Yoshimune,

as a good Confucian ruler, felt it incumbent on him to give the
people a flawless calendar, and his scientific training permitted
him to recognize that the current one was carelessly made and full
of mistakes.

A Kyoto silversmith named Nakane Genkei was recommended
to Yoshimune as a calendar expert, and thereupon was invited to
Edo for an examination. Nakane's responses pleased the shogun so
much that he was requested to punctuate for Japanese reading a
recently imported Chinese calendar study.[19] Nakane executed the
order, but on presenting the punctuated book, reported that it was
only an extract from a longer Western study, and that unless he
could see the complete work, it would be impossible for him to
give a clear explanation of the meaning of the text. A copy of the
Chinese version of the original was eventually secured, on the
basis of which Nakane compiled his calendar. He was still not
satisfied with his work, however, and informed the shogun that it
would be necessary to consult other Western books in order to
gain a real understanding of the correct methods of making calendars. The prohibition placed on all books containing the word for
"Lord of Heaven" or the name of Matteo Ricci prevented Japanese scholars from advancing in their studies. Nakane concluded
his plea with the suggestion that if it was the shogun's desire to
place calendar making on a scientific basis in Japan, the severe
restrictions on the importation of Western books in Chinese translation would have to be relaxed.[20]

Yoshimune's decree of 1720 represented a necessary first step
toward a knowledge of Western science, but the number of books
in Chinese on the subject was very limited. It was not until 1740
that Yoshimune decided to encourage the study of the Dutch language, when he ordered Noro Genjō and Aoki Konyō to learn the
language, the former for scientific purposes, the latter in order to
make a dictionary. The two men did not begin their studies until
the following year, when they were given some lessons by the interpreters accompanying the Dutch embassy to Edo. Since they were
able to receive instruction only during the few days of each year
that the Dutch were in the capital, it is small wonder that their

progress was slow.[21] Noro managed by 1750 to compile his *Japanese Explanations of Dutch Botany* (*Oranda Honsō Wage*) from conversations with members of the Dutch embassies and from translations made for him of European botanical studies. Aoki's dictionary was not completed until 1758. Although this was not an impressive work, especially for a prominent scholar, it was of considerable historical importance.

More significant than these achievements of Noro and Aoki was the cachet of respectability given to Dutch studies. It was no longer possible to dismiss "barbarian learning" as an unworthy pursuit when, with the encouragement of the shogun, two of the most distinguished men in the country were devoting themselves to its study. Dutch learning was thus extended from the small circle of Nagasaki interpreters to the shogun's palace itself, and before many years had elapsed there were students of the West in every part of Japan.

2. The Rise of Barbarian Learning

Comparatively few people in eighteenth-century Japan ever saw a foreigner. Those who lived in Nagasaki might occasionally have come across Chinese merchants and sailors, and those who lived along the road to Edo might even have caught a glimpse of a Dutchman in his palanquin being hurried off on the annual mission to the capital, but most Japanese regarded foreigners (and particularly Europeans) as a special variety of goblin that bore only a superficial resemblance to a normal human being.

The usual name given to the Dutch was *kōmō* or "red-hairs," a name intended more to suggest a demonic being than to describe the actual coloring of the foreigners' hair.* The Portuguese had also at one time been declared by the shogunate to possess "cat's-eyes, huge noses, red hair and shrike's-tongues,"¹ but the words "red-hairs" by themselves came to mean only the Dutch, and they were always portrayed by Japanese artists with suitably tinted locks. One might imagine that personal observation would have persuaded the Japanese that the foreigners were actually not so

---

* It is difficult to say precisely what was meant by "red-hairs." The Chinese were the first to call Westerners by this name, probably because the Europeans' hair was so much lighter than their own as to suggest the red-haired demons of Buddhist paintings. The Japanese adopted the Chinese term, although individual writers who actually had seen Dutchmen sometimes said that their hair was yellow or brown, certainly much more likely colors.

terrifying to behold, but one visitor to a Dutch ship reported: "When we went aboard, the captain and many others took off their hats to salute us. They have dark, sallow faces, yellow hair, and green eyes. They seem to appear from nowhere, and are just like goblins and demons. Who would not run away from them in fright?"[2]

As time went on, however, more sophisticated people attempted to disprove the fanciful descriptions of the Dutch that were in common circulation. "People say that the Dutch have no heels, have eyes like animals and are giants," related one man, "but the fact is that people of every country differ somewhat, and just because the Dutch do not resemble us, we must not say that they are like animals. We are all products of the same Creator." This writer felt that it was not worth the effort to deny the rumor that when Dutchmen urinate they raise one leg like dogs.[3]

Not only in the matter of personal appearance were the Dutch considered to be very strange creatures; the fact that they were unacquainted with traditional Chinese teachings caused some educated men to classify them as animals on those grounds alone. A daimyo once asked Honda Toshiaki how it was that the Dutch, whose ignorance of the writings of the sages clearly marked them as animals, were nevertheless able to produce such fine articles. Honda answered wryly that even animals are capable of surprising skills.[4] Shiba Kōkan (1747–1818), another leading student of Western learning, replied to a similar query, "If what you say is true, human beings are not as clever as beasts."[5]

People like Honda or Shiba, with enlightened ideas about the Dutch, were by far the minority. For most, "Oranda" (the Japanese rendering of Holland) stood for all that was new and outlandish. When the poet and novelist Saikaku began to write verses in a vein that seemed eccentric to his contemporaries, they referred to his "Oranda," irrational, style. "Oranda" was sometimes also used in an agreeable sense to describe things that were the last word in fashion, but most frequently the term simply meant nonsense. Even the children of Nagasaki at their games cried "That's the Dutch way!" when something was done wrong.[6]

The few people like the official interpreters who came into di-

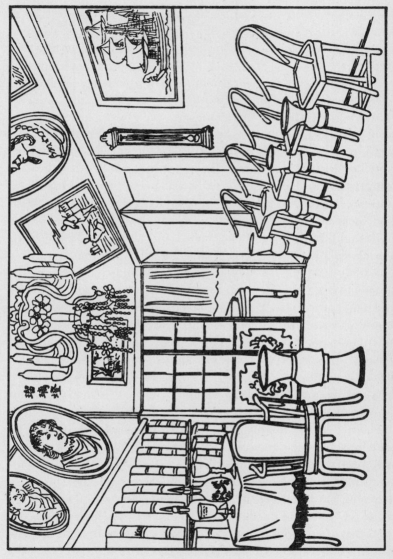

2. Shiba's Drawing of Dutch Factory Director's Room

rect contact with the Dutch do not appear to have made the most of their opportunities. Their attitude was one of extreme inquisitiveness mixed with a fondness for the exotic. One would like to call this attitude one of "intellectual curiosity," but a glance at any of the books of interviews with the Dutch reveals the haphazard nature of their questions. "Who is the commanding general in Holland?" "Do you have false teeth in your country?" "Are there big rivers in Holland?" "What is meant by 'mummies'?"[7] Such was a typical series of questions, and however carefully they were answered, virtually the same things would be asked of the next group of Dutch to be examined.

It was Japanese love of the exotic that led to the collection of all manner of European curiosities, ranging from watches to strange animals. Dutch books and scientific instruments were bought at high prices by wealthy amateurs, not for their intrinsic interest but as oddities. The scholar Ōtsuki Gentaku (1757–1827), justifying trade with the Dutch, gave a long list of useful objects imported from Holland,[8] but in practice only Dutch medicines and cloth were widely known or used in Japan.* Economists complained that the importation of Dutch goods led to extravagance. One man drew up a table of degrees of increasing luxury in dress: the parvenu went from cotton to pongee, to silk, to brocade, to Chinese embroidered cloth, and finally to Dutch woollens, the most unusual and therefore the most desirable of all fabrics.[9]

The Nagasaki interpreters shared in the general fondness for foreign things. They were delighted, for example, to attend a Dutch New Year dinner, finding every dish fascinating if not exactly to their taste.[10] Some of the interpreters were proud to have a foreign-style room in their house. When Shiba Kōkan visited Nagasaki in 1788 he ate Chinese moon-cakes in a Dutch room, a happy blend of exoticisms. Shiba, however, was much less enthusiastic about Dutch interior decoration than the interpreters. He recorded a visit to the factory director's room: "There was a row of chairs, next to each of which was a silver spittoon standing about two feet high, looking like a flower-vase. On the floor-mat-

---

* Ōtsuki's list included watches, telescopes, saffron, ivory, powdered sugar, cloves, pepper, velvet, and various types of medicine and cloth.

ting was a rug with a flowered pattern, and a glass chandelier
hung from the ceiling." While Shiba was contemplating the room
with faint distaste, the director came in, a long pipe in his hand,
and greeted the Japanese. "Isn't this a splendid place?" he exclaimed complacently. Shiba replied "I am dazzled," but to himself remarked that the Dutch seemed to think Japanese very primitive not to go in for such decorations.[11]

Only a few of the interpreters attempted to make scholarly use
of their contacts with the Europeans. In 1763 an interpreter named
Kitajima Kenshin completed a work called *Explanations of the
Dutch Celestial and Terrestrial Maps,* based on Dutch originals
of 1700. Kitajima was not content, however, with translating
Dutch cartographical theories; he advanced one of his own, that
Japan formed a special section of the globe, together with Ezo,
Tartary, Korea, the Ryukyus, Formosa, Luzon, Java, etc.[12] He
named this region *Fortis Jamato.*

Kitajima was aided in the preparation of his work by the interpreter Nishi Zenzaburō, one of the most gifted scholars of Dutch
of the time. In 1767 Nishi undertook the ambitious project of
single-handedly compiling a Dutch-Japanese dictionary. Had this
laudable effort been completed, the study of Dutch would certainly have been greatly facilitated, but Nishi died the following
year, having progressed no further than the letter B.[13]

Nishi is also known as the man who discouraged the two physicians Maeno Ryōtaku (1723–1803) and Sugita Gempaku (1733–
1817) when they informed him of their desire to learn Dutch. It is
clear that some of the interpreters jealously guarded the study of
Dutch as a family secret, and this factor may have been behind
Nishi's declaration that it was virtually impossible to learn the
language. Maeno, who had already had some instruction from
Aoki Konyō in Dutch without making much headway, resolved
nevertheless to go to Nagasaki to learn what he could. He made
the trip about 1770 and returned with a number of Dutch books
and a phrase-book containing a few hundred words. But he was
unable to do much more than to spell out the words in the learned
books he now possessed.

Sugita had been so discouraged by Nishi's advice that he entirely abandoned the idea of studying Dutch, but he found his interest in Western medicine aroused anew in 1771 when he was shown two textbooks of anatomy. The owner indicated that he was willing to sell, and Sugita examined the books closely. "I couldn't read a word, of course, but the drawings of the viscera, bones, and muscles were quite unlike anything I had previously seen, and I realized that they must have been drawn from life. I wished with all my heart that I might somehow acquire this book . . . but at the time I was so poor that it was entirely beyond my means."[14] Sugita's clan leaders came to his rescue and bought him one of the books.

The work Sugita acquired was *Tafel Anatomia,* written in 1731 by the German physician Johann Adam Kulmus.[15] Once in possession of the book, Sugita was anxious to test its validity with actual experiments, but at the time the only persons in Japan who performed dissections were the *eta,* or pariah class. These unfortunate people served as butchers, tanners, and furriers, occupations felt to be beneath the dignity of normal citizens, and dissections were considered to be their proper task. Doctors occasionally hired the services of an eta for this purpose; some years before Sugita's time, two court physicians had written a study based on eight dissections they had witnessed in which they attempted to reconcile the discrepancies between the anatomical drawings in Chinese texts and their actual observations. This they did by declaring that on deep reflection they had come to the conclusion that there must be physiological differences between Chinese and Japanese.[16]

As good luck would have it, a friend wrote to Sugita one day in April 1771 that a certain doctor was to have a dissection performed on the day following. The scene was the execution ground at Kotsugahara, and the subject was a fifty-year-old woman nicknamed "Old Mother Green Tea," who had been put to death for some great crime. Sugita asked some of his friends, including Maeno Ryōtaku, to be present. When Maeno appeared the next day, he was also carrying a copy of *Tafel Anatomia,* one of the books he had obtained during his stay in Nagasaki. Sugita's description of what followed deserves to be quoted at length:

We all went to the place in Kotsugahara prepared for the anatomy lesson. The dissection itself was to be performed by an eta named Toramatsu, who was reputed to be skilled in this art and who had promised to come. On the day of the dissection, however, he suddenly took ill, and an old man of ninety years, said to be his grandfather, appeared to take his place. He was a robust old man, and told us that he had been performing dissections since his youth and had cut up a good many people in his time.

The dissections that had taken place up to this time had been left to the eta, who would point to a certain part he had cut and inform the spectators that it was the lungs, or that another part was the kidneys. Those who had witnessed these performances would go away convinced that they had seen all there was to be seen. Since, of course, the name of the organ was not written on it, the spectator would have to content himself with whatever the eta told him. On this day, too, the old eta pointed at this and that, giving them names, but there were certain parts for which he had no names, although he had always found such things in the same place in every corpse that he had ever cut up. He also remarked that none of the doctors who had previously witnessed his dissections had ever wondered what these parts were.

When Ryōtaku and I compared what we saw with the illustrations in the Dutch book, we discovered that everything was exactly as depicted. The six lobes and two ears of the lungs, and the three lobes on the right and four lobes on the left of the kidneys, such as were always described in the old Chinese books of medicine, were not so found. The position and shape of the intestines and stomach were also quite unlike the old descriptions.[17]

Sugita and Maeno, by now convinced of the superiority of the Dutch anatomy text, decided to translate it. The only aids to translation they possessed, however, were the crude vocabularies Maeno had been given in Nagasaki. The two men, together with a colleague named Nakagawa Junan, spent the next four years working on the translation, often spending many hours attempting to determine the meaning of a single word. It was difficult not only to discover what a Dutch term meant, but also to find a suitable Japanese equivalent. Sometimes they used the old words, such as were found in Chinese books of medicine; at other times they were forced to invent new expressions because the Chinese terms did not designate precisely the same things as the Dutch words. Eventually, however, the translation was completed, and it was decided to publish it. Sugita and Maeno knew that a rather trivial book entitled *Tales of Holland*,[18] published in 1765, had been confis-

3. Sugita Gempaku

cated and the blocks destroyed because the Dutch alphabet had
been reproduced in its illustrations. To smooth the way for their
new book, therefore, they had copies presented in advance both
to the court of the shogun in Edo and to the imperial palace in
Kyoto. Then, when they were assured that there was no objection
from any quarter, they released the book to the public in 1774, the
first work to be translated from the Dutch and openly circulated.

The importance of *Tafel Anatomia* is not to be measured merely
in terms of whatever advance it made possible in Japanese medicine. It started a great wave of interest in Dutch learning of every
description, although medicine continued to be the chief subject
of study. Most fortunately, this sudden increase of interest in Western learning coincided with the term as factory doctor of C. P.
Thunberg, whose stay in Japan has already been mentioned. When
the Japanese discovered that Thunberg was far more learned than
any of his recent predecessors, they plied him incessantly with
questions both at Nagasaki and at Edo when he visited the capital.
Thunberg recorded how the Japanese looked up to him "as an
oracle, whom they suppose capable of giving them information
upon every subject,"[19] but at last the inquisitiveness that had so
characterized their earlier dealings with the Dutch had been given
a direction. Although questions on scientific matters did not pre-
clude the possibility of inquiries on trivialities, some useful purpose was now served by the interrogations.

Thunberg was much impressed by the zeal and determination
of the Japanese physicians who visited him in Edo, but he had a
low opinion of their professional skill. So poor was their knowledge of internal medicine, he declared, that it was only by chance
that they ever cured anyone. It is amusing to read how, for example, the Japanese doctors would spend a full quarter of an hour
feeling the pulse in each wrist of a patient, although Thunberg's
insistence on the virtues of bleeding as a cure in a "host of circumstances" reminds us that Western medicine, too, had its shortcom-
ings. But for the Japanese believers in the new Western science
there was little room for doubt, and the physicians went ahead
with phlebotomies, albeit with trembling fingers.[20]

It was about this time that the Japanese name for foreign studies came to be *rangaku* (the *ran* being extracted from "Oranda") in place of the old *bangaku* or "barbarian learning," indicating the new dignity in which they were held. Numerous aspiring young men went to study with Maeno and Sugita. By this time Maeno had become very skilled in Dutch and had written several books to aid beginners, but the most important textbook was the *Ladder to Dutch Studies* written in 1783 by Maeno's pupil Ōtsuki Gentaku.[21] In this work Ōtsuki's brief survey of Dutch grammar and pronunciation, valuable though it was, took second place to the real purpose of the book, the defense of Dutch studies per se. The new *rangaku* for the first time was declared to be as worthy of the superior man's attention as traditional Chinese philosophy.

The clash between *rangaku* and Confucianism, which first occurred at this time when Dutch studies were assuming prominence, lasted for many years without a clear victory for either side. Earlier men such as Aoki and Noro were by training Confucianists, and Sugita himself had written that *rangaku*'s rise would have been impossible had it not been preceded by Chinese studies, but the Confucianists were quick to attack when they thought they saw a dangerous rival. Ōtsuki defended Dutch studies:

Ever since in recent years Dutch learning has risen, there has been a tendency for Confucian scholars to reject it, declaring that barbarian theories should not be adopted. What is the meaning of such criticism? Dutch learning is not perfect, but if we choose the good points and follow them, what harm could come of that? What is more ridiculous than to refuse to discuss its merits and to cling to what one knows best without hope of changing?[22]

Ōtsuki's attitude appears sensible enough to us, and the reader may wonder why the same man could not both study Dutch science and preserve the traditional virtues of filial piety, benevolence, decorum, and the rest. However, behind the question of the value of Dutch studies as such lay the key issue of Chinese intellectual supremacy. The established formula for Tokugawa Japan had been the combination of Chinese learning and Japanese "spirit." Most of the numerous Japanese Confucianists of the time attempted to demonstrate that the intellectual attainments of

China were balanced by the superior Japanese spiritual virtues, and that perfection in both would make the best of all possible men. Rangaku had no place in this scheme of things; whatever Japan lacked in the way of learning was to be supplied by China. In other words, the Japanese had to choose between Chinese and Western knowledge as the complement of their own spiritual heritage; it was not possible simply to add rangaku to what already existed without profoundly disturbing the prevailing mode of thought.

The first counterblow by the partisans of Dutch learning to the criticisms of the Confucianists took the form of an attack on China itself, not because of any hostility to Confucian morality or toward the Chinese people, but because it was felt that there was room for only one learning. Ōtsuki used the new geographical knowledge to attack China's claim to be the center of civilization:

Hidebound Confucianists and run-of-the-mill doctors have no conception of the immensity of the world. They allow themselves to be dazzled by Chinese ideas, and, in imitation of Chinese practice, laud the Middle Kingdom, or speak of the Way of the Middle Flowery Land. This is an erroneous view; the world is a great sphere on the surface of which are disposed the various nations. Although boundaries are determined by nature, each people gives an honorific name to the homeland. China is called the Middle Land, the Middle Plain, the Middle Flower, the Middle Kingdom, or else the Flowery Capital, the Divine Continent. Similarly, Holland calls Germany, her motherland, "Middelland," and our country proclaims itself to be "Nakatsukuni"—"The Land in the Middle." England uses the location of her capital as the starting point in counting degrees of longitude, and must also have a corresponding manner of naming her country.

In terms of size, Egypt, a territory of Africa, should be termed the center of the world. This would mean that China and Japan are at the eastern end of the world, and Holland and the other European nations at the northwest. But what excuse is there for us to adopt the proud usage of China and speak of the Middle Flowery Land, or of Flowery People, Flowery Ships, Flowery Things, etc.? For long years we have been imitating them, senselessly delighting in their ways without thinking of anything else. This has led to our excessive stupidity with respect to geography, and to a limitation on the knowledge we have gained with our eyes and ears. Thus it is that there are people who know only the names of China and India, and some extreme cases who think that Holland is a Chinese possession. Some even consider every foreigner, apart from the Chinese, to be a barbarian unworthy of comment. How crude and how narrow such learning is![23]

Variations on the same theme are found in the prefaces to the *Ladder to Dutch Studies* written by Ōtsuki's friends.[24] "Our former sovereigns had commerce with all countries, seeking out the best things in each place. They did not choose between 'Chinese' and 'barbarian,' and that is why both Confucianism and Buddhism are found in Japan." The same writer (Kuchiki Ryūkyō) noted that the compilers of the *Chronicles of Japan* referred to the Chinese as "barbarians," and that they were so classed in the first Japanese census. Another preface writer, Ogino Kyūkoku, declared that Chinese learning was dead, and that its best traditions were now maintained by the Dutch. Dutch learning, which was based on actual facts and not on empty theories, must therefore be studied by Japanese. In these prefaces, then, the method of attack was already shifting from the imputation that Chinese were not better than other people to the more positive statement that they were not as good as the Japanese or Dutch.

The emergence of this attitude is of the greatest significance in the history of Japanese thought. From the beginnings of civilization in Japan, the model had always been China, directly or indirectly. Inevitably Chinese ideas had been considerably modified in Japan, and some Japanese aesthetic and spiritual concepts were never vitally affected by Chinese example; but by and large China was admitted to be the fount of all wisdom, and such Japanese claims for recognition as existed generally took the form of "Even though we are a small country, we are just as good as China in many ways." With the rangaku movement, however, the unique claims of China to distinction were denied: "The sun and moon shine on every place alike." Japanese scholars began to doubt the value of all that had been believed for more than a thousand years.

The protest against Chinese learning assumed a different form among the advocates of *kokugaku,* or native learning, whose rise to prominence roughly paralleled that of the Dutch scholars, and who were much influenced by them. It was the attempt of the devotees of kokugaku to discover in the native literature of Japan and in the Shinto religion a complete culture, and thus to free Japan of all dependence on China. The lengths to which such men went to prove their thesis were sometimes comical, notably in their

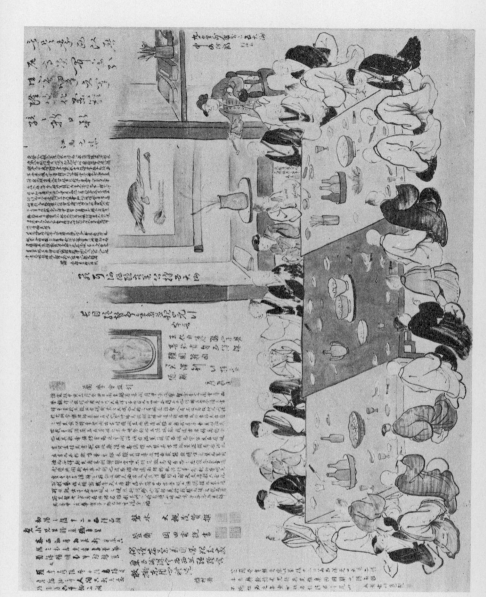

4. Celebrating
the Dutch
New Year

efforts to demonstrate that the Japanese possessed writing before the introduction of Chinese ideographs, but equally in their fanciful etymologies. A school founded on so insecure a base was naturally eager to gather to itself whatever outside support there might be, and the kokugaku scholars readily adopted the anti-Chinese arguments of Ōtsuki and others. It was even announced that rangaku itself was a necessary element in the training of the scholars of Japanese learning. The students of rangaku for their part neither welcomed nor rejected their strange allies; in general, their attitude was vaguely respectful toward Shinto, but they knew enough about the rest of the world to realize that Japan was neither the leading nor the most ancient nation.

The Confucianists, who were the common target of the partisans of Japanese and Dutch learning alike, responded acrimoniously, and were perhaps driven further than they intended in the direction of uncompromising orthodoxy. Toward the end of the eighteenth century the government was persuaded by the court scholars to forbid the teaching of any but the strict Chu Hsi school of Confucian philosophy, and though in the nineteenth century the importance of Western learning became increasingly evident, the restrictions on it grew even more severe.

It would be unfair, however, to suggest that all Confucianists were uncompromising enemies of progress. Ōtsuki himself quoted with approval the remarks of Shibano Ritsuzan (1734–1807), an orthodox Confucian scholar who nevertheless saw some value in Western learning. He stated that even barbarians incapable of reading Chinese books might possess the ability to make deductions from their personal observations that were valid for all mankind.[25] This rather grudging admission of the possible merit of foreign learning referred primarily to European medicine, the one branch of rangaku that escaped official wrath in the difficult days of the early nineteenth century. The study of Dutch medicine was in any case the object of most of the men who turned to rangaku, but when it became dangerous to dabble in other types of foreign learning, some men became doctors in spite of themselves in order to continue their Dutch studies with impunity. Only gradually did

Western science gain supremacy in all fields. By this time Confucianism and the old Japanese "spirit" had drawn together, and the new dichotomy of "Eastern morality and Western techniques" was made by innumerable Japanese writers.

In the eighteenth century, with which we are primarily concerned here, there was greater freedom for the students of Western learning. Ōtsuki, who had begun as a doctor, became so proficient in Dutch that he decided to devote himself chiefly to the language. In 1789 he opened the first Dutch Language School in Japan, the Shirandō in Edo. Between 1789 and 1826 the school had ninety-four pupils, chiefly men interested in medicine but also men of other professions.[26] Similar schools were later founded in other parts of the country. The total number of people who learned Dutch both at these schools and in other ways is impossible to ascertain, but it is true to say that most of the interesting, if not the influential, men of late-eighteenth-century Japan were attracted by the new learning, some only out of curiosity, others with deep conviction. As Sugita wrote in 1815, at the age of eighty-two, when looking back on the development of the studies that he had done so much to promote:

They say that one drop of oil cast into a wide pond will spread out to cover the entire surface, and this may well be so. In the beginning, there were just the three of us—Maeno Ryōtaku, Nakagawa Junan, and myself—who came together to make plans for our studies. Now, when close to fifty years have elapsed, this learning has reached out to every corner of the land, and each year new translations seem to be brought out. This is a case of one dog barking at something only to be echoed by 10,000 dogs barking at nothing.[27]

3. Strange Tales from Muscovy

Rangaku might have remained a purely academic discipline, the stepping-stone to greater knowledge of European science, had it not been for the threats to Japan's peaceful isolation that caused some Japanese to turn to Dutch learning for guidance as well as information. These men were interested not so much in Dutch medicine or astronomy as in discovering how the European example could help keep Japan safe from invasion by making the nation strong and economically sound. In the writings of such men as Honda Toshiaki one finds numerous references to the chief outside stimuli to Japan in the late eighteenth century, the letters sent by Baron von Benyowsky and the return to Japan of the castaway Kōdayū.

The Adventurer's Warning

Few more curious personages are to be found in the pages of modern history than Baron Moritz Aladar von Benyowsky, whose career led him from Hungary, the land of his birth, across Asia to exile in Kamchatka, to the coasts of Japan and China in a stolen vessel, to Europe and America, where great dignitaries lent support to his chimerical projects, and finally to death in Madagascar after an attempt to establish himself as "Ruler of all Rulers." His lies and intrigues seem to have had little other motivation than a desire to create mischief, and this he did in all quarters of the globe.

In his lengthy memoirs, Benyowsky described, or imagined, his adventures in picturesque detail. We are told not only of his capture in battle by the Russians, of his terrible journey in chains across the wilds of Siberia, and of his life in Kamchatka during the winter of 1770–71, but of beauteous damsels who could not resist his manly charms, and of the high honors his bravery and ability won for him. Interesting though a full account of his career would be, we need concern ourselves here only with Benyowsky's brief visit to Japan and the incidents immediately surrounding it.

It was in May of 1771 that Benyowsky, weary of his exile, engineered a revolt among the convicts of Kamchatka and managed to gain control of a small vessel lying in the harbor. Typically, he proclaimed the purpose of his actions to be the overthrow of the "usurper Catherine II," thus seeking to impart greater dignity to what must have been a rather sordid uprising. But this ambitious project was driven from Benyowsky's mind by more pressing considerations: his badly equipped vessel was soon short of provisions, and it seemed doubtful that the crew would survive the journey back to Europe, much less have the energy to restore the rightful prince to the Czardom of All the Russias.

Fortunately for Benyowsky, land was sighted on July 8, 1771, or about two months after the escape from Kamchatka. The adventurer had much to say concerning his experiences in Japan at the "Bay of Usilpatchar," as he fancifully called the landfall. There he was royally received by the great "Ulikamhy," of whom he was informed "that he was King of the province, and had married one of the daughters of the Emperor; that he was one of the most learned men in the country, being acquainted with astronomy in the highest degree, and that his soul was endued with celestial qualities, having never done harm to any one; that he was adored in his own province, and desired in all the others."[1]

Benyowsky's account of the festivities that attended his visit, of his philosophical discourses with the enlightened Japanese mon-

arch, and of the delightful manners of the natives would arouse
our suspicions merely from what we know of the usual Japanese
treatment of foreigners, but we also happen to have proof of the
fictitious nature of "Ulikamhy" and all his court. One of Benyowsky's shipmates kept a record of the voyage from Kamchatka, and
he related in a much less colorful manner that far from receiving
lavish hospitality, the strangers were warned by the Japanese,
"who passed their hands across their throats, thereby wishing to
intimate to their unbidden guests that they, one and all, hosts and
guests, would have their throats cut if they allowed them to come
on shore."[2]

The harbor where Benyowsky's ship had anchored was in Awa,
in southeastern Japan. The lord of that domain, anxious to get
rid of his unwanted visitors, presented them with liberal amounts
of rice, water, and salt. He also accepted, and eventually passed
on to the shogun, two letters written in German and addressed to
the Dutch factory director in Nagasaki.[3] Benyowsky, who had
posed as a Frenchman in Kamchatka,* now assumed the guise of
a commander in the navy of Her Imperial Roman Majesty, that
is, the Empress of Austria, and claimed the help of the Dutch as
an ally and friend of the "high-mighty and illustrious states of
Holland." He apparently hoped that Dutch intercession with the
Emperor of Japan would enable him to remain in the country
long enough to conclude some profitable trading. But four days
after his arrival in Awa, Benyowsky yielded to the menacing ges-
tures of the natives and departed. After a brief stay at nearby
Tosa, he next anchored at Ōshima, off the southern tip of Kyushu.

While in Ōshima Benyowsky sent the factory director four more
letters, three of them to express his gratitude for the provisions
the Japanese had given him at Awa and Ōshima. The last of the

---

* J. J. B. de Lesseps related his surprise at the cool reception he was accorded
by the Kamchatka officials when he first arrived. He discovered that this treatment resulted from "the disadvantageous impression which they had imbibed
of the character and genius of our [French] nation, originating in the perfidy
and cruelty exhibited in the person of the famous Beniowsky in this part of the
peninsula. This slave called himself a Frenchman, and acted like a true Van-
dal." *Travels in Kamtschatka* (London, 1790), I, 156.

letters, by far the most important, gained great celebrity in Japan as "Benyowsky's Warning," and was aptly called the "first piece of national defense literature."

Highly Illustrious, High, and Wellborn Gentlemen, Officers of the Highly Esteemed Republic of Holland:

Unkind fate, which has for some time been driving me here and there on the sea, has brought me for a second time into Japanese waters. I have come ashore here in the hope that I might possibly meet with your high excellencies, and obtain your help. It has been a great misfortune for me not to have had the opportunity of speaking to you personally, for I have important information to disclose. I have deemed it necessary because of my general respect for your illustrious states to inform you in this letter of the fact that this year, in accordance with a Russian order, two galliots and a frigate from Kamchatka sailed around Japan and set down all their findings in a plan, in which an attack on Matsma [Hokkaidō] and the neighboring islands lying under 41°38′ N. Lat. has been fixed for next year. For this purpose a fortress has been built on the Kurile island nearest to Kamchatka, and ammunition, artillery, and a magazine have been readied.

If I could speak to you personally, I might reveal more than writing permits. Your high illustriousnesses may make such preparation as you please, but my advice, as an ardent well-wisher of your illustrious republic and a co-religionist, would be that you have a cruiser ready if you can. With this I further commend myself and am as subscribed, your most obedient servant

BARON ALADAR VON BENGORO*
Army Commander in Captivity

20 July 1771 on the island Usma

When I went ashore I left there a map of Kamchatka which may be of use to you.

We may wonder what reason Benyowsky had for sending such false tidings to the Dutch. Of their untruthfulness there can be no doubt. Far from planning aggressive moves against Japan, the Russians had all they could do to hold together their Pacific empire, which had never consisted of much more than a wretched colony in Kamchatka (where vodka was the most plentiful commodity), a handful of traders in the Kuriles, and a string of tiny

---

* Benyowsky, in the guise of an Austrian officer, adopted this Germanic version of his name in writing to the Dutch, and he was thus known also to the Japanese. Benyowsky's name was more properly Benyovszky, but it was by the former spelling that he was known in England.

outposts in America, sometimes marked by such revealing names
as Massacre Bay. Benyowsky was certainly aware of these facts, but
a passion for the truth was never one of his attributes. Perhaps he
hoped to ingratiate himself with the Dutch by disclosing the supposed Russian plot, though if this was his motive it is hard to see
what he expected to gain.

In any case, Benyowsky's departure from Japan a month before
even his first letter had reached the Dutch deprived him of the
pleasure of witnessing the confusion he had aroused. The Japanese, unable to read Benyowsky's German, turned his letters over
to the Dutch factory officials for translation. To aid in the identification of the mysterious foreigners, they also produced a pair of
trousers and a shirt that had been bartered by some of Benyowsky's
crew at Tosa, but the Dutchmen remained baffled about the nationality of the pretended officer of the Holy Roman Empire. It
was eventually suggested that the ship might have been a Spanish
galleon on the way to Mexico from the Philippines, the only European vessel known to be near Japanese waters.

For many years afterward, the meaning of Benyowsky's letters
was discussed by earnest Japanese, and indeed his warning started
a new type of thinking about the problems of war. Apart from the
two abortive attempts by the Mongols to invade the country in the
thirteenth century, Japan had never known the fear of an attack
from abroad, and military defense planning had been confined to
problems that might arise in such internal warfare as had beset
the country before the establishment of peace in 1600. The sudden revelation of an external threat to Japan's security necessitated a great change in strategy, and led to a serious agitation in
favor of increased military preparations.

The group of national defense enthusiasts who drew inspiration
from Benyowsky's warning was at first limited in size by the secrecy
with which his letters were surrounded. It was impossible, however, to prevent the interpreters and Dutchmen who had taken
part in the translation from confiding the contents of the messages
to interested visitors. Hirazawa Kyokuzan (1733–91), who journeyed to Nagasaki in 1774 as a member of a daimyo's entourage,

5. Baron von Benyowsky

カレナン
掛版 かけゑ
當今女主ヱカテリナの像

6. Catherine the Great

left the earliest Japanese account of the foreign ship that several years before had touched at Awa. He was told that the letters revealed the captain of the ship to be a Russian under orders from his country to survey the waters of Japan in preparation for a Russian attack. It was gratitude for the provisions and firewood received at Awa that had prompted the captain to make his startling confession. "Then he set sail, and nobody knows where he went."[4]

Three years after his return to the capital, Hirazawa set off for Hokkaidō, apparently to ascertain the truth of the rumors he had heard of Russian infiltration. It was not often that men of letters journeyed to the lonely northern island; not only did reports of its dismal climate discourage visitors, but suspiciousness and even hostility toward outsiders were well-known traits of the Matsumae clan, which ruled the island. Hirazawa received surprisingly friendly treatment, however, presumably because it was clear that his visit was in the nature of a literary excursion and not an official tour of inspection. He related to the clan leaders the terrible warning of Benyowsky, and urged them to adopt new defense measures, but his alarm was not shared by his hosts, who were doubtless confident that the bravery of the Japanese warrior was still a fair match for foreign guns.[5]

Another visitor to Nagasaki who was stirred by Benyowsky's letters was Kudō Heisuke (1734–1800), a doctor who visited the city in 1780 in order to study Dutch medicine. While he was there he became friendly with the interpreters and eventually with the factory director himself, who confided many state secrets to him. Kudō learned, for example, that the Dutch considered Japanese policies to be highly inept in that they had permitted the Russians to extend their grasp to one after another of the Kurile Islands. Kudō was nevertheless inclined to discount reports of Russian designs on Japan, declaring that he believed them to have been invented by the Dutch traders in order to preserve their trade monopoly. Discussing an encounter between Russian traders and Matsumae clan officials of several years before, he wrote, "I cannot believe that Russia intends to wage war on us. No importance

could have been attributed by the Russian government to the incident that took place in Ezo. I think it must rather be that the
Russians have heard of the abundance of precious metals in Japan
and wish to trade with us."[6]

But Kudō could not be entirely tranquil; the news of Benyowsky's visit had upset him greatly. He wrote, "We do not know
what Benyowsky had in mind when he sailed around Japan surveying our coastline, but we must not ignore the fact that he did
so. A detailed inquiry should be made into what happened."[7] This
suggestion, together with his other findings, was included in Kudō's book *A Study of Red Ainu Reports* (by "Red Ainu" he meant
"Russian"), completed in 1781. The work was later brought to the
attention of Tanuma Okitsugu, then virtual dictator of Japan,
who was so impressed by it that he ordered the Matsumae clan to
submit a report on the situation in the north. The clan leaders
responded in vague and mystifying terms, hoping to satisfy the
government without revealing their military weakness, but Tanuma rejected their report and directed that a small expedition be
sent to Ezo, Karafuto, and the Kuriles to obtain firsthand information.

The mission of 1785–86 was described in the *Ezo Miscellany,* a
short, factual work which, far from confirming Kudō and other
enthusiasts who had vaunted the wealth of Ezo, related in detail
the actual hardships of life in that desolate region. The members
of the expedition were also able to confirm rumors of Russian activity in the Kuriles, but only in the most negative way. On the
island of Uruppu they came across one miserable party of "Red
Ainu" who had been living there for six years. The contrast between the condition of these lonely men and the stories that the
Japanese had heard of the fearsome Russian threat to Ezo made
one of the party ask the Russians about what had happened to
Benyowsky. "Oh," replied a trapper, "he sailed off to America
with a fleet of eight big ships."[8]

By the time the mission to the north had returned to Edo, Tanuma was out of power, and his successor showed himself to be
without interest in the explorer's information. The *Ezo Miscel-*

lany, like so many other useful books written about this time, was consigned to oblivion in the government archives. But the repercussions of Benyowsky's visit were far from ceasing at this point; the most important product of his stimulus to Japan, the *Kaikoku Heidan (Military Talks for a Maritime Nation)* by Hayashi Shihei (1738–93), did not appear until 1791.

Of all the late-eighteenth-century students of the West, Hayashi gained the greatest fame during his lifetime, both because of the intrinsic interest of his work and because of the sensational aspects of his career. For readers of today, however, the rangaku scholars who devoted themselves to the study of European arts or history are likely to appear the most congenial, and Hayashi's almost exclusive preoccupation with military science counts in his disfavor. His work is nonetheless of exceptional importance in Japan's discovery of the West.

Hayashi came from the north of Japan, the home of many of the most intransigent of Japanese thinkers. Although his interest in things European was at first restricted to Dutch horsemanship, to study which he visited Nagasaki in 1775, he soon moved on to a more general consideration of European ways, possibly under the influence of his friend Kudō Heisuke.[9] After two more trips to Nagasaki he was filled with new ideas, and his impatience at the intellectual isolation in which Japan was living grew ever more intense. His visit of 1782 resulted in the compilation of his first major work, a geography of Korea, the Ryukyus, and Ezo. He chose this subject because he believed that all Japanese, regardless of their wealth or education, should be acquainted with the geography of these countries. The work contains some interesting things, but it is now commonly treated as a preliminary study for the epoch-making *Kaikoku Heidan,* which begins:

What is meant by a maritime nation? It is a country not connected by land to any other, but bordered on all sides by the sea. There are defense preparations that are suited to a maritime nation, and that differ in kind from those prescribed in Chinese military works, as well as from those traditionally taught in Japan by the various schools. . . .

Military preparation for Japan means a knowledge of the way to repel foreign invaders, a vital consideration at present. The way to do this is

by naval warfare; the essential factor in naval warfare is cannons. To be
well prepared in these two respects is the true requisite of Japanese defense, unlike the military policies appropriate to such continental countries as China and Tartary. Only when naval warfare has been mastered
should land warfare be considered.[10]

It may seem only too obvious to the reader that Japan, an island
nation, required a navy, but at the time Hayashi wrote these
lines Japan did not possess a single warship or, for that matter, a
single vessel of any great size or pretensions. Military science
meant only the art of civil warfare in the mountains and valleys
of Japan, and the tactics that were studied were chiefly those found
in such ancient Chinese texts as the celebrated *Art of War* by Sun
Tzu. These works had not dealt with the problems of an invasion
by enemy ships, since China's chief worry had always been the
violation of her land frontiers by hordes of savage tribesmen; the
respect for Chinese precedent was so great in Japan that no one
since the half-forgotten days of the Mongol invasions had stopped
to consider the military implications of the fact that Japan is surrounded by water.*

To combat this reliance on Chinese example, Hayashi felt it
necessary to discredit China in the eyes of the Japanese. This he
attempted to do by depicting the Chinese as potential enemies to
Japanese independence rather than as bringers of enlightenment,
their traditional role. The Manchu dynasty, he asserted, had cor-
rupted the good ways of the Chinese people.

It is not improbable, I believe, that some future Manchu ruler, profiting
by a period of internal peace, will engage in rash foreign ventures, hoping to emulate the old achievements of the Mongols. If this happens, the
Chinese will be moved chiefly by greed, and the benevolence of the Japanese government will not win them over. Nor will they be intimidated
by Japanese military prowess, for their attacking armies will be enormous.[11]

It is hard to say how seriously Hayashi meant this argument to
be taken; probably it was intended simply as a warning against the

---

* I mean, of course, defensively. Before the country was closed, armed Japanese ships had ranged about the East. The inferiority of the Japanese navy had
worried Hideyoshi, and indeed had been one of the causes of the failure of his
Korean campaign. But Japanese military thinkers never considered the possibility that foreign ships might attack Japan.

complacent assumption that the Chinese could be counted on to behave themselves like gentlemen. The real threat to Japan, as Hayashi often remarks, was Russia.

Russia in recent years has become the mightiest of the nations of Europe. Her armies have extended their conquests to the distant territories of Tartary, to the land of Siberia, and even as far as Kamchatka. To the east of Kamchatka, however, there is no territory worth taking, and that is why there are indications that Russia has turned her attention toward the Kurile Islands. As early as 1771 an adventurer named Baron Moritz Aladar von Benyowsky was sent from Muscovy to Kamchatka, and from there to Japan, where he visited various harbors. He sailed halfway around Japan, sounding the depths of the different ports. Especially of note was his stay in the province of Tosa, where he left a letter for the Dutch director resident in Nagasaki. His motives for coming here are to be hated and feared.[12]

Hayashi's apprehensions of the possibility of a Russian attack were intensified by the high opinion he had formed of European military techniques.* Unlike the Chinese, who relied heavily on elaborate stratagems, or the Japanese, who placed their confidence in native courage and proficiency in close fighting, the Europeans considered firepower the most important element in warfare. They had invented many unusual weapons, including the airship, which was designed primarily to terrorize the enemy soldiers.[13] The Westerners excelled particularly in naval warfare and built ships of exceedingly fine construction. Hayashi had been informed that Benyowsky's vessel was "powerfully built, like a small fortress,"[14] rather excessive praise, we may think, for the small galley Benyowsky commanded. Hayashi believed that European ships were so superior to Chinese ones that Japan could not possibly find guidance in naval matters except from the West.

Behind the greatness of the European nations, Hayashi saw their wonderful laws, which kept them peaceful and orderly. "Nations sometimes invade each other's territories and attempt for years to hold these conquests, but it never happens that soldiers of the same country fight among themselves. Japan and China have yet to attain this stage."[15]

---

* Hayashi in his writings includes a drawing of a *luchtschip* that he had seen in a *Kriegsboek,* presumably some Dutch military work. He declared his intention of making an airship and testing it, when he had the time.

It was also by virtue of the wonderful laws* that so many Europeans had been inspired to conquer distant lands. The great European tradition of learning (dating back perhaps 6,000 years) and the general familiarity of Europeans with the sciences of astronomy and geography made this ambition easy to satisfy even without recourse to arms. Japan must not comfort herself with the thought that the Europeans were too far away to invade her. If Western armies did not themselves come to Japan, there was always the possibility that the Chinese and Manchus, who had become increasingly friendly toward the Europeans, might also adopt the wonderful laws and experience the same desire for territorial expansion. Then the overwhelming military power of China could easily be brought against complacent, indifferent Japan.[16]

What remedy existed, then, against attack either by Europeans or by European-inspired Chinese? Japan must build her defenses. Every part of the coastline of Japan should be fortified with naval batteries such as already were found in Nagasaki. This might seem an impossibly difficult task, but it could be completed in fifty years. "A frontierless sea road leads from the Nihon Bridge in Edo to China and Holland. Why is it that there are defense installations only in Nagasaki?"[17]

Before any more positive military steps might be taken, however, the samurai had to be reeducated. As a result of the protracted period of peace, they had forgotten about the art of war and had surrendered themselves to debilitating luxuries. Schools must be established for instruction in both military and cultural subjects, for without literary attainments a soldier is no better than a barbarian. Such institutions would eventually produce men versed in both disciplines, rare though they have been in the course of history. Many Japanese generals had become famous, but with only two exceptions they had all lacked the necessary cultural abilities to make them truly great men: these were the legendary Emperor Jimmu and Tokugawa Ieyasu. China could boast of a few such men, but the greatest of those endowed with both literary and

---

* What exactly he meant by "wonderful laws" (*myōhō*) is not clear; quite possibly it was Christianity.

martial talents was the Empress Catherine of Russia, who had "spread her virtue and extended her power."[18]

The *Kaikoku Heidan,* Hayashi's contribution to the solution of Japan's military problems, caused the author a great deal of trouble. He apparently sold maps and even prints of his drawing of a Dutch ship in order to raise funds to pay the printer.[19] The first volume was published in 1787 in his native city of Sendai; difficulties held up the rest of the work, and only four years later did the whole appear. No more than thirty-eight copies were actually bound into book form, but one of them fell into the hands of an enemy. Hayashi was denounced as a disseminator of false reports and as a danger to the state; eight months after the publication of his book he was arrested and sent to Edo, where he was imprisoned. This unhappy turn of events can hardly have come as a great surprise to Hayashi, who had self-consciously written in the preface to the *Kaikoku Heidan*:

The teachers of military science for many generations past have all based their doctrines on Chinese textbooks, which naturally has meant that they have fallen into Chinese ways and have been ignorant of the proper defenses for a maritime nation. I am the first person to have discussed this matter that has excited my deep concern. My extensive investigations into the subject have yielded the information incorporated in this book. But I know that no ordinary citizen is permitted to disclose such facts even if he possesses them; this silence is taken as a mark of circumspection. Since I am a single man who likes to act when he is convinced of something, I have not given a second thought to the possibility of incurring the displeasure of the authorities. I have therefore listed without ornamentation those factors that have made it easy for any invader from Benyowsky on to attack Japan. My purpose in compiling this book has been to inform the authorities of what is necessary to the defense of a maritime nation. This is why I have undertaken to discuss so grave a problem in spite of the humbleness of my position and the smallness of my virtue. I realize that I have gone far beyond my station and that I shall not escape punishment. But it is the author's words that matter, not his person.[20]

Hayashi was arrested by order of Matsudaira Sadanobu, chief of the state councillors, on the grounds that he had published a book dealing with affairs of state and advocating the violation of existing laws. On being informed of his arrest, he recited a poetical epigram, the first of several famous ones composed toward the end of

his life: "Will this head fly or won't it? Spring will soon be here."[21]
Hayashi remained for almost six months in an Edo prison before
this question was answered for him. During this time he received
messages of sympathy and even promising offers of escape, but he
stoically declined to shirk his punishment. The counsel ultimately
prevailed that Hayashi was an ignorant person whom it would be
pointless further to interrogate, and an order was given that he be
returned to Sendai for confinement. The blocks of the *Kaikoku
Heidan* were ordered to be destroyed.

After his return to Sendai, Hayashi was allowed to live in relative comfort in his brother's house, but he had fallen into a melan-
cholic state and took no pleasure in anything. He gave himself the
sobriquet of "The Hut of the Six Withouts" (*Rokumuan*) from a
poem he composed at this time: "I have no parents, no wife, no
child, no printing-blocks, no money, and nothing to be happy
about."[22] He lived for another year in this state of depression before he expired of chagrin.

Hayashi's crime in the eyes of the shogunate was not that he had
ventured to criticize the government, but that he had published
views considered inimical to the internal security of the state.[23] As
Kaempfer, the learned German, had put it a century before, "Liberty of Conscience, so far as it doth not interfere with the Interest
of the secular Government, or affect the peace and tranquillity of
the Empire, hath been at all times allow'd in Japan, as it is in
most other Countries of Asia."[24] Honda Toshiaki, for instance,
had profited by the "Liberty of Conscience" to write criticism of
the government far more severe than Hayashi's, but was prudent
enough not to publish his manuscripts. Matsudaira Sadanobu was
actually not opposed to Hayashi's principal ideas, as is demonstrated by the fact that he afterwards ordered a strengthening of
shore defenses and himself made a tour of inspection of the eastern
coasts;[25] he simply could not tolerate the insubordination Hayashi
had shown in appealing publicly to the nation for support of his
cause. The punishment that Hayashi received does not appear to
us to have been very severe, but Matsudaira thereby succeeded in
discouraging other independent-minded persons from publishing

their opinions (and, incidentally, gave Hayashi a measure of fame denied to more cautious contemporaries).

It cannot be pretended that the *Kaikoku Heidan* was inspired entirely by Benyowsky's visit and letters, but the essential points of the book—the danger from abroad and the need for sea defense—had their origins in Hayashi's speculations on the meaning of the adventurer's mysterious voyage. A European counterpart to the *Kaikoku Heidan* may perhaps be found in the memoir written in July 1776 by the French diplomat Jean-Benoit Scherer and presented to the French foreign ministry.[26] According to this strange document, word had leaked out from the Russian embassy in London of an English plan for a joint Anglo-Russian attack on the Japanese Empire. The combined fleets of the two countries would be placed under the command of Captain Cook, who would rendezvous with the Russians at Kamchatka under pretext of searching for a northern passage. Russia, Scherer's document went on, had promised to help the British with the prosecution of the American Revolutionary War if the campaign in Japan were successful, and England in turn agreed to help Russia by "amusing Germany by a war that she would have her allies make" if this were necessary. Japan would be helpless to resist the Anglo-Russian invaders because, Scherer had learned, almost all weapons in the country had been melted down to make building material. The only way of forestalling this attack would be to send a French fleet under Bougainville to supply the Emperor of Japan with arms with which to repel the foreigners.

The reader may perhaps already have guessed the source of Scherer's strange information. It was none other than Benyowsky, who, not content with having upset Japan with his prophecy of an impending Russian onslaught, sought to hoodwink the great statesmen of Europe with an elaborated version of the same story. Scherer acknowledged his debt to Benyowsky, and suggested that Bougainville's fleet pick up the adventurer in Madagascar on its way to Japan so that it might profit by his profound knowledge of the island empire. But the French foreign minister, the Comte de Vergennes, was sceptical about the reliability of the memoir, and the student of history was thus robbed of the pleasure of reading of a French fleet sailing into Edo harbor with arms for the astonished Japanese. That would have been a spectacle worthy of Benyowsky.

The Return of the Castaways

In 1637 it was decreed that no Japanese subject might leave the country or, having left it, return;[27] this meant Japanese were kept from learning of the outside world except as directed by the government. Before this edict there had been flourishing Japanese colonies in the Philippines and such distant places as Siam and Java, and Japanese mercenary troops had been widely used both by Asiatic monarchs and by the new European rulers of the East. But with the prohibition on overseas ventures and on the construction of oceangoing ships, only isolated groups of Japanese Christians were left outside the country, and the Japanese soon lost their mastery of seamanship.

It should not be thought, however, that there was no longer any shipping within the confines of the Japanese Empire. According to Honda, ninety ships carrying rice alone entered Edo harbor every day, and many more were constantly navigating inshore waters with cargoes of produce from the farming provinces on their way to Osaka and Edo. Such ships were small, poorly constructed, and inexpertly handled, for the skippers no longer knew the old lore of the sea and had not yet learned the new science of navigation. When typhoons occurred it was inevitable that some ships should be lost at sea and others wrecked on distant coasts. Honda described the helplessness of such vessels when they were carried out to sea by a storm.

Even when the weather improves, the crew are at a loss to tell in which direction to head, and the ship floats about helplessly. As a last resort they cut off their hair and make vows to Buddha and the gods. Then they take out pieces of paper on which have been written the names of the twelve directions, roll them up into balls, and put them into a basket with a hole in its lid. (This they call "drawing lots.") The captain and crew, in tears, fervently call on Buddha and the gods of heaven and earth to indicate the direction. They grasp the basket in their hands and strike

the lid. Then, when one of the pellets jumps out, they pick it up, their
eyes blinded by tears of joy, and cry that it is the direction vouchsafed by
Buddha and the gods. They then set their course by it, and go completely
astray.[28]

Japanese ships were sometimes carried northward by the Black
Current to Kamchatka or the Aleutian Islands, and even to the
western coast of North America. Other ships were driven by tropi-
cal storms as far south as Annam. From time to time castaways
from shipwrecked vessels were returned to Japan, as in 1685, when
the Portuguese, attempting to restore friendly relations with Japan,
brought to Nagasaki twelve Japanese who had been shipwrecked
near Macao. The authorities were naturally suspicious of Portuguese motives, but after examining the ship and finding no religious articles or commercial wares aboard, accepted the castaways
and rewarded the Portuguese for their efforts with thirty sacks of
rice. The old distrust of Catholicism persisting, the Portuguese
were ordered never to visit Japan again, and the attempt to renew
trade relations failed.[29] The Chinese and Dutch, who still enjoyed
this privilege, also occasionally returned shipwrecked Japanese
sailors, probably in the hope of ingratiating themselves with the
government.

Most of the castaways, however, never saw their native land
again, either perishing under the attacks of hostile natives or in-
termarrying with them and losing their Japanese identity. Of
such happenings we have, of course, no record, but from the end
of the seventeenth century there had been a number of Japanese
shipwrecked in Kamchatka, some of whom later gained considerable fame. In 1697 Vladimir Atlassov, the conqueror of Kamchatka, came across a Japanese sailor named Dembei living in a native
village. Presumably because of difficulties in communication, Atlassov did not at first learn the stranger's nationality. He related

that a Prisoner, who came over Sea in the Bussi [a kind of whaling ves-
sel], had a peculiar Language; he wore small Whiskers, and had black
Hair, and by his Visage did not look unlike a Greek. He said farther,
that this Stranger wept as soon as·he saw an Image among the Russians,
by which he gave them to understand that they had the like in his Country. Wolodimir had this Man two years with him, in which Time he had
learn'd something of the Russian Tongue; And having been two Years,

before Wolodimir's Arrival, among the Koroeiki, he spoke at first in that Tongue, by an Interpreter; He said he was an Indian, and that in their Country there was a great deal of Gold, and whole Houses of China: Their Kings liv'd in Silver and gilt Palaces. Wolodimir had, likewise, taken a Piece of Silver-Coin from the Koroeiki, about one Sixth of an Ounce in Weight, which this Stranger affirm'd to be his Country-Coin. He said, that they used no Sables, no other Furs, for Linings, in India; But that their Cloaths were made of all Sorts of Stuffs, quilted with Cotton. Atlassow said, that this Stranger travell'd with him, 6 Days Journy, from Anadirskoi to Liski, where he fell sick, and his Legs swell'd, for which Reason, he was brought back to Anadirskoi Simovia. He gave him the Character of a Man of good Sense and Breeding.[30]

Dembei's true identity was eventually discovered, and he was taken to St. Petersburg, where he was presented to Peter the Great in January of 1702. The Czar made various inquiries about Japan and later ordered that Dembei be sufficiently instructed in the Russian language to permit him to explain the grammar of Japanese to "four or five adolescents."[31] Three years later was founded the Japanese Language School, which lasted in spite of many vicissitudes until 1816, when it became impossible to find anyone willing to study Japanese.[32]

Since it was obvious that the newly organized school could not survive the death of Dembei unless replacements for him were available, it was decreed that if any Japanese were shipwrecked on the coast of Kamchatka, one of them should be sent to St. Petersburg. During the following century or more, wrecks occurred with sufficient frequency to keep the school provided with a teacher most of the time. The castaway-professors were generally trained for a few years in the Russian language, baptized, given Russian names and wives, and then installed in their academic duties.

It may be imagined with what consternation the Japanese government learned (in 1781) that a school had been established in Russia for the purpose of teaching the Japanese language. "Japan's secrets are being revealed to the foreigners!" was the general cry. There was little justification for such alarm; the school was certainly one of the most ineffectual ever created. When Kōdayū, the most famous of the castaways, was asked to correct a dictionary compiled by one of his predecessors, he was surprised to find that most of the words were in patois and of a coarse nature.[33] The students, discouraged by the ineptness of the instruction, had to be offered special inducements to stay on, but nothing could make them learn usable Japanese. On the few occasions when their services were required, the graduate interpreters were totally unintelligible in their adopted language, as one might expect when a Russian attempted to speak an illiterate Japanese fisherman's tongue. The lowest point of the school was reached near its end, when it was discovered that two Russians who had been studying Japanese for nineteen years were still unfamiliar with the elements of the language.*

The language school had not been created, as the Japanese feared, to facilitate an invasion of Japan. It was rather an expression of the eighteenth-century passion for exploration, which caused governments and individuals to spend great sums of money on voyages of discovery. When, for example, Captain W. R. Broughton sailed round the island of Ezo and along the eastern coast of Japan (thereby causing much commotion among the inhabitants), it was not to acquire new colonial possessions for England, but because Broughton was "a navigator who was zealous to extend the bounds of geography, and who was well aware that little was to be done in any other part of the Pacific Ocean."[34] This disinterested predilection for geographical knowledge was difficult for Japanese to understand, and indeed before long it was to give way to the nineteenth-century ideas of Captain Krusenstern, who wrote after his voyage of 1803–4: "With regard to taking possession of Aniwa [a cape and bay at the southeast end of Saghalien], this could be done without the smallest danger, as the Japanese, owing to their total want of weapons of every description, would scarcely think of resistance. . . . I am convinced that this conquest would not cost a single drop of blood."[35]

When Kōdayū appeared at the Court of St. Petersburg in 1791,

---

* The incompetence of the Russian interpreters of Japanese may have been exaggerated. Kudō Heisuke and Satō Genrokurō both described interpreters, the descendants of Japanese castaways, who could speak and even write Japanese. See Ōtomo Kisaku, *Hokumon Sōsho* (Tokyo, 1943), I, 213–14, 303.

Russian interest in Japan had dwindled almost to the vanishing point. The last major Russian-sponsored voyage of discovery in the area of Japan had been Captain Martin Spanberg's of 1738–39. He had been instructed to overcome the "inveterate Asiatic unsociableness" of the Japanese by returning any castaways who happened to be in Kamchatka and by other demonstrations of amity, but his brief contacts with Japanese officials did not come to anything.[36] In the years after Spanberg's expedition occasional flashes of interest in Japan had saved the moribund language school from extinction, but by the time of Catherine the Great, neither the desire to improve existing maps nor the hope of commercial advantage drew people's attention toward the island empire. Territorial aggrandizement, such as Captain Krusenstern was to suggest, does not appear to have been widely considered.

The most important event in Russo-Japanese relationships up to the end of the eighteenth century was the visit to Russia and return to his native country of Kōdayū, a ship captain from Ise, whose career will be described below. The earlier Japanese castaways in Russia of whom we have record were pathetic but colorless sailors, at first bewildered by the unfamiliar society they had accidentally entered, and then swallowed up by it, almost without a trace. Kōdayū, however, was a lively and intelligent person, able to hold his own and more in the strange circumstances in which he found himself. Consider the description of Kōdayū by Lesseps, a French traveler who met him in Kamchatka in 1788:

> His figure has nothing in it singular, and is even agreeable; his eyes do not project like those of the Chinese; his nose is long, and he has a beard which he frequently shaves. He is about five feet in stature, and is tolerably well made.
> His superiority over his countrymen was calculated to make him be distinguished; but this circumstance has less weight than the vivacity of his temper and the mildness of his disposition. . . . The freedom with which he enters the house of the governor and other persons, would among us be thought insolent, or at least rude. He immediately fixes himself as much at his ease as possible, and takes the first chair that offers; he asks for whatever he wants, or helps himself, if it be within his reach. . . .
> He is possessed of great penetration, and apprehends with admirable readiness every thing you are desirous to communicate. He has much

curiosity, and is an accurate observer. I was assured he kept a minute journal of everything he saw, and all that happened to him.... His repartees are in general sprightly and natural. He employs no concealment or reserve, but tells with the utmost frankness what he thinks of every one.[37]

Lesseps also informs us of the veneration in which Kōdayū was held by his men. We can only imagine that he was a source of great strength to them during the trials they had already endured. In January 1783 Kōdayū's ship, the *Shinshō Maru*, had set sail from his native port of Ise for Edo with a cargo of rice.[38] The first night out the ship was caught by a severe storm and driven far off its course. For seven months the small vessel wandered about the ocean, and it must have seemed to the crew that they were fated never to see land again, when one day, the fog suddenly lifting, a lookout descried the island of Amchitka in the Aleutians. The overjoyed men made all speed to get ashore, little realizing that this bleak island with its perpetual fog and cold was to be a worse prison than ever was the *Shinshō Maru*.

Four years passed on Amchitka. As companions in their loneliness the Japanese had two Russian fur trappers as well as a number of Aleut natives. When at length a sealing vessel came to transport the furs to Kamchatka, it was decided to take along the surviving Japanese. Of the sixteen original crewmen only nine were left.

Kamchatka proved no great improvement over Amchitka. The Japanese led a wretched existence there, hungry or suffering worse calamities most of the time. This Russian possession was then one of the dreariest places in the world, having fallen into such disrepute that "even its name is hardly pronounced without a mixture of horror and disgust; it is looked upon as a country in which hunger, cold, poverty, in short every species of misery is concentrated."[39] Three more Japanese died in Kamchatka before the rest were removed to Irkutsk in Siberia, the site of the Japanese Language School since 1753.

It seems likely that had it not been for the energy of Kōdayū the surviving Japanese would have spent the rest of their days in Siberia. Three times Kōdayū requested permission to return to

Japan, only to be informed that the Empress desired the Japanese to settle in Russia and become merchants; she herself would give them money for this purpose. Kōdayū was still not daunted. He became friendly with Erik Laxman, a Finnish scholar living in Irkutsk, and interested him in the plight of the Japanese. Laxman agreed to accompany the five remaining castaways to St. Petersburg, there to petition the Empress for authorization to leave Russia. The Japanese were delighted at this turn of events, but just then two of them were taken so seriously ill that they could not make the journey. Thinking they were on the point of death, they both adopted the Russian faith. As Kōdayū explained:

When people die in Russia who have not received the teachings of the Church, they are not buried in holy soil, but are treated much like dead animals. For this reason, when Shinzō was very ill and thought he was certain to die, he was converted to the Russian faith. Then, to his surprise, he recovered, and he bitterly regretted not being able to return to Japan with me.[40]

Kōdayū, his two companions, and Laxman set out from Irkutsk in January 1791 and traveled day and night at the greatest possible speed to St. Petersburg. But the unhappy castaways were doomed to still another delay: three days after their arrival Laxman fell gravely ill, and was forced to remain in bed for three months. Kōdayū's affection for his benefactor made him devote all his energies to tending him—"and thus it was I thought no more about our petition."

It was not until October of that year that Kōdayū was granted an audience with the Empress, but already he was well known to the fashionable world of St. Petersburg. Invitations and presents poured in from all quarters; everyone was desirous of meeting a Japanese, especially so engaging a one. Kōdayū bore these attentions with dignity and amiability, fully living up to his new role of a "noble savage." Certain court officials of a more practical nature began also to consider the benefits that might accrue from trade with Japan, but Catherine herself at first remained very sceptical on this subject. Only after meeting Kōdayū and hearing in detail Laxman's arguments on the great commercial opportunity that repatriating the Japanese might afford did she change her views.[41] In 1792 she issued an edict to the Governor of Siberia directing him to return Kōdayū and his two companions to Japan in the manner outlined by Laxman's memorial. She ordered him further to select certain merchants to go along on the journey, and specified presents that the governor was to offer the Japanese authorities in his own name. Possibly the fear of a rebuff from the Japanese caused the Empress to divorce herself from direct connection with the mission and to order instead that it be placed under the command of an official of minor rank.

The ship *Ekaterina,* under the command of Lieutenant Adam Laxman, the son of Kōdayū's friend, sailed from Siberian waters on September 13, 1792, with the three castaways aboard. The port of Nemuro in Ezo was reached on October 17, and Laxman sent ashore letters in Russian and Japanese announcing the reason for his visit. The local authorities in Ezo were thrown into great confusion by the arrival of these unexpected guests, and advice was frantically sought from Edo. In the meantime, Laxman was hospitably received and even invited to use the governor's bath.

When Laxman's letters were delivered to Matsudaira Sadanobu, he was at a loss what to do.[42] The meaning of the Japanese message was clear in spite of certain faults of orthography: the Russians intended to proceed to Edo and negotiate for trade. Matsudaira, good Confucianist that he was, looked to precedent for guidance. The last attempts by European nations to secure trading privileges in Japan had been made by England in 1674 and by Portugal in 1685. Both nations had been refused, the English because their queen was Portuguese, the Portuguese because their nation was detested as the source of the Christian heresy.[43] In the case of the Russians, however, there could be no question of a Portuguese alliance, and their variety of Christianity was apparently harmless. Moreover, Matsudaira appreciated the Russian kindness in having returned the castaways, and felt that their behavior in the affair had been exemplary. He asked the opinions of three advisers, who variously responded: (1) that the castaways should be accepted and the Russians then ordered to leave at once; (2) that the Russians should be asked to negotiate in Nagasaki; and (3) that Ezo should be opened for trade.[44]

In the end, Matsudaira fell back on another precedent. In 1727, the King of Cambodia had sent presents to the shogun, asking for trade. The presents had been refused, but the Cambodians were issued a permit to enter Nagasaki harbor.[45] Matsudaira felt that the Russians' request was analogous enough to invoke this precedent, and thus he could treat them legally and with the proper etiquette. If the Russians, like the Cambodians, failed to pursue their trade efforts, at least they would not have been insulted by a refusal. If they did seek trade in Nagasaki, there would be time to reconsider when they came. Laxman was accordingly informed that he would have to make his request for trade at Nagasaki, the normal place for dealings with foreigners. The Russian envoy was issued a document permitting him to call at that harbor, and although he was warned that no favorable response could be promised, it seems likely that had he sailed immediately to Nagasaki an agreement might have been reached.* Laxman, however, being reluctant to go beyond the limits of his authorization, decided to return to Russia for further instructions.[46]

During the course of these negotiations, the three Japanese castaways had disconsolately waited for the day when they might be allowed to go back to their homes. Laxman at first refused to part with them until he was received at Edo. He gave in only when the shogunate made it clear that unless the castaways were released on the spot he would have to take them back to Russia with him. By this time one of the three Japanese had died of scurvy.

The Russian ship departed, and Kōdayū, restored to his native land, was again very much a center of attention. He was summoned before the shogun, who examined the books and presents he had brought back and interrogated him about his life in Russia. The

---

* Japanese scholars differ very considerably about the degree of success of Adam Laxman's mission. Some believe that he all but opened Japan to Russian trade; others declare that the permit to visit Nagasaki was only a polite face to the unalterable conservatism of the shogunate. Laxman himself was pleased with his accomplishments, and the Empress Catherine II permitted him to include a Japanese sword in the family coat of arms.

shogun's questions were asked at random, and suggest that he was more interested in displaying his own knowledge of Russia than in learning new things from Kōdayū. The interrogation sometimes took the form: "There is a great clock in the castle tower of Moscow. Have you seen it?" Similar inquiries about the statue of Peter the Great and a famous Muscovian cannon were followed by "Have you ever seen a camel?"[47]

The scribe of the interview between the shogun and Kōdayū was Katsuragawa Hoshū, a physician of considerable attainments who at one time had been given instruction by Thunberg, the Swedish scientist. Dissatisfied with the fragmentary interrogation he had witnessed, Katsuragawa resolved to make fuller use of the knowledge that Kōdayū had gained in the West. Day after day he questioned the former ship's captain about every detail of his experiences in Russia. The ninth volume of his report, for example, contains articles on sleighs, sedan chairs, boats, military equipment, swords, musical instruments, silverware, lacquer, books and printing, hourglasses, compasses, billiards, umbrellas, chess, tiles, glass, soap, and many other subjects.[48]

Certain information that Kōdayū could probably have furnished does not appear in Katsuragawa's book. News of the French Revolution, for instance, must certainly have reached Kōdayū's ears while he waited in St. Petersburg for his audience with the Empress, but no mention of it is made, either because it did not occur to Katsuragawa to ask about such matters or because he was unwilling to include potentially dangerous thoughts in his work.

Within the limitations he imposed upon himself, however, Katsuragawa did a magnificent job of drawing out from Kōdayū's recollections the most comprehensive picture of a European nation yet obtained in Japan. Our respect for Kōdayū's powers of observation is also increased; little of interest in Russia appears to have escaped his eyes. But once he had told his story and demonstrated his proficiency in writing Russian script, there seemed to be little left for him to do. People were of course curious about his experiences, but the government feared he might indiscriminately reveal matters best kept secret. He was given a generous pension

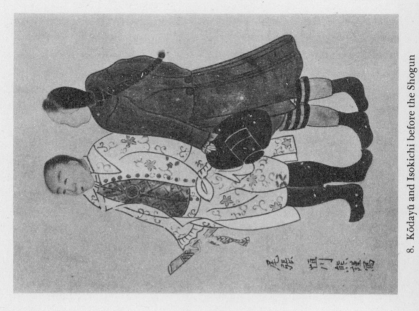

8. Kōdayū and Isokichi before the Shogun

7. Kōdayū in Nemuro

as a reward for his exploits, allowed to marry the wife of his choice, but ordered to retire to the herbary of the shogun. There, a virtual prisoner, he spent the years until his death in 1828 (at the age of 77) quietly cultivating his garden.[49]

In the isolated world of Japan the return of one of her citizens from abroad was an event notable enough to merit discussion for many years. Kōdayū's stories caused the fears about Russian southward expansion to be joined (though not replaced) by an intense admiration for Catherine the Great and her rule. Matsudaira and other important men in Japan waited with impatience for Laxman's ship to appear in Nagasaki harbor. It seemed that a new era might soon commence, one in which Japan would be emerging from her isolation of long standing. Why, the Japanese wondered as the years went by, did the Russians not come back? They could only suppose that the question of trade between the two countries was as important a consideration to the Russians as it was to themselves. The Court of St. Petersburg, however, entertained small hopes of commercial profits from Japan; besides, urgent matters closer to home demanded their attention. The repercussions of the French Revolution and the rise of Napoleon were so keenly felt in Russia that little attention could be spared for the minor matter of trade with Japan.

Not until 1804 did the Russians make use of the permit that Laxman had received. In October of that year, Captain Krusenstern's ship, the *Nadezhda,* bearing Ambassador Rezanov, sailed into Nagasaki harbor to ask for trade. For six months the Russian ambassador was kept waiting while leading figures in the capital debated over the policy to be adopted. Matsudaira Sadanobu, now out of power, attempted to persuade the government to deal with the Russians, and his opinions were shared by most of the enlightened men of the day. It was only after months of uncertainty that the reactionary leadership of the shogunate decided to send the Russians away. The decision aroused sharp outcries; some writers declared that the treatment of the foreign ambassador had been disgraceful, even inhuman. "The Russians must think we are animals!" declared Shiba Kōkan.[50]

It is difficult to estimate precisely the lasting results of the two major challenges from abroad in the late eighteenth century—Benyowsky's warning and the return of Kōdayū. The country remained closed to the foreigners even after these events, and official policy became if anything more reactionary. Yet some political changes had occurred, and thought within the nation had been intensely stimulated. Among the changes we may note the assumption of direct control over Hokkaidō by the shogunate, beginning in 1799, and the establishment of a magistracy (*bugyō*) at Hakodate. Two northern clans were ordered to defend Hokkaidō, the Kuriles, and Saghalien, and exploration parties were sent out by the government to survey these domains.

The rangaku movement had led Japanese chiefly toward the scientific achievements of the West. Contact with Russia made Japan aware that her isolation might soon be broken, and gave new impetus to the movement to make the nation technically and militarily the equal of Europe. However, the powerful conservatism of the leaders of the government resisted all pleas for change. To shake the rigid Confucian structure of Tokugawa Japan would require still greater and more compelling pressure from outside.

4. The Call of the West

The early rangaku scholars had demonstrated that Dutch learning was of value. Later scholars had disputed China's claim to being the center of the world, and by the last decade of the eighteenth century there were some who elevated Europe to the position of Japan's model in all things. To them Europe was that part of the world whose long years of civilization had taught the folly of war, whose people lived in splendid houses free from the dangers of fire and robbery, and whose rulers devoted themselves entirely to benevolent plans for the welfare of their subjects. This portrait of life in eighteenth-century Europe may make us smile—it would certainly have made Voltaire smile—but it was not much further removed from reality than contemporary European descriptions of wise Persians or Chinese. The purpose of such fanciful accounts of distant countries was in both cases the same: to call attention to deficiencies at home by praising the superior ways of little-known foreigners, and thus to create desire for reform and progress.

But before an examination of the intrinsic superiority of Western achievements might be undertaken, it was necessary for the friends of European civilization to prove the great pedigree of the Western nations. Their European equivalents wrote admiringly of the timeless antiquity of China. Timelessness, however, was not the point emphasized by Japanese lovers of European science and precision; most sought to state exactly how much older Europe was. "Which of the nations of the world was first to become civilized?" asked Honda Toshiaki, and himself replied that it was Egypt, whose civilization dated back over 6,000 years. China, he added, was only about 3,800 years old, and Japan could boast of a mere 1,500 years since the Emperor Jimmu founded the country.* It was only to be expected, he concluded, that young nations like China and Japan should fail to exhibit the perfection in their institutions that Europe had long before attained.

The foundation of Holland was most precisely dated by Japanese writers who, unacquainted with the Christian significance of Western chronology, imagined that 1787, or whatever the year happened to be, marked the number of years since that event.[1] Honda, though second to none in his admiration for Holland, did not believe the country was quite so old; the Western date, he asserted, was based on the year of birth of a compassionate and efficient Roman emperor named Alexander, who had devised the calendar, among other notable achievements.

Regardless of the dates employed by the pro-European scholars to prove their theories, the greater antiquity of the West was always invoked to demonstrate its superiority in every way to the East. Shiba Kōkan declared that Germany was the oldest of all nations and added: "The foundation of Japan has been a matter of very recent times. That is why learning here is so shallow, and thinking so lacking in profundity."[2] Honda complained that although six thousand years' experience had gone into the making of every European institution, Japan nevertheless chose to ignore the ways of the West in favor of less highly evolved Chinese usage. Japan was "an isolated island," a small country of no great age or learning. Now was the time to adopt the practices of the "parent nations" of Europe.

* It is curious that Honda gave 1,500 years since the Emperor Jimmu. This figure is surprisingly close to the one modern scholarship has fixed. By traditional dating it would have been almost 2,500 years since the foundation of the country. Honda Toshiaki, *Seiiki Monogatari* in *Honda Toshiaki-shū* (Tokyo, 1935), p. 129.

The argument that "with age comes wisdom" was a clever one, although rather specious in this instance. A more pertinent general argument in favor of Western ways was that of utility. Western writing (or architecture or calendars) was pronounced to be more efficient and convenient, and therefore more desirable, than its Japanese equivalent. Another claim was that some Western customs appeared to contribute to the prosperity of the European nations and therefore ought to be adopted in Japan. But even though such arguments were more plausible than the one based on the comparative ages of civilizations, they were not incontrovertible, and as a last resort the six thousand years of European civilization could always be invoked.

The battle over the merits of Western learning was carried into almost every imaginable field by the rangaku scholars and their associates. Some of the major topics they debated will be considered below, together with the opinions to which they gave rise, particularly those of two champions of the West, Shiba Kōkan (1738–1818) and Honda Toshiaki (1744–1821).*

Painting

Nowhere was the new attitude toward the West more strikingly shown than in the field of painting. During the days of the Portuguese there had been a certain amount of painting in the Western style, chiefly of religious subjects, done in Japan, but little permanent influence had resulted from it, and the main techniques had to be learned afresh in the eighteenth century. *Ukie,* a Japanese adaptation of Western perspective, was first used by the print makers, notably Okumura Masanobu (1686–1764), but for reasons of design rather than to achieve greater realism, later the chief desideratum. In the middle of the eighteenth century, Maruyama Ōkyo (1732–95) founded a school of painting that also borrowed certain European techniques, but neither the innovations of Masanobu nor those of Ōkyo sufficed to make them Western-style

* Honda's views on economics are the subject of the following chapter. Excerpts from his two leading books, *Tales of the West* and *A Secret Plan of Government* (both 1798), are given in the Appendix, pp. 175–226.

62   *The Call of the West*

painters; an untrained critic might be hard put to find anything
specifically un-Japanese in their works.

The first artist to have painted in a thoroughly European manner was Hiraga Gennai (1729–80), a talented eccentric with a
penchant for writing books with indecent titles. Hiraga visited
Nagasaki in 1753 in order to study Western painting, but he soon
extended his interests far beyond this field. Shiba Kōkan recorded
how Hiraga, fascinated by a Dutch zoology book in the collection
of one of the Nagasaki interpreters, sold all of his household possessions, including his bedclothes, in order to purchase the volume.[3] In addition to being a noted mineralogist, Hiraga was one
of the first in Japan to understand the workings of electricity, and
the first (in 1764) to produce asbestos. Though Hiraga was play-
wright, novelist, scientist, mining expert, potter, and political
writer by turns, his greatest contributions were probably in the
field of painting, not so much in the works he himself produced as
in the influence he exerted on younger men.

Hiraga's first successes as a teacher of painting were in Akita,
where he had been invited in 1773 to investigate mining possibilities. Hiraga did not confine himself to prospecting, but gave lessons in Western-style painting to some of the local samurai. When
his first pupil, Odano Naotake (1749–80), appeared for a lesson,
Hiraga asked him to draw a flour dumpling from above. Hiraga
rejected the finished sketch with the words, "You can't tell whether
it's a tray or a cartwheel," whereupon he taught Odano the principles of shading. Odano learned how to delineate objects by light-
ness and darkness of color, rather than by line alone as was customary in Japanese painting. The skill Odano eventually acquired
is apparent in the illustrations that he drew for Sugita's translation
of *Tafel Anatomia,* but his early death prevented him from developing into a major artist.[4]

The daimyo of Akita, Satake Yoshiatsu (1748–85), noting the
progress made by Odano in Western art, asked Hiraga for lessons.
Satake became one of the outstanding painters in the European
style. He proclaimed his view of art: "For painting to be of any
use whatever, it must resemble the object it portrays. If one paints

a tiger in such a way that it looks like a dog, the lack of resemblance becomes comical. Those lofty spirits who claim that one should paint conceptions and not mere forms lose sight of the practical uses of painting."[5] This was an attack on the traditional schools of painting, which regarded the close depiction of real forms as "artisan's work" and insisted that the "spirit" of the subject must be portrayed. But, Satake argued, such a view of art was not practical, not at all what Westerners meant by the term.

Honda Toshiaki, though no artist, was interested in Western painting for its practical value:

"Why is it that European painting differs from Chinese and Japanese painting?" someone asked.

I replied, "European paintings are executed in great detail, with the intention of having them resemble exactly the objects portrayed so that they will serve some useful function. There are rules of painting that enable one to achieve this effect. The Europeans observe the division of sunlight into light and shade, and also what are called the rules of perspective. For example, if one wished to draw a person's nose from the front, there would be no way in Japanese art to represent the central line of the nose. In the European style, shading is used on the sides of the nose, and one may thereby perceive its height."[6]

Ōtsuki Gentaku was more lyrical in his praise of a flower picture by the Dutch artist Willem van Royen, painted in 1725:

In the shapes of the flowers, the forms of the fruits, and the design of the birds and insects, there is such realism in the colors, such precision in the positions, such brilliance, that one feels exactly as if one were seated in some celebrated garden whose exquisite perfumes scented one's sleeves. Ah, the skill with which life has been copied may indeed be called robbing the art of the Creator.[7]

The most important exponent of Western painting in the late eighteenth century was Shiba Kōkan. In *A Record of Kōkan's Repentances*, he describes his career:

Now that I am over seventy years old, I have first realized the errors of the years of my prime. From my boyhood days I used to plan how I might satisfy my ambition, becoming famous by my skill in some special art. I wanted to leave behind a reputation that would survive even after I died. I first thought I would make swords, for swords (the soldier's most precious possession) are passed on to later generations. I thought in this way I would enjoy renown with posterity, but the country is now well governed and at peace, and though famous old swords are still worn by the samurai for ornamental purposes, nobody wants new swords. Besides, the sword is a deadly weapon used for slaughtering people. That is why I repented of that career.[8]

Shiba traced his later employment as a maker of dagger hilts, as an apprentice painter, and finally as a highly successful forger of prints of the *ukiyoe* artist Suzuki Harunobu. Perhaps "forger" is too strong a word, for the composition of the pictures, if not the style or signature, was Shiba's own. But not content with these easily won laurels, he turned to the study of Chinese painting, in which he quickly achieved proficiency. Then as now the Chinese style required the mastery of certain conventions: leaves must not be drawn as an artist saw them, but as described in textbooks of painting; and every element in a landscape was prescribed, from the "dragon's spine" of the mountains to the number of strokes of the brush to be used in depicting the figure of a traveler crossing a tiny bridge.

Shiba had no trouble with these conventions and before long was teaching the secrets of Chinese painting to others, notably the chief officials of the Lord of Sendai. After Shiba had given an illustrated lecture on Chinese techniques that quite dazzled his audience, he was summoned before the lord himself, among whose entourage he created a great impression by drawing in the Chinese style a Japanese man and woman. He was kept painting for twelve hours by the delighted spectators, and a brilliant future was freely predicted for him.[9] These events took place before Shiba was thirty.

In the meantime (in 1763) Shiba had met Hiraga Gennai, from whom he began to learn of Western oil painting. The first subjects he attempted in the European style were landscapes, especially of Mount Fuji. Thus even while his fame as an artist in the Japanese and Chinese styles was reaching its height, he was devoting himself increasingly to Western painting. His original preference for these new techniques apparently arose from his love of Fuji and his desire to paint the celebrated mountain in all its aspects. The Chinese-style painters would have nothing to do with so Japanese

9. Self-Portrait of Shiba Kōkan

a mountain as Fuji, and instead filled their pictures with nameless Chinese mountains copied from old masters or from textbooks. Artists of the traditional Japanese schools of painting were also incapable of portraying Fuji as it actually looked, preferring a vague and misty "delineation of the spirit" of the mountain. For such Japanese artists Shiba had nothing but contempt: "People talk of Japanese painting, but it is derived entirely from China, and even when its exponents are drawing Fuji, Japan's celebrated mountain, the methods they employ are Chinese. Nothing whatever has been invented in Japan."[10]

Shiba noted that cheap prints of Fuji sold at the way stations to Edo were very popular with members of the Dutch embassies to the capital; from this he concluded that the mountain must be the most beautiful in the world. This strengthened his determination to do greater justice to the true beauty of the peak than any previous artist. What he sought in his pictures was not to illustrate the grandeur of nature and the smallness of man or to make any other spiritual point, but to depict as exactly as possible the mountain's appearance. He gave his theory of art:

What is remarkable in painting is that it enables one to see clearly something that is actually not there. If a painting does not truly portray a thing, it is devoid of the wonderful power of the art. Fuji-san is a mountain unique in the world, and foreigners who wish to look upon it can do so only in pictures. However, if one follows only the orthodox Chinese methods of painting, one's picture will not resemble Fuji, and there will be none of the magical quality in it that painting possesses. The way to depict Fuji accurately is by means of Dutch painting.[11]

Western oil painting, he added, was not a polite accomplishment of dilettanti, like Chinese calligraphy, but was "an instrument in the service of the nation."

This remark suggests another use that its admirers discovered in Western art—its educational value. Many Japanese, including the Shogun Yoshimune and Matsudaira Sadanobu, had been impressed by the detailed illustrations found in Dutch botanical and zoological works. In such books it was obviously essential that an object's true appearance rather than its "spirit" be shown. Shiba and Honda were also struck by the pedagogic use made of symbols in Western art. Shiba related how the Dutch taught morality with their symbols (*zinnebeelden*), and Honda was at great pains to unravel the symbolism of a Russian map:

There are human figures on this Russian map. The woman is the Empress Ekaterina. There is also a letter E with plants sprouting from it like an aureole. This must mean that the light of virtue is cast on the four continents from the E. The four nude figures each represent a continent, and this means that all the continents will in the future belong to Russia. To have presented a map with this significance to the Japanese officials was a bold plan of the Russians to test whether they could conquer Japan.[12]

Honda was certainly extracting the full meaning of each symbol!

Painting became for such men a practical means to an end rather than "art for art's sake." This didactic view of the purpose of art was closer to the views of the Confucian moralists than to those of eighteenth-century European painters (who were enchanted with the decorative Chinese art), but Honda and Shiba would have been pained to be told so. Chinese painting had become for Shiba no more than a set of artistic clichés; to him only Dutch art possessed the vitality that brought it close to the lives of the people. Honda went a step further in pronouncing it the best medium for popular instruction, contrasting Dutch books of information illustrated by explanatory diagrams with the Chinese and Japanese tradition of esoteric learning passed down from teacher to pupil.

One of the works to which Honda referred was the *New and Complete Dictionary of the Arts and Sciences* (1769)[13] of Egbert Buys, a book of great importance in Shiba's career. When, about 1780, he began the study of Dutch, at first with Maeno Ryōtaku and later with Ōtsuki Gentaku, he went over those parts of Buys' encyclopedic dictionary that dealt with the arts.[14] This study enabled him in 1783 to rediscover the art of engraving, lost in Japan since the days of the Jesuit missionaries. Although Shiba's engravings had the merit of being pioneer experiments, they were judged to be far inferior to Dutch ones. Matsudaira Sadanobu accordingly sent a protégé to Nagasaki in 1799 to learn the art directly from the Dutch. This man was so successful in his maps of the world that Matsudaira gave him the sobriquet of Aōdō—"Hall of

11. Oil Painting by Shiba Kōkan

Asia and Europe"—and it is by the name of Aōdō Denzen that this first great Japanese engraver has since been known.[15]

Shiba used often to visit the Dutch embassy while it was in Edo. On one of these occasions the factory director Isaac Titsingh, who contributed so much to the development of scientific interest in Japan, gave Shiba a copy of the *Great Painter's Book*[16] by Gerard de Lairesse, which caused Shiba to plunge deeply into the study of oil painting. Apart from the help he received from Hiraga Gennai, it is not clear just what training he had. Another writer described the training of a Dutch painter thus: "The Red-Hairs are extremely proficient in painting. Everyone who learns this art first studies carefully the anatomies of men and women and learns to draw naked people. Later they draw clothed people as well."[17] This may have been the procedure Shiba adopted. In any case, he decided in 1788 to visit Nagasaki in the hope of improving his knowledge of Western painting. He visited a group of Japanese artists who were experimenting with oils and pronounced their work to be very poor.[18] After he had returned to Edo, he described his journey in a diary illustrated with delightful little drawings in the Japanese style, as if Shiba thought his first manner better suited to an informal narrative than the painstaking accuracy of the Dutch style.

Shiba continued to paint until the end of his life, although his main interest shifted first to science and then to philosophy. His reputation as a painter is today very high, and his pictures are proudly displayed by museums. The dispassionate observer might find his works interesting rather than beautiful, but his technical skill is quite evident. Shiba's work is also important because of his influence on many later Japanese artists, including Hokusai (who in turn influenced the French impressionists, to make the circle of borrowing complete). Whatever one may think of contemporary Japanese painting in the Western style, it is clearly the descendant of Shiba's experiments and of his passion for usefulness and truth.

Writing

During the period 1592-1614 the Jesuit Mission Press had issued a number of Japanese books, for the most part religious tracts, printed in Roman letters. Like much else that had come with the Portuguese, however, the Western alphabet had faded from the memory of the Japanese by the late eighteenth century. It is true that Arai Hakuseki, in one of his accounts of interviews with the Italian priest Sidotti, had written in 1713 of the simplicity and excellence of the alphabet,[19] but it was only with the growth of Dutch studies that Western writing became a matter of great interest to Japanese intellectuals. The pioneer work was the *Tales of Holland* (1765) by Gotō Rishun, in which the alphabet was given in normal print, script, and Gothic letters, together with a brief description.[20] The ease with which the alphabet might be learned was extolled in Ōtsuki's *Ladder to Dutch Studies* (1783). One essay in *Miscellaneous Chats about the Red-Hairs* (1787) by Morishima Chūryō attacked the use of Chinese characters as a method of reproducing the sounds of Japanese. Morishima emphasized how foolish the Dutch thought the Japanese system of writing, a serious accusation to the increasingly self-conscious Japanese:

> In a Dutch book that describes the customs of all countries, the use of Chinese characters is ridiculed in these terms: In China a character is used for every object and thing. Some characters have only one meaning, whereas others are used to express ten or twenty ideas. There are probably tens of thousands of them. Even though the natives of China study them day and night, so earnestly that they forget about sleeping and eating, they are unable to learn in the course of a lifetime all the elements in their country's writing. This means that few people can easily read books written in their own tongue. This is the height of the ridiculous. In Europe, twenty-five letters are not considered inadequate.
> I believe that in the olden days writing was simple, and no characters were ever used. In later times, Chinese characters were borrowed to indicate the fifty sounds of Japanese. In subsequent generations Chinese characters came to be used for meaning as well as sound, and the national custom of using only a few easy characters was abandoned in favor of the complicated and troublesome Chinese system. Why was this?[21]

The distinction drawn by Morishima between the spoken sounds of Japanese and the symbols used to represent them is a fundamental one in the history of the language. As he stated, Japanese sounds were first written by using Chinese characters phonetically; from these phonetic signs was evolved the Japanese syllabary, or *kana*. But the use of characters to express both Japanese and Chinese words is very old. A very rough analogy may be made between the use of Roman letters to represent the sounds of old English, and the increasing adoption of words from the Latin language to make modern English. Just as some English scholars chose to display their learning by the use of difficult Latin expressions and allusions, so Japanese scholars did with corresponding Chinese terms. Similarily, there were both Englishmen and Japanese who wrote their serious works in the classical language, finding the native tongue incapable of all the desired nuances.

The attack on the use of Chinese characters in part reflected the generally anti-Chinese sentiments of the advocates of European learning. Honda, for example, decried those scholars whose reputation for learning was based entirely on their ability to read Chinese characters. He said that the amount of time required to learn the tens of thousands of characters could be put to better use. "Instead of attempting to win a name as a scholar by one's mastery of Chinese characters, it is more sensible to use our Japanese kana and to concentrate on the meaning."[22]

The Japanese party of exploration that visited the Kuriles in 1786 was impressed by the ease with which the Russian alphabet could be taught to the natives, and the advantages of an alphabet for pedagogic purposes were often mentioned by progressive-minded persons. Shiba felt that the restrictions on learning imposed by the necessity of first mastering the complicated (and, for Japanese, superfluous) Chinese characters had prevented the development of science in Japan.

Human beings from the age of two can say "Papa" and "Mama." As they grow up, they naturally acquire familiarity with many words. No one has to study how to pronounce the sounds of *tenchi*, but no one can read the characters for the word without learning them. Chinese characters are used in both China and Japan, and without studying them it is impossible to read books or to understand the teachings in the classics. However, in Japan the pronunciation that is employed is basically the native one. Ordinary conversations are invariably in native words, and there are no characters for many of the expressions.

The Western nations, instead of characters, use signs that merely indicate the pronunciation. Is it not a waste of time to read books first without understanding the meaning and only then to ask a teacher about

it? In the West they use the sounds of their own language as the basis
of writing, and they have but to look at a book if they wish to study the
principles of heaven and earth. It is like reading Japanese kana. No
distinction is made between elegant and common language. One can
learn all the fundamental principles without a teacher.[23]

Shiba showed his acquaintance not only with Western script but
with the Korean, Manchurian, and Indian alphabets. It was apparently his view that each nation should have an alphabet (or
syllabary) of its own. For the Chinese, the use of characters might
be most practical, but for the Japanese the native kana was greatly
to be preferred, since it suited the words of ordinary speech much
better than any other system. Honda Toshiaki, who also advocated
the use of kana in preference to Chinese characters, felt that the
Western alphabet was still better. For one thing, the kana signs
were twice as numerous as the letters of the alphabet, which made
them less convenient. For another, the kana could not represent all
possible sounds, unlike the versatile alphabet. Most important, the
alphabet was used by almost all the countries of the world, and
was thus better suited than any more localized system to the needs
of a nation with international trade.

In Honda's view Japanese writing, like Japanese painting, was
an invitation to dilettantism instead of a practical tool. He wrote:

If a careful study is made of their system of writing and ours, it will become apparent which is correct and which false. The failings in our way
of life cause people to spend most of their time in idle and elegant pursuits, the number of which constantly increases. They are forgetful of
themselves, and when they reach old age it is too late for them to repent.
It was fortunate for the Westerners that they foresaw this eventuality
and took steps to avoid a system of writing so profitless to the nation.[24]

The struggle to eliminate the use of Chinese characters is still
going on today, 150 years after the pleas of Honda and Shiba were
first written, with not much greater chance of success than before.
The chief obstacle in the path of pure kana or romanized script
would appear to be the enormous number of homonyms originally
borrowed from the Chinese, but which are now as much a part of
normal Japanese as, for example, "electrical" or "moment" are of
English. The advocates of native learning attempted to purify the

language of Chinese-derived words and thus remove this obstacle, but the results are as startling as if the English words given above were to be replaced by "amber-crafty" or "eye-blink," words of a purely native character.

At the end of the eighteenth century the use of Western script was restricted to a small number of enthusiasts. Shiba was fond of signing his paintings "K. Shiba," in the Western manner, and other artists used Dutch words, sometimes in meaningless combinations as decorative elements in their works. Ordinary people regarded Western writing as something outlandish and utterly bewildering. Captain Vasili Golownin, a Russian who was captured by the Japanese in 1811, recorded:

> They considered a specimen of Russian writing as great a curiosity as an inscription in Japanese would be looked upon in Europe, and shewed us a fan upon which were inscribed four lines of a popular Russian song, signed by a person named Babikoff, who, it appeared, had visited Japan along with Laxman. Though these lines must have been written twenty years before we saw them, yet the fan was as clean and fresh as if perfectly new. The owner kept it wrapped up in a sheet of paper, and set so much value upon it that he would scarcely suffer it to be opened.[25]

Thus the practical Western script managed to furnish yet another amusement for the Japanese dilettanti.

Books

It is not surprising that there are but few references to European belles lettres in the writings of Honda, Shiba, and others of their time. Dutch novels or plays would have been far too difficult for the average rangaku scholar to understand.[26] Besides, the emphasis was always on the practical value of Western learning, and this might have been difficult to establish in the case of light fiction. Honda even denied that such books existed: "The custom in Europe is to consider utility to the state the first essential. There is accordingly an academy that examines all books before they are printed in order to ensure that nothing of a frivolous or indecent nature is published."[27]

Shiba, however, was familiar with one work of Western literature, *Aesop's Fables*. This famous book had first appeared in a

Jesuit-sponsored translation of 1593, but like other publications of
the Portuguese period, it was no longer known in the eighteenth
century when Shiba discovered a copy in the Lord of Kii's library.
He translated a few of the fables into Chinese and made up others
in Aesop's manner.[28] The particular appeal of the fables for Shiba
—he said, but we may not believe him—lay in their didactic value,
their use as "symbols." In this way he managed to salvage something practical from an otherwise merely entertaining book.

Part of another Western literary work was known to Hirazawa
Kyokuzan, who heard the following tale while he was in Nagasaki:

Some ten years ago a ship was stranded on an island, and two men of
the crew went ashore to look for water. There they encountered a giant
over ten feet tall with one eye in the middle of his forehead. The giant
was glad to find the two men. He seized them and took them off with
him to a rocky cavern. The giant sealed the entrance to the cave with a
huge boulder. Inside there was another giant, the mate of the first one.
The cave was spacious, with cracks in the rock serving as windows. There
were many beasts inside.

One of the giants went out, and the opening was shut as before. The
other giant caught the two men and stared at them for a long time. Suddenly he seized one of them and began to eat him from the head down-
ward. The other man looked on in terror and astonishment as though
he were watching demons in a nightmare. He could not think how he
might escape. While the giant was devouring half of the first man, the
other covered his face and could not bear to look. The giant then fell
into a drunken sleep, snoring like thunder.

The man pondered how he might safely escape. Finally he made up his
mind and gouged out the giant's eye with his dagger. The giant let out
a great cry and ran wildly about in his rage, groping around for the man,
who was lying flat on the floor of the cave. The giant, unable to find the
man because of his blindness, opened the entrance to the cave a little and
drove out the animals. One by one he let them out, apparently hoping
by this means to catch and kill the man. The man was trapped, but he
quickly caught hold under the belly of a huge boar. The giant let the
animal out, not realizing the trick that had been played on him. The
man was able to escape to his ship, which at once set sail.[29]

Hirazawa was relating this bit of the *Odyssey* as the actual experiences of a certain man, but he was not wholly inclined to believe
the tale. According to Western atlases he had consulted, there was
indeed a land of giants, but no mention of their being cannibals.

It is interesting to speculate how Homer's story found its way to Nagasaki in 1774. Probably it was told to the Japanese by one of the more literate Dutch factory employees, but perhaps it had arrived in a more complicated way across the breadth of Asia. Hirazawa claimed not only to have heard this version of the Polyphemus episode, but also to have read less elaborate variants of it in books of travels and strange tales. It was the most likely type of European literature to be rendered into Japanese; the first translation of a European novel (completed in 1850) was the *Record of Wanderings* "written by an Englishman, Robinson Crusoe."[30]

With few exceptions, however, the books imported to Japan up to the end of the eighteenth century were of an obviously practical nature. Among the most popular works were the dictionary of Buys mentioned above, and the Chomel *Encyclopaedia,* a copy of which Titsingh gave to one of the interpreters. In later years Sugita Gempaku and other outstanding rangaku scholars began a translation of Chomel's work, but after thirty-five years of hard work the project was finally abandoned.

The principal interest was in Western scientific books, as is clear from an account of an auction of the effects of a Dutch merchant attended by the interpreter Nishi Zenzaburō and some of his colleagues in 1762. Although they bought a number of souvenirs, they failed to acquire any of the auctioned books, even though these included a sea atlas, dictionaries, law books, and Kaempfer's *History of Japan.*[31] Apparently the only books that Japanese desired at the time were works of medicine, natural history, astronomy, and physics. By the end of the century there were quite good collections of scientific European works in different parts of Japan, including one begun with some qualms by Matsudaira Sadanobu:

I began about 1792 or 1793 to collect Dutch books. The barbarian nations are skilled in the sciences, and considerable profit may be derived from their works of astronomy and geography, as well as from their military weapons and their methods of internal and external medicine. However, their books may serve to encourage idle curiosity or may express harmful ideas. It might thus seem advisable to ban them, but prohibiting these books would not prevent people from reading them. There is, moreover, profit to be derived from them. Such books and other foreign things should therefore not be allowed to pass in large quantities into the hands of irresponsible people; nevertheless it is desirable to have them deposited in a government library. If there is no one to read them, however, they will merely become nests for insects. I informed the Governor of Nagasaki that if such works were acquired by the government, they would not be dispersed throughout the country, and could thus be consulted if there were any official need of them. This is how it happened that foreign books came to be purchased.[32]

Other libraries were in the possession of individual Nagasaki interpreters, one of whom, Shizuki Tadao (1760–1806), made what was probably the most remarkable translation of the eighteenth century; this was his *Rekishō Shinsho (New Book on Astronomy)*, a textbook on physics and astronomy translated between 1798 and 1803 from the Dutch version of an English work of a century before. Although Shizuki disclaimed being anything more than a "tongue man," his work was no mere translation but a fresh study of all the available material on the subject, designed especially for Japanese readers. In addition to works by John Keill (1671–1721), the author of the original text of the *Rekishō Shinsho*, Shizuki read studies by Newton and Napier in Dutch translation and other European scientific books in Chinese versions. Ōtsuki Gentaku declared Shizuki to have been the most skilled of the interpreters, and the excellence of the *Rekishō Shinsho* would seem to confirm his opinion.

Shizuki distinguished himself also with his translation of part of Kaempfer's *History of Japan*. This section in Kaempfer's text was entitled "An Enquiry, whether it be conducive for the good of the Japanese Empire to keep it shut up, as it now is, and not to suffer its inhabitants to have any Commerce with foreign nations, either at home or abroad."[33] Shizuki's rendering was more simply entitled "On the Closure of the Country," and its purpose was to show that a celebrated European believed it wisest for Japan to continue her policy of isolation. This was perhaps the sole example of a Western book being cited to prove that the traditional Japanese ways were best. It was more commonly assumed that European writers on returning to their countries from Japan wrote accounts ridiculing the backward ways of the Japanese.

It may seem strange that Shizuki, an outstanding scholar of Western science, was at the same time an advocate of national isolation, but no necessary contradiction was involved. Ōtsuki Gentaku, for example, believed that the Japanese must master Dutch learning, but once this had been accomplished no further traffic with the West would be required. Honda's admiration for the West was always tempered by his fear that the foreigners might learn too much about Japan, and he showed himself more partial to isolationism than we would expect of so progressive a man. Shizuki must have shared with these two men the belief that it was essential to preserve Japan's free option as to what she would borrow from the West; opening the country would mean admitting undesirable foreign ideas as well as useful scientific learning.

Shizuki's contributions as a translator were not equaled by any of the other rangaku scholars, and indeed the seeming absence of translations in an age of great curiosity about the West is quite remarkable. Apart from *Tafel Anatomia* and a few officially requested renderings of short geographical and historical works, the eighteenth century did not produce any significant translations. This may be attributed in part to a feeling that all persons seriously interested in the West would learn Dutch, in part to the fear that once the laborious work of translation had been accomplished it would be impossible to have the manuscript printed because of strict government censorship. We know that some translations were circulated privately. Honda, for instance, was so proud of his translation of a Dutch textbook on navigation that he intended to present it to all Japanese ship's captains. He wrote, "It ought to prove the most valuable thing on the ship."[34] But neither this nor any other of Honda's translations enjoyed any wider renown than among the circle of his friends, and such must also have been the fate of Dutch books translated by other scholars. It is perhaps as well for the reputation of some of the rangaku advocates that such works have not been preserved; many of the curious misapprehensions of foreign history and geography current in the eighteenth century must have had their origin in mistakes of translation or interpretation.

The period of haphazard translation was brought to a close in 1803 when the shogunate established an office at the Edo observatory for the translation of Dutch astronomical and surveying works. In 1811 a similar office with more general translation duties was created.[35] From this time on, scientific books were regularly acquired and rendered into Japanese.

A word may be said at this point about the knowledge of European languages other than Dutch in eighteenth-century Japan. By the middle of the century there were no longer any Portuguese interpreters at the Deshima factory, and whatever interest in European languages existed was channeled into the study of Dutch. In 1779, however, when the Shogun Ieharu ordered Maeno Ryōtaku to translate the inscriptions on a set of engravings in his collection, Maeno discovered to his dismay that they were in Latin:

The great lord ordered me to translate the inscriptions on the Western pictures, and I have respectfully undertaken the task. They were made in France, but the text is in Latin, the language from which French was derived. It is both elegant and concise, and capable of expressing profound meanings. Therefore, no one who is not learned, be he French or Dutch, much less from Nagasaki, is familiar with it.[36]

Maeno conscientiously went ahead with his task even though he had few other aids than a Latin-Japanese dictionary some 150 years old. Since he had no knowledge of Latin grammar, his interpretations of the quatrains describing each of the pictures left something to be desired. For example, the Latin word *est* was rendered "animal food," with the imaginable consequences to the sense of the poem. Maeno bravely struggled on, translating the inscriptions into both Japanese and classical Chinese, with which language he thus identified the high cultural level of Latin.

The return of Kōdayū in 1792 meant that there was at least one Japanese quite familiar with the Russian language. He brought with him a number of books, and he may have translated some, though of this we have no record. In 1811 Captain Golownin spoke with a "learned academician" who "employed himself in translating from the Russian a work on arithmetic, published at Petersburgh for the use of the public schools, and which had been brought to Japan by Kodia [Kōdayū]."[37] But even before Kōdayū's time there were Japanese in the Kuriles who knew a little Russian, learned from trappers in the region or perhaps in Kamchatka. When Captain W. R. Broughton visited Ezo in 1796, one of the Japanese who questioned him claimed to have been in St. Petersburg.[38]

Organized instruction in other European languages began in 1808 when the factory director Doeff gave lessons in French to six pupils. In the following year a group of Japanese began the study of Russian and English, and from that time on these languages were regularly studied.[39] In 1826, when Kondō Morishige compiled a list of foreign books in Japan, he enumerated many grammars and dictionaries of English and other non-Dutch European languages, as well as works of science, history, and literature that had been accumulating in the country during the preceding half century.[40] Kondō's impressive list demonstrates how grossly Japanese knowledge of the West before Perry's arrival has been underestimated by some historians.

Religion and Philosophy

If there was one point on which virtually all Japanese intellectuals of the late eighteenth century were agreed, it was the uselessness of Buddhism and the degeneracy of the Buddhist clergy. This attitude is surprising in view of the fact that every person was required by law to be associated with a Buddhist temple, and a man who had spent his life denouncing every aspect of the religion (like Honda Toshiaki) was almost certain to be interred after his death within temple grounds.

Diverse groups such as the Confucianists and the rangaku and native-learning scholars each had different reasons for finding Buddhism so detestable; but common to all was the view that the Buddhist monks were ignorant and lawless. The large numbers of temples and priests would suggest that the religion was in a flourishing state; it was claimed, however, that not one in a hundred of those who took the vows did so from a sincere desire to espouse the principles of the Buddha.[41] According to believers in the supremacy of the native Japanese learning, the foreign character of Buddhism itself made it inevitable that the monks should lead unworthy lives; other scholars felt that the priests' sorry state resulted from their abandonment of the true intent of basically good Buddhist laws. Shiba Kōkan began one of his numerous diatribes on the latter theme with the sentence "Monks nowadays are the idlers of the nation and do not practice the calling of true priests."[42]

When we examine the variety of Shiba's views on Buddhism, they may strike us as a confused potpourri of everyone's criticisms, probably because his habit of grouping together short essays written at different times makes it impossible to follow the chronological development of his ideas. It is interesting nevertheless to observe the tortuous line of his opinions, from careful suggestions for restoring Buddhism's dignity to violent attacks on the religion. He stated, for example, that a proper understanding of Buddha's teachings could benefit the nation greatly. Learning, he said, was the essential requirement of a priest. "He who wishes to become a true minister of Buddha's faith need only have the proper mental qualifications. He need not enter a temple or shave his head."[43] The enlightened priest would not read the sutras for their literal meanings but as symbols of higher truths. This was very demanding, but if priests were recruited among mature, educated men instead of among farm youths, before long there might be great religious leaders who could penetrate to the inner truths and redeem Buddhism in the eyes of the nation.

From this view, found in several of his essays, we move on to this:

Confucianism and Buddhism may briefly be characterized as follows. The former lays down the principles of benevolence, righteousness, decorum, wisdom, and sincerity to guide man in daily living, enjoining him to obey them during his life. The latter views man's life as a brief dream, and teaches him not to worry about a mere fantasy.[44]

Stronger still:

Everyone, high and low alike, should study the Way of the Sages. One should read the *Analects* and the *Great Learning* over and over. People should not study Buddhism. It is a false teaching. The origin of the various Buddhist sects is to be found in the Christianity of the West. This was the foundation for Sakyamuni's teachings.[45]

And to make the confusion complete:

There should be in our divine land no other creed but that of the Great
Goddess of Ise. Buddhism is a heterodox Indian religion and a teaching
foreign to us. It is not the proper creed for the Land of the Gods, and
the nation has been too long in prohibiting it.[46]

There is hardly a statement on religion by Shiba that is not con-
tradicted elsewhere in his writings. In the convolutions of his
thought we can trace the spiritual confusion of a sensitive man
who had been deeply affected by the new foreign learning. Shiba
was perfectly willing to admit the superiority of Western science—
"China and Japan have no science"—and he castigated the Japanese for their emotional, "womanish" preference for the trappings
of religion over the bare truths of science. Yet, however great his
admiration for European learning, and we must remember that
Shiba was not only a painter but an outstanding popularizer of
science, he felt that there was something spiritually unsatisfying in
its teachings. He managed in some way to obtain information
about the Christian religion, thinking that it might form the complement to the scientific knowledge of the West, but Christianity's
superficial resemblances to Buddhism persuaded him that it was
essentially the same religion, later adopted by Sakyamuni and
transmitted to the nations of the East.[47] For a while he considered
the possibility that Buddhism, in spite of the ludicrous errors of
fact in its religious writings, aimed at higher truths not expressed.
In the end he abandoned this idea, summarily rejecting both Buddhism and Christianity as foreign. Confucianism and Shinto attracted him for a time, but the behavior of professional Confucianists alienated him from that philosophy, and he was soon put
off by the primitive nature of Shinto.

After all these unsuccessful attempts at finding a religion or
philosophy that could satisfy his spirit as Dutch learning did his
mind, Shiba fell into a kind of misanthropy that made one Japanese writer liken him to Schopenhauer.[48] He is more apt to remind
us of Heraclitus or one of the other early Greek thinkers in the
specific tenets of his philosophy, and it is quite possible that he
read about their theories in some Dutch work. Shiba believed that
fire was the primordial principle, and that from it had come water.

The primal nature of fire had caused the Shintoists to make the sun their chief goddess, and the Buddhists also identified their central deity, Dainichi, with the sun. In the world formed by the interaction of fire and water, man cut a poor figure: "It is entirely a matter of personal preference that man considers himself the most excellent of creatures."[49] Shiba even contrasted the meanness of man with the cooperation and fairness exhibited by the ants, but man's scientific achievements, which enabled him to measure the grandeur of the universe, distinguished him above other creatures.

> Heaven and earth were formed by the energy of fire and water. These two principles fill space and give life to all things, and all things live in them. Compared with the vastness of the heavens, man does not seem even as great as a tiny insect. Man may imagine that he enjoys long life, but the swiftness with which his life ends may be likened to that of the autumn cicada that knows not the spring, or the mushroom born in the morning that withers by nightfall.
>
> And yet, man is the marvel of creation, for he knows the immensity of the heavens, he has measured earth's limits, and he has traveled to its most distant shores, never ceasing in his running, leaping, moving. Everywhere on the globe grows the insect called man, and his numbers are beyond reckoning. Each of these creatures has eyes, a nose, and a mouth, similar to all others but different, and possesses aspirations of his own. . . . There is no such thing as a friend of the same mind. Though we may laugh together over such a book of idle words as this one, we will soon diverge in our desires. Though we are alike, we are unalike.[50]

At the end of his life Shiba lost interest in all the things that had formerly given him pleasure, and turned to the nihilistic teachings of Taoism. On his deathbed he is reported to have said, "Even if someone wanted a painting, I would not draw it. If a prince summoned me, I would not go. I am weary of Dutch learning, astronomy, and thinking up new inventions. Only Lao Tzu and Chuang Tzu give me any pleasure."[51]

Shiba was typical not only of the more sensitive thinkers of his time but of similar men in the days following the Meiji Restoration of 1868, when the first flush of enthusiasm for the West had given way to disillusion and dissatisfaction. Men in such a state are likely to turn first to old beliefs, as Shiba did, for the wisdom they need in their time of trouble. Shiba was passionately devoted to the new learning and was a great pioneer on its behalf, but though science taught him the potentialities and limitations of man, it did not satisfy his religious end ethical preoccupations. Rejecting one set of beliefs after another, he finally found comfort in the Way which cannot be named.

In sharp contrast with Shiba's twists and turns, we have the direct and positive views of Honda Toshiaki on the subject of religion. He applied to it his universal test: "What use does it have?" In the case of Buddhism there was no doubt in his mind. Japan, already at a disadvantage because civilization had been slow in spreading eastward from its source in Egypt, had suffered from the impact of this religion. "Japan was then a young country, and practical learning had yet to develop. This outside interference further hindered the growth of knowledge. Buddhism usually has the effect of causing people to waste their time in utter ignorance."[52] Honda was particularly severe toward Buddhism, but he also showed little sympathy for the other religious teachings followed in Japan, always because of their lack of practical value for the nation.

There are indeed Confucian books of wisdom, but the scholars derive no use from them. Buddhists read their scriptures, but since it is their practice to chant them in the original Sanskrit, they sound rather like the croaking of frogs. As for Shinto, it is the rule to speak of its profound mysteries, but these do not appear to be of any help to the ordinary people.[53]

Honda's wholesale rejection of traditional Japanese beliefs came from his conviction that conditions in Japan had to be changed. All institutions that contributed to these conditions must therefore be eliminated, and their place taken by the institutions of more successful countries.

In general, one may say that Japan is at a standstill, while Russia is moving ahead. Because of our tendency toward ineptitude in all things, Russia has become master of standstill Japan's Kamchatka. The reason the barbarians of islands east, south, and west of Kamchatka all seem to be attracted like ants to the sweetness of the Russian order is that the Russians have made capital out of their experiences of struggle and toil during the past 1,500 years.[54]

The only religion that escaped Honda's severe criticism was Christianity. It is true that he sometimes waved the bloody shirt of the forbidden religion in order to win support for certain proposals, such as his desire to have a clearly defined frontier established between Japan and Russia, but on the whole he was friendly to the Christian religion. He had been informed that important Chinese had adopted Christianity, finding it a religion far preferable to Buddhism, and he wondered if that were not the secret of the prosperity of China's port cities.[55] If so, Christianity would be the one religion with a really practical value.

Though Honda deplored the supposed Portuguese plots to invade Japan, he greatly admired the Catholic priests who had visited the country. He related the history of one of them at some length. "He had been selected by the Emperor of Rome to sail to Japan and to give instruction in the Catholic religion as well as in the principles of natural government. It was not his mission to prepare the people for a conquest of the country, as the Portuguese had done, but to transmit the benevolent and merciful institutions of the Roman emperor."[56] The shogunate had unfortunately refused to heed the priest's words, and after forty years of imprisonment in Japan the virtuous foreigner died without having accomplished anything. Honda believed that the "principles of natural government" that the priest had sought to convey to the Japanese might yet serve as a remedy for the otherwise hopeless situation prevailing. "Whoever puts it into effect will leave a name for all generations to come as a great leader. The benevolent and merciful system of the Emperor of Rome will naturally be founded. If this happens, the two nations will enjoy friendly relations, ships will go back and forth between them, and considerable profits will accrue to both countries." Honda concluded his account with the words "It was unfortunate and unkind that this person, who could have helped the nation, was cruelly neglected during the forty years he lived in Japan."[57]

Honda's admiration for Christianity was not based on any detailed knowledge of its theology, but rather on the fact that it appeared to be the faith of prosperous and well-governed foreign nations. The only Christian work he quoted was the *Seven Conquests* by Didacus de Pantoja (1571–1618), an anecdotal account written in Chinese about virtuous persons who conquered the seven sins and wicked ones who did not. From this book Honda apparently learned little more than that in the West no man, not even an emperor, might have a concubine; this, he felt, was eugenically most desirable.* But neither Honda nor any of the other scholars of foreign learning were really much interested in Christian doctrine.

It remained for the Shinto propagandists, especially Hirata Atsutane (1776–1843), to employ the theological resources of Christianity in the general attack on Buddhism. Hirata, who will be dealt with at greater length in a later chapter, praised the European nations as splendid places, "which have established the limits of human knowledge and recognize the grandeur of God."[58] In this fact, he believed, was to be found the true meaning of Western learning, and not in scientific achievements. This view was not shared by most of the enthusiasts for Dutch learning, however, who turned to the West for practical information rather than for transcendent truths.

Science

The early interest in Dutch medicine had lesser counterparts in the Japanese studies of botany, zoology, physics, and other European sciences. Some of these have already been discussed; of the others, perhaps the most interesting are astronomy and geography.

* Honda believed that in the West it was always felt desirable for relatives (the closer the better) to marry in order to keep the good qualities of a family intact. "If no suitable spouse may be found within a family, and a person from another family is taken, people declare that this calamity bespeaks the wrath of God. It is usual in such cases among the lower classes to point the finger of scorn at such marriages. Thus, even if a family has a great many children, it is attempted not to contract marriages more remote than with cousins, or with aunts and uncles if their age is suitable. This is considered to be destiny, and such marriages are praised all the more highly." Honda Toshiaki, *Seiiki Monogatari* in *Honda Toshiaki-shū* (Tokyo, 1935), p. 188. Honda's disciple Mogami Tokunai quoted the *Seven Conquests* approvingly, though he imagined that laughter was one of the seven deadly sins. See Minakawa Shinsaku, *Mogami Tokunai* (Tokyo, 1943), pp. 234–35.

The most important development in Japanese astronomy of the late eighteenth century was the introduction of the Copernican theory. As early as 1778 the philosopher Miura Baien (1723–89) was informed by one of the Nagasaki interpreters of the theory adopted in the West "that the sun does not move and the earth is not stationary," and in 1788 Shiba learned the same thing on a visit to Nagasaki.[59] Five years later he published a popular account of the Copernican theory; his ideas were developed in successive works until the *Explanations of Copernican Astronomy* appeared in 1808.* A preface to the work describes the distrust with which the Copernican theory was at first received in Japan, and Shiba's dominant role in persuading intellectuals of its validity.[60] Honda mentioned how, when he saw Shiba's first description of the Copernican theory, he was reluctant for a time to accept the new idea, but after consulting older works of astronomy he perceived its correctness. Once having entered the circle of believers, Honda poured scorn on those who still clung to the traditional astronomical conceptions.

Everyone in Europe now knows about this theory, which was first given to the world some 280 years ago, but Chinese and Japanese do not even dream of such things. I can understand why people might suppose that the sun causes the day and the night, but some declare that every day a new sun comes into being, travels from east to west, and then disappears; others think the sun burrows under the earth each day to reemerge in the east and travel westward. Even the most learned men of Japan have wasted their time because they were unable to accept the truth.

In recent years, however, European astronomy has been introduced to Japan. People have been astonished by the theory that the earth is actually whirling about, and no one is ready to believe it. In Japan even great scholars are so amazed by this notion that they assert, "If the earth were in fact spinning about, my rice bowl and water bottle would turn over, and my house and storehouse would be broken to bits. How can such a theory be true?"

It is entirely to be expected that disbelievers are by far the majority.

---

* This was the *Kopperu Temmon Zukai.* In the earlier *Oranda Tensetsu* Shiba wrote as if he believed the sun moved around the earth, and only in conclusion did he express preference for Copernican astronomy. See *Oranda Tensetsu* (Edo, 1796), II, 5–12. By 1808 he was fully convinced of the newer theory.

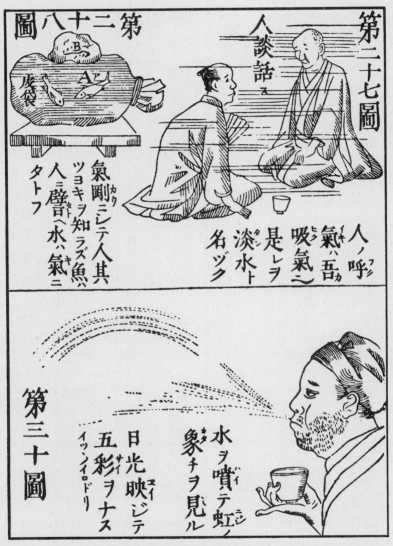

12. A Page of Shiba's Scientific Demonstrations

Even in Europe the Copernican theory was not at first accepted; only after outstanding men had resolutely subscribed to it was everyone finally converted.[61]

The opposition to Copernican astronomy came principally from reactionaries who were against any new ideas, particularly foreign ones, and from Buddhists, some of whom continued to write anti-Copernican treatises until late in the nineteenth century. Among scientifically-minded men, however, the Copernican theory found far readier acceptance in Japan than it had in Europe. This was partly because, as G. B. Sansom has said, "the beliefs of China and Japan were neither geocentric nor anthropocentric,"[62] and partly because the prestige of Western science was such that any of its theories, however strange or distasteful, was certain to find ready acceptance among all the leading intellectuals. By 1811 even the officials in remote Hokkaidō with whom Captain Golownin spoke accepted the Copernican theory,[63] and it was not long before Japanese were claiming to have invented the theory themselves.*

For most Japanese, as Honda complained, astronomy was no more than a means of improving the calendar. By contrast, his own great interest in the science arose from his desire to perfect the art of navigation in Japan, a knowledge of which was essential if Japan were to trade with the far-flung nations of the world.† Geography was also necessary to the would-be navigator, and the two sciences were very closely associated in Honda's writings.

Honda's geographical information was better than that of most of his contemporaries, but it suffers from curious weaknesses, all apparently connected with his propaganda for empire. Chief of

* The scholars of native learning, equating the sun with the deity Ame-no-minaka-nushi no kami, "the god who rules the center of the heavens," claimed that the Copernican theory was one of their most ancient beliefs. Other scholars, such as Asada Gōryū, claimed to have discovered the theory independently. See Tōkyō Kagaku Hakubutsukan, *Edo Jidai no Kagaku* (Tokyo, 1938), pp. 7, 57; and Boleslaw Szczesniak, "The Penetration of the Copernican Theory into Feudal Japan," *Journal of the Royal Asiatic Society*, 1944, p. 58.

† Honda, along with his pupil Sakabe Kōhan, is often credited with founding on a scientific basis the studies of astronomy and navigation in Japan; he also holds a place in the history of Japanese mathematics. See David E. Smith and Yoshio Mikami, *A History of Japanese Mathematics* (Chicago, 1914); and Hayashi Tsuruichi, *Wasan Kenkyū Shūroku* (Tokyo, 1937), II, 102–3.

these was his "science of latitudes and longitudes," which he thought enabled one to predict exactly the climate of a place merely by knowing its latitude. From this premise he argued, for example, that Kamchatka must have the same climate as England, and hence that it could be developed into as thriving a country. It is hard to say whether this was a genuine error on his part arising from a lack of information, or merely a device for persuading people of the truth of his thesis. Honda also vastly overrated the size and desirability of certain islands he had marked for Japanese expansion; this error seems more clearly attributable to his propagandistic efforts.

In general, if we can believe the writings of Honda and his fellow opponents of vulgar errors, people in Japan at the end of the eighteenth century had only the vaguest notions of geography. It was still almost universally believed that the earth was flat. China and Korea were regarded as actual though distant countries; Russia lay on the borders of reality, somehow threatening Japan to the north, and such countries as India and Holland were like the "Island of Devils" of the Japanese storytellers. The information about European countries that was likely to filter down to the ordinary people was of such a nature as to confirm their belief in the fantastic character of those remote lands. Hirazawa Kyokuzan believed that in England the dead were not buried but stored in mountain caves "where they do not rot even after a thousand years, so that their descendants can recognize them." He also heard (a distortion of the story of St. Patrick and the snakes of Ireland?) that there were no rats in England; those that came ashore from ships died as soon as they touched English soil.[64]

Against a background of such tales, whatever their origin, Honda's geographical knowledge appears quite respectable. We do not know all the sources of his information, but he was certainly familiar with Johann Huebner's *Geographie,* a famous eighteenth-century work that had gone through many editions in Europe. What he knew of the Kuriles and other northerly regions, on the other hand, was learned either from his own experiences or from those of his friends, and was thus of greater significance in the history of geography in Japan. At a time when several European expeditions had failed to determine whether Saghalien was an island or was connected to the north with the mainland of Asia, the Japanese explorer Mamiya Rinzō (1775–1844) discovered the channel that makes Saghalien an island.* Maps by Japanese cartographers were eagerly sought by Europeans when such expeditions as Captain Broughton's called at Hokkaidō. Gradually, under the leadership of such rangaku enthusiasts as Honda, geography developed from a collection of strange stories about faraway lands to a science that could command the respect of Europeans.

* Mamiya and two fellow geographers, Mogami Tokunai (1754–1836) and Takahashi Kageyasu (1785–1829), are dealt with at length in Chapter 6.

5. Honda Toshiaki's Economic Theories

The biographical information we have about Honda Toshiaki (1744–1821) is disappointingly limited even for an age as reticent about the details of individual lives as his was. Our chief source is a short account in the nature of an encomium written in 1816 by Uno Yasusada, one of his pupils.[1] Uno bestowed on his teacher the usual praiseworthy traits of virtuous Japanese: Honda had simple tastes, wore thin clothing in winter, and slept only four hours a night. Uno failed, however, to discuss matters that interest us far more, such as the circumstances of the composition of Honda's chief works, or the relation of Honda to other figures of his time.

We are told that Honda was born in the northwestern province of Echigo, where his father, a samurai, had taken refuge after killing a man. The geographical factor in Honda's life was important, for his interest in the northerly regions was first inspired by stories he heard from people of his province who had visited Hokkaidō or who had farmed there during the summer. In a memorial written in 1792, Honda stated:

I was born in northern Echigo, and when I grew up I used to mix with sailors, even occasionally going to sea with them. I became well acquainted with the geography of Ezo and with the customs and nature of the

Ainu. From that time until now, when I am fifty years of age, I have
never ceased day or night to think of ways of developing the region.[2]

As a second son, Honda was under less obligation than the eldest
to remain in Echigo with his family and to carry on its line. He
appears to have had early ambitions of engaging in public affairs,
and to this end he decided to go to the capital. At the age of eighteen he arrived in Edo, and soon afterward began the study of
mathematics under Imai Kanenobu, heir to the school of Seki
Kōwa, greatest of all Japanese mathematicians. He also studied
astronomy and fencing. By the age of twenty-three he had become
proficient enough to open a school of his own in the district of
Otowa. The subjects he taught were mathematics, astronomy,
geography, and surveying.[3]

He apparently lost interest in these sciences, however, and en-
trusting the work of teaching at his school to his pupil Sakabe, he
devoted himself almost entirely to political studies. He traveled
widely throughout Japan examining geographical and social conditions, supply problems in various regions, and the general situation in the country. Personally coming into contact with bandits
and highwaymen, he learned of the circumstances that forced men
to turn to such pursuits, and he evolved plans both for preventing
losses at their hands and, more important, for eliminating the
causes of banditry itself. Everywhere he found poverty and misery,
with their attendant evil of infanticide. The one solution he
thought of was trade, not only within the country but with the
nations of the entire world.

The first step toward achieving the kind of trade that Honda
sought was a knowledge of navigation. To improve his ability in
this science, he studied Dutch, becoming proficient enough in the
language to be able to read and translate a work on navigation. In
his books Honda referred constantly to Dutch learning, but we do
not know how much he actually knew of the language. None of his
longer translations survive, but certain mistakes in Dutch that he
made in his other works suggest that his grasp of the language was
not very secure. In any case, he was presumably capable of handling the short descriptions linking navigational tables. His advice

to would-be students of Dutch was perhaps revealing of his own limitations: he said that it was best to begin with mathematical texts, for then one could always make some sense of the numbers at least.

Honda does not appear to have had any close friends among the rangaku advocates. His correspondence is directed instead to two liberal Confucian scholars of Mito, Tachihara Suiken (1744–1823) and Komiyama Fūken (1764–1840).[4] In his letters to them Honda expounded his views on the problems that concerned him most, and in return he received their criticism. Tachihara, the more distinguished of the two, was the general supervisor of the Mito historical bureau, which was then compiling the *Dai-Nihonshi,* a monumental history of Japan. Honda and his friends also exchanged books, Tachihara apparently having even sent him prohibited Christian works that had been preserved in Mito. In 1799 at their request, Honda secretly made a journey to Hitachi, where he drew up a program for increasing local prosperity.[5]

In 1801 Honda went to sea on a tour of the north as captain of the *Ryōfū Maru.* This may not have been his first journey to this region. Apart from the jaunts he took as a young man, he may have gone as far as Kamchatka in 1784, as his biographer Uno claimed.[6] In 1785 he persuaded the shogunate expedition to the northern islands to take him along, but at the last moment he fell ill and Mogami Tokunai took his place. In any case, his enthusiasm for the north, which earned him the pen name of Hokui— "northern barbarian"—seems to have abated considerably after his voyage on the *Ryōfū Maru.* The account of his journey, which we might expect to be filled with descriptions of the wonders of the north, is little more than a ship's log. This sudden change of feelings, if indeed there was one, may have stemmed from his disillusionment after actually seeing the bleak islands he had so often praised. In 1808, when it was suggested that he make another trip to the north, Honda, pleading his advanced age, requested that Mogami again go in his stead.

Honda entered the service of the Lord of Kaga in 1809 in the capacity of adviser on foreign affairs. Among other duties, Honda built warship models that he displayed and operated on a theatrical stage within the castle enclosure. The Lord of Kaga was apparently very interested in Honda's ideas and continued to support him until 1816, although Honda actually left his service after only six months. Many samurai from Kaga went to study with Honda in Edo; the most famous was Zeniya Gohei (1771–1852), who became an outstanding advocate of foreign trade and, less prudent than his teacher, died in prison.*

Little was recorded concerning Honda's personal life. Nothing, not even her name, is known of his wife. He had a daughter, Tetsu, who was proficient in Confucian studies (unlike her father) and showed a special talent for music.[7] Honda died in Edo in 1821. A century after his death, on February 11, 1924, his merits were at last recognized by the Japanese court; as a result of the favorable attention his writings were beginning to attract at that time, he was posthumously granted a junior fourth rank.

During his lifetime and for many years afterward, Honda's chief writings were known only to a small group of friends and students. He also wrote a few memorials to Matsudaira Sadanobu in which he outlined his views on various problems, including the development of Ezo, but these naturally had no wider circulation than the manuscripts of his other works. Honda was accordingly little known in his time, and one comes across few references to him in nineteenth-century accounts. In 1888 a version of his *Tales of the West (Seiiki Monogatari)* was published as a supplement to a Tokyo newspaper,[8] and three years later the first printed edition of his *A Secret Plan of Government (Keisei Hisaku)* appeared. Others of Honda's manuscripts have been printed in recent years, but a complete edition of his writings does not exist.[9]

The dating of Honda's writings is sometimes difficult, since they were not printed during his lifetime. Most of them were written

---

* The direct cause of Zeniya Gohei's imprisonment was his son's ill-fated attempt to develop marshland, but this may merely have been a pretext; his wealth and power, the results of his commercial ventures (including foreign trade) had aroused envy and hostility. See Matsukaze Toshisada, *Zeniya Gohei Shinden* (Kyoto, 1930), pp. 77–80; and Charles David Sheldon, *The Rise of the Merchant Class in Tokugawa Japan* (Locust Valley, N.Y., 1958), pp. 152–60.

in the decade 1790–1800, and his two chief works were completed in 1798. The following is a list of his most important works; they are found in the collection *Honda Toshiaki-shū,* edited by Honjō Eijirō.

Ezo Miscellany (Ezo Shūi), 1789

Views on the Development of Ezo (Ezo Tochi Kaihatsu Guson no Taigai), 1791

Memorial on the Development of Ezo (Ezo Kaihatsu ni Kansuru Jōsho, 1792

Explanation of Natural Government (Shizen Jidō no Ben), 1795

Tales of the West (Seiiki Monogatari), 1798

A Secret Plan of Government (Keisei Hisaku), 1798

Statement on Government (Keizai Hōgen), c. 1800

Waterways (Kadō), 1800

On Ships (Chōkiron), 1801

The economic thought of Honda Toshiaki forms the most important part of his work, in spite of the magnitude of his achievements in the field of science. Unlike his contributions to mathematics and navigation, however, Honda's economic writings remained unknown for many years and exerted no immediate influence on his time. His ideas were perhaps of too great originality to have won favor in any event, but they did not spring into being without antecedents. We must look into the history of economic ideas of the Tokugawa period in order to appreciate Honda's particular contributions.

The Tokugawa Economy

The two factors that dominated all others in the economic and social life of Honda's time were the persistence of peace and the closure of the country. The first of these created the peculiar problems of the era; the second prevented them from being solved. The numerous economic writers of the time (including Honda) never failed to pay tribute to the wisdom of Tokugawa Ieyasu in having established the foundations of a peace lasting for more than two hundred years, but however pleasing this situation might appear, it brought with it serious problems. It was paradoxical that Tokugawa Japan, founded as a military state, should have experienced one of the longest periods of uninterrupted peace that any country has ever known. An even greater paradox was the maintenance of an idle and decadent military class, the samurai, to protect the people from the nonexistent perils of war. The division of the nation into four classes—samurai, farmers, artisans, and merchants (in descending order of importance)—had been officially recognized. The samurai were accorded the highest rank because of their importance in defending the country, but after so long a period of peace, their military function had come to seem almost meaningless.

Scholars attributed to the samurai various other duties, including the instruction and guidance of the commoners, whose ignorance was at first assumed and later encouraged. They were to serve as models of virtue and frugality for the entire nation. But as time went on, the samurai proved themselves unworthy of their high responsibilities. They did not devote themselves in time of peace to the study of the literary arts, but since they were compelled to spend much of their time in Edo, indulged in all the pleasures the capital afforded. They showed few qualms about leaving the farmers on their country estates to get along as best they could without models of proper conduct. Not only did the samurai forfeit their moral leadership of the nation; their extravagant habits frequently caused them to run up heavy debts with the city merchants. If a daimyo* was short of cash after selling his stipend of rice, he would commonly extract more taxes from the already suffering farmers in his domain. This behavior sometimes led to uprisings, especially in the closing years of the Tokugawa period, but on the whole the Japanese farmers were docile and lived in quiet misery.

Most samurai could see no way out of their predicament. Not schooled in the practical realities of business life, they were taught to despise everything that savored of trade as a low seeking after

* The daimyo were, of course, a special class of samurai who ruled over fiefs of varying dimensions. Writers on economics seldom distinguish between the ordinary samurai and the daimyo in their discussions of the military class, and it is sometimes difficult to know whether their statements apply to both groups indiscriminately.

profit. Thus, though they might be so heavily in debt as to feel it necessary to address the merchants they met in the street in terms of great politeness (instead of the brusque tones of the superior), the samurai were convinced by training that all their difficulties were the result of the businessmen's striving for profit; if only everyone would follow their example of placing righteousness before other considerations, all problems would soon be solved. This attitude might be described as properly Confucian, but to a realistic person like Honda it was absolutely infuriating.

The incapability of the samurai cost them their position of leadership in all but name. Preeminence among the four classes naturally did not devolve on the farmers, traditionally considered the second highest class. Although the farmers were always lauded as "the foundation of the nation" and the source of life-essential food and clothing, in practice they were treated far worse than the artisans and merchants, who ranked below them. The farmer was the sole regular taxpayer in Japan, and new measures were constantly being devised to increase the amounts he paid. Although such measures usually assumed the guise of (and may actually have been intended as) benevolent laws to relieve the plight of the suffering tillers of the soil, the farmers' condition grew only worse. They were exhorted to work harder and produce more, but if ever they did enjoy a bumper harvest, the price of rice was likely to be so low as to cancel out most of the profit, and increased taxation would take care of the rest. In addition to their normal woes, the generation of 1770–90 saw an unprecedented series of natural disasters—volcanic eruptions, floods, epidemics, drought—that brought about severe famine conditions.

Yet in the midst of their misery the farmers were incessantly enjoined to abandon their ways of extravagance and self-indulgence. Such admonitions were made in part because of official resentment of any improvement in the standard of living of the farmers, however slight. The discovery that farmers now had mats on their floors drew forth the same cries of horror from eighteenth-century Japanese economists as the unrestrained drinking of tea by English farmers did from English writers.[10] A second cause for com-

plaint about the farmers' extravagance stemmed from the fact that
some of them, finding it impossible to make a living on the soil,
had gone to the cities for employment. This was laid to their love
of luxury rather than to necessity. A century before, Kumazawa
Banzan (1619–91), the great Confucian scholar, had noted, "If
there happen to be one or two rich families among fifty or a hundred poor ones, people are sure to say that the farmers are well-off
and extravagant. . . . There are so many farmers that even if one or
two come from each village and are seen in the cities, they appear
to be numerous."[11]

The discussions by philosophers and economists of the unhappy
lot of the farmers did not go beyond superficial expressions of pity
and the recitation of Confucian platitudes about benevolence and
righteousness. Honda realized how sterile such discussions were,
and attempted to discover some formula for national prosperity
more feasible than the old "Work harder, spend less." There was
perhaps nothing wrong with this time-tested dictum, but except in
the rare instances of capable management of domains by enlightened men, no amount of hard work or thrift on the part of the
farmers seemed to improve their lot: improvement itself was not
necessarily considered desirable.

The third of the classes, the artisans, was the least important and
least discussed. The artisans were classed with the merchants as
"townsmen" (chōnin), and most of the attacks on the merchants
were thus leveled in part at the artisans as well. There was, however, the general feeling that since the artisans actually produced
something, they were not quite as culpable as the profit-grabbing
merchants. The agitation against extravagance was nonetheless directed against the livelihood of the artisans for, apart from certain
imported wares, most luxury goods were produced by this class. On
these grounds a few writers protested against the sumptuary measures of the shogunate, which were, practically speaking, the only
economic policies recognized by the Confucian-minded rulers.
These men believed that the money spent on objects of luxury
went into the hands of craftsmen and was thus not thrown away.

The government has ordered that there be no more gold- or silver-leaf
made. It has also decreed that the manufacture of especially beautiful

toys and dolls be discontinued. Although I speak with trepidation, I believe that this is an inept policy and presently will usher in a decline in Japan. If I may be permitted to conjecture the reasons behind these decrees, I imagine it is the government's deep-seated judgment that luxury in society is the cause of misery, and that to use foil on useless articles such as children's toys is to waste gold and silver. But the persons who are willing to pay high prices for such articles are not poor people, but always great or wealthy ones, and thus it amounts to putting money into circulation.[12]

The modern reader may find little to choose between the proponents of sumptuary laws and those who believed in the public benefits of private extravagance. Honda's attitude was characteristically independent: he felt that it was desirable for a ruler to be liberal in his patronage of the artisans, not merely because this circulated money but because it encouraged the production of fine articles that could serve as suitable material for export.

The merchants, whose position was officially the lowest and who were the target of attack of virtually every lawgiver and philosopher, had managed by the late eighteenth century to rise nevertheless to the position of greatest power. In vain were sumptuary laws levied against them; if they were forbidden to wear silk, they would line their cotton garments all the more gorgeously. The books, theater, and art of the time were all designed to please their tastes. A special philosophy for businessmen was evolved, the so-called "teachings of the heart" (*shingaku*), which preached that it *was* possible for merchants to show benevolence and to shun excessive profit-grabbing.[13] This philosophy did not have any noticeable influence on the ways of most of the merchants, and the criticisms to which they were subjected grew all the more bitter in the late eighteenth century. Hayashi Shihei declared, "Townsmen have no other function than to siphon away the stipends of the samurai," and another writer called them the "weevils of the state."[14] This was a new view of the businessmen; previously they had been thought contemptible because they ran after gain, but not useless.

Although all writers deplored the avarice and general baseness of the merchants, few offered any specific solution to the problem. Some thought the samurai should assume the functions of the merchants, believing that the innate probity and righteousness of the warrior class would protect it against falling into the evil ways of tradesmen. Honda was in favor of this rather naïve proposal, but he extended it to the operation of vital services, not merely by virtuous samurai in place of wicked businessmen, but by the government itself. Only the government, he felt, was qualified to perform such functions. His may not have been an entirely practical answer to the question of what was to be done with the merchants, but it impresses us as more sensible than the moral diatribes of other eighteenth-century writers.

In spite of its faults and inadequacies, the organization of Japan into four social classes was favored by writers of every shade of political belief, from the most conservative Confucianist to dissidents like Honda. Schemes were often brought forward to ensure the maintenance of society along the rigid lines of samurai, farmers, artisans, and merchants, but in point of fact there was a constant mixing of the classes that was impossible to prevent. Farmers drifted into the towns to become artisans and merchants, while the samurai mended their difficult financial positions either by contracting marriage alliances with the merchants or by setting up in trade for themselves. This mobility of the classes was made possible by the fact that the class system was a political expedient and not an article of religious belief. It was possible, though extremely difficult, for the son of the humblest farmer's family to rise to a high position; at the same time the fall from glory of samurai was a feature of Tokugawa history.

Above the four classes stood the government, feudal in origin and still preserving many feudal customs but essentially a modern centralized state. In the early part of the eighteenth century, control of the government was still in the hands of the shogun, a member of the Tokugawa family, which had come into power after the Battle of Sekigahara in 1600. The shogunate exercised varying degrees of authority over the country; in the central part of Japan, close to the seat of its power, there was no question about the finality of its decisions, but often in remote regions in the south or north of the country obedience was given the shogunate to the extent that it was consonant with the plans of the local barons. To control the barons a system known as *sankin kōtai* had been established, under which the various daimyo were required to spend alternate years in Edo, and to leave their families there as hostages. This system had an additional advantage for the shogunate in that it necessitated large expenditures by the daimyo, who were thus forced to maintain establishments both in their provinces and in the capital. These provisions, however, worked greater hardships on the small nobles than on the powerful "outside lords."*

By the late eighteenth century, political power had left the direct control of the shogun and passed into the hands of advisers. The most noteworthy examples of this type of political figure in Honda's time were Tanuma Okitsugu (1719–88) and Matsudaira Sadanobu (1758–1829). It is difficult to make a fair appraisal of Tanuma today. The histories of the period were all written by people opposed to him and desirous of pleasing his successors. He is inevitably referred to as "notoriously corrupt," and certain delightfully ingenuous remarks are attributed to him, such as: "Gold and silver are so precious a treasure that they may scarcely be bought with human lives. If someone is so desirous of serving his government that he will part with even such a treasure, it is clear that his purpose must be loyal. The strength of his purpose may be measured by the size of the present."[15]

Although Tanuma's regime has been characterized as a "government by bribery," and its extravagance is legendary, it seems to have been very like later shogunate administrations. When economic troubles arose, resort was had to the two usual shogunate expedients, sumptuary laws and manipulation of the coinage. The sumptuary laws were quite strict but had little apparent effect, and the currency debasement only caused inflation. Tanuma, however, was not content with these time-honored panaceas for eco-

---

* The "outside lords" (*tozama*) were those who opposed the Tokugawa family at the Battle of Sekigahara in 1600. Those who supported the family were known as *fudai*. The sankin kōtai system is the subject of Toshio Tsukahira's *Feudal Control in Tokugawa Japan* (Cambridge, Mass., 1966).

nomic ills. Marsh reclamation was begun under his orders, and
the settlement of Ezo projected.[16] Tanuma was also interested in
how the West might help Japan. He extended his patronage to
Hiraga Gennai's European studies. Later he requested the Dutch
to send carpenters from Batavia to instruct Japanese workmen in
the building of bigger ships for the Osaka-Nagasaki trade, and it
appeared to Isaac Titsingh, factory director at the time, that the
country might soon be opened to European ships. Japanese sailors
had already received training in the handling of Dutch boats.[17]

But Tanuma's administration was dogged by natural calamities
that he was powerless to control. The worst of these was the erup-
tion of Asama-yama in 1783, which was followed by a terrible famine. In 1784 Tanuma's son was assassinated, and it became apparent that his regime could not last much longer. The suffering due
to the famine was blamed on the government, and Tanuma was
eventually forced to resign in 1786.

His successor was Matsudaira Sadanobu, of whom there has already been considerable mention. Matsudaira's avowed intention
was to go back to the policies of his ancestor Tokugawa Yoshimune. This entailed a complete repudiation of all of Tanuma's
projects, including the obviously constructive ones. Like Tanuma
he issued sumptuary laws, but unlike Tanuma he chose to restore
the value of the coinage (as Yoshimune had done). He was so determined to return to the glorious old days that it was a matter of
indifference to him if his policies caused widespread depression in
the cities. The honesty of his regime was admirable, but wits of
the time complained that "fish don't live in clear water," and there
was longing for the old muddiness of Tanuma's day. Matsudaira's
policies were not much more successful than Tanuma's in spite of
his personal integrity, and he resigned in 1793 after only six years
in power.

Matsudaira's failure was not due to any lack of ability on his
part. His writings show him to have been a man of great intelligence. His weakness was indicated by Shiba Kōkan, who said of
Matsudaira that he was "very learned and clever but knew next
to nothing about geography."[18] Ignorance of geography kept him

from following Tanuma's tentative plans for opening the country and developing Ezo; Matsudaira was therefore unable to extricate Japan from her economic difficulties. As long as it was forbidden to trade with foreign countries, there was no means of dealing effectively with the alternating problems of famine and surpluses, and as long as transport facilities within the country remained hopelessly inadequate, there would continue to be great inequalities of distribution. Geography, including its adjunct sciences of surveying and navigation, was the key to the solution of both the internal and external problems of Japan, as Honda Toshiaki preeminently realized.

Trade within and without the country on a large scale was also the only way to stabilize the price of rice, by far Japan's most important crop. Instead of adopting this solution, however, Matsudaira followed the example of Yoshimune and attempted to lower the price by deflation. This policy was successful enough when there were small or moderate crops, but when there was a bumper harvest, deflation helped drive the price of the rice to a dangerously low level. At this point inflationary measures might be taken to force the price upward, but generally the only persons to profit by these contradictory policies were the merchants (and artisans), who unlike the samurai and farmers did not rely on rice for their livelihood.

Another favorite remedy for the rice problem was the "ever-normal granary."[19] This ancient plan called for the government to purchase rice at high prices in years of plenty, to store it, and then to sell it in lean years at lower-than-market prices. The scheme had an appealing simplicity, but though it was tried from time to time in both China and Japan, it never succeeded in the long run. It could work only if fat and lean years followed each other fairly regularly; a series of bountiful harvests would exhaust the capacity to buy rice, and the storehouses would be emptied by any prolonged famine. The system also required honest administration, and this was not always available.

The final means to which the government had recourse in dealing with high commodity prices was to command them to fall.

Yoshimune issued decrees to this effect in 1724 and 1726—with little practical effect, as might be imagined.[20] Honda clearly showed the futility of such attempts to control prices.

These measures were surpassed in fatuity by the official interpretation of the causes of the economic distress. Everything was attributed to the merchants' want of righteousness. One good Confucian hopefully suggested that if even only ten percent of the merchants would have consideration for the samurai and farmers, and show their righteousness by selling at lower prices, they would enjoy such popularity that all the other businessmen would be forced to lower their prices too.[21] Kumazawa Banzan, who was wise enough to recognize that the gradual switch from a rice economy to a money economy had been responsible for the merchants' increasing power, could think of no better solution than the restoration of the old rice standard.[22]

Honda's Proposals

Honda Toshiaki was not immune to the traditional economic ideas that were constantly being proposed as entirely new programs. At different points in his writings he advocated both the inflation-deflation plan and the "ever-normal granary" plan, but these were temporary expedients for him. His main economic program is to be found in the "four imperative needs" that he enumerated in his *Secret Plan,* namely gunpowder, metals, shipping, and colonization.* These words in themselves do not fully explain Honda's goals. He was interested in explosives primarily for their use in blasting new channels for rivers, part of his program of improved transport and flood control, rather than for their military purposes. By metals he meant both precious metals, which in mercantilistic fashion he wished to attract to Japan, and base metals, the use of which he advocated in place of wood in order to reduce losses from rot and fire. Shipping and colonization were the key points in his plan and will be treated at length.

Honda, either independently or under Hayashi Shihei's influ-

* A translation of parts of Honda's *Secret Plan* appears in the Appendix, pp. 176–204.

ence, had become convinced that Japan must face up to her geographical situation as an island nation and not imitate the continental customs of China. Hayashi had stressed the necessity of a navy and familiarity with naval tactics; Honda emphasized the benefits that would come from merchant shipping. The prosperity of Holland and England, both maritime nations, made it clear to him that only through foreign trade could Japan attain lasting prosperity. This trade required ships of sufficient size and strength to withstand long voyages, and a knowledge of navigation that would permit Japanese captains to guide their vessels to any port in the world. By such trade it would become possible for Japan to "obtain what we lack for what we have," a familiar phrase of Honda's.

Honda insisted that shipping be government-owned. He thought it disgraceful that under existing conditions people's lives were at the mercy of the merchants; if they so chose, the owners of the rice ships that daily supplied Edo with its food could starve out the city. The government, on the other hand, would act in the interests of the people and use its ships to move rice from the growing areas to the cities. Honda noted that sometimes in one part of Japan surpluses of grain were left to rot on the ground, while in another part of the country there might be a famine. Two reasons for this condition existed: the fewness of navigable rivers (which should be remedied by widening and clearing rocks from streams by means of explosives), and the lack of shipping. By eliminating these conditions the government could move surplus grain to areas where it was needed, thus benefiting both the growers, who would otherwise lose the value of the rice, and the starving people in the famine-stricken areas.

Such measures, Honda believed, would help relieve existing conditions, but greater national prosperity would eventually cause an increase in population by removing the reasons for infanticide. Even when every part of the land was brought under cultivation there would not be enough food, for though the land is limited in size, the population can grow indefinitely. The only solution to this problem was to expand the territory available for cultiva-

tion by overseas expansion, at first to islands close to Japan, later
to islands historically Japanese, such as the Kuriles and the Bonins,
and finally to Kamchatka, the Aleutians, and North America.
These regions at present might be under Russian or other foreign
domination, but since Japan was far better situated geographically
to rule them, it ought not to be difficult to regain what carelessness
in the past had permitted to be taken away. When an empire had
been won for Japan, her prosperity would be unequaled. The capital of Japan should then be moved to Kamchatka because of its central location and because it was potentially a richer place than
Japan itself. Food and other products from the new dominions
would flow into Japan in return for the benefits of civilization.
Then Japan would be acclaimed Mistress of the East, the counterpart of England in the West.

As this summary of the "four imperative needs" indicates, Honda's plans for "governing" were quite different from the traditional
Confucian advocacy of hard work, frugality, and righteousness. He
did not, of course, reject all the old conceptions. He declared it essential that the four classes of society be maintained. However, this
did not prevent him from insisting that merit and not class be the
qualifying factor in appointing persons to official positions. His
bitterness toward the merchants did not differ greatly from that
of other writers, but he recognized the necessity of trade. Honda's
prescription for unscrupulous businessmen was not that they
should be taught benevolence, nor that it was desirable to revert
to an age when money was unknown, but that they all be kept
under strict government supervision. For the farmers he showed
sympathy based on firsthand experience of their sufferings.

The difference between Honda and other contemporary writers
on economics was his pragmatic approach. His chief concern was
always the practical benefits that might be obtained from any policy. He was by no means indifferent to ethical issues, but it was
not enough for him that a ruler be steeped in Confucian lore; he
must also be a skilled man of science familiar with the new techniques of civilization. It was for this reason that he exalted the
Empress Catherine of Russia above any of the sage emperors of

China or martial heroes of Japan. Honda's impressions of the Empress's life were exceedingly garbled, but it is obvious what qualities he thought she possessed. They are illustrated by an anecdote twice related by him. Some twenty years ago, he said, the Empress of Russia heard about a lake in Siberia that used to overflow every August and flood the countryside. She accordingly issued a proclamation asking her people to suggest some means of eliminating this danger. One man stated that he knew of a way, and the Empress granted him an audience. When she heard his plan she declared "Heaven has sent you to me," bowed twice to heaven, gave the necessary orders to her ministers, and then retired into her palace.*

Here, then, was the model ruler in action. When she was informed of something afflicting her people she at once attempted to discover a remedy by appealing to the entire nation. Capable men among the lower classes as well as persons close to the government were encouraged to offer their suggestions. Then, when she had heard the wise man's scheme and judged it to be feasible, she did not hesitate to grant all the necessary funds. The Empress Catherine thus implemented her ethical interest in the affairs of her people with the necessary practical steps. No wonder, concluded Honda, that the Russian domains have increased so greatly that they now include Kamchatka and the Kuriles! Half of the world belongs to Russia, and most of it won not by force, but by the wisdom of the Empress Catherine. "True possessions are gained through acts of virtue; countries that submit to force of arms do not yield in their hearts."

Honda discussed the ways Japan might follow Russia's example under three main headings: foreign trade, population, and colonization.

Foreign Trade. As we have seen, at the end of the eighteenth century Japan's foreign trade was restricted to China and Holland. There was no legal reason why ships could not come to Japan

---

* Honda attributed many curious feats to the Empress Catherine, including the conquest of Tartary by an army of elegantly attired Amazons led by herself. See *Keizai Hōgen* in Honda Toshiaki, *Honda Toshiaki-shū* (Tokyo, 1935), p. 103.

from such countries as Siam or Annam as they had earlier in the century, but the Japan trade had become steadily less profitable for foreigners. The only export of any consequence was copper; Thunberg described it as the finest known, containing much gold. However, ever since Arai Hakuseki had written the *Short Account of Specie* (about 1708) there had been increasing feeling on the part of Japanese intellectuals against the export of this metal. In his work Arai had given highly exaggerated figures about the amounts of gold, silver, and copper that had been sent abroad and had lamented its loss, declaring that metals were the "bones" of a country, which once removed would never grow again.[23] Honda accepted both Arai's figures and his conclusion. By his time the government had severely limited the export of copper, but Honda found it inexcusable that even relatively small amounts of this article of permanent value should be traded for the perishable fripperies brought in by the Chinese and the Dutch.

Apart from his condemnation of the export of copper, Honda did not devote much attention to the Nagasaki trade or suggest what functions it might best fulfill, for he regarded it as an entirely negative arrangement. He was convinced that Japan should not be content to let foreign countries bring their wares to her; she should follow Europe's example and herself seek out trade in all quarters of the globe. The first step in Japan's new and aggressive policy of foreign trade should be the establishment of commercial relations with Russia. "Places should be set aside on Etorofu and Kunashiri where Japanese goods can be traded for Russian ones. In this way there can be peaceful trade, and we shall gain knowledge about both the Russian people and their country, knowledge that will certainly prove beneficial."[24]

In his desire to promote trade with Russia, Honda had been anticipated by Kudō Heisuke, who had written:

Trade with Russia will be a good way to help foster the development of Ezo. If Ezo can be brought under Japanese control, all of Ezo's products including precious metals will be available to us. Trade with Russia necessarily cannot be confined to Ezo. Nagasaki and all other important ports should also be opened to Russian trade.[25]

Kudō's proposal that the major ports of the empire be thrown open to Russian ships was extraordinarily liberal in its intention, but it was quite contrary to Honda's idea of foreign trade. Honda looked back wistfully to the old days when Japanese ships had sailed to the countries of southeast Asia, and he deplored the later edicts that had destroyed the Japanese merchant marine. For him it was essential that trade be carried out on Japanese ships; this was necessary not only as a matter of prestige but also for the profits of carriage by sea. Whether Japan was open or closed to foreign ships was a matter of indifference to him; he was interested only in seeing to it that Japanese ships took advantage of the accessibility of foreign ports.

Honda was aware of the problem of finding suitable Japanese goods for export if copper were not to be sent abroad. His solution took the following form:

As part of a national policy, every effort should be made to promote the production in this country of articles that are of as fine manufacture as possible. If such efforts are made, individual industries will be encouraged, and attempts to improve the quality of Japanese products will follow. In that way many articles famed for their excellence will be produced in this country. This will help us gain profit when trading with foreign nations.[26]

Honda saw Japan as an advanced country, one whose exports were manufactured goods, rather than a less developed country having only raw materials to offer for trade abroad. Shiba Kōkan, by contrast, believed that trade with Russia would be a good way to dispose of Japan's surplus rice at a profit. He quoted a Chinese philosopher to demonstrate the futility of attempting to dispose of rice when there is a glut.

Huai Nan-tzu wrote, "One does not sell firewood in a forest, and one does not vend fish on a lake. That is because there is more than enough on the spot."
Since there is not any Japanese rice in other countries, we should load big ships with it and sell it in Russia and elsewhere. We could then obtain goods from other lands such as medicines and valuable manufactures that we do not possess here.[27]

Honda differed from Shiba also in the matter of the benefits to be derived from foreign trade. He was less interested in the natural products or manufactures of other countries than in their precious metals—their permanent treasures. He described in detail the prosperity of the port of Amsterdam, dwelling especially on the number of ships that come in from abroad (including Japan) each year laden with gold, silver, and fine copper. The importance given by Honda to precious metals recalls the mercantilism still popular in the Europe of his time, and it is worth noting how exactly his theories tallied with the definition of mercantilism as "a set of doctrinal tendencies which overemphasized the precious metals, foreign trade, manufacturing, the desirability of a dense population, and state action in economic matters."[28] One is tempted to suggest a European origin for Honda's program, but this is not at all likely. His desire to obtain precious metals from other countries, for example, is the counterpart of Arai's fear that Japan was losing her own precious metals in trade with China and Holland. The other points of resemblance to European mercantilism have similar Japanese origins, but they were all brought to their logical conclusions and welded into a system by Honda's original efforts. Mercantilism was an old story to eighteenth-century Europe, but for Japan it was a great discovery.

Population. Honda's theory of population is developed at greatest length in his *Tales of the West.* In brief, it was Honda's belief that the natural rate of increase of the population of Japan was 19.75 times in 33 years,* and that only administrative deficiencies kept the rate lower. If parents were able to feel a reasonable amount of security in the future of children they brought into the world, there would no longer be abortion or infanticide to cut down the population. The increasing population would then outstrip the growth in food supply, and it would be necessary for Japan to acquire foodstuffs from abroad, both by trade and by colonization. Honda's final picture of Japan, in other words, was of a strong manufacturing country supported by an empire that produced raw materials.

Honda's views on population have led to his being called "the Japanese Malthus." They also resemble somewhat the theories of

---

* See p. 115 below for an explanation of Honda's calculation.

Hung Liang-chi, known as "the Chinese Malthus." By examining the writings of the Englishman and the Chinese, we may be able to understand Honda's ideas more clearly, and to realize the inapplicability of the sobriquet.

Malthus published his first *Essay on Population* in 1798, the same year Honda's *Tales of the West* was completed. Malthus believed "that population, when unchecked, goes on doubling itself every twenty-five years, or increases in a geometrical ratio" while subsistence increases only arithmetically. The checks of which he wrote were misery and vice; he recognized no others at first, but later admitted a "preventive check" arising from "the distinctive superiority in his [man's] reasoning faculties, which enables him to calculate distant consequences."[29] In countries like the newly founded United States of America, where there was little misery or vice, the predicted increase in population had occurred. Eventually, Malthus concluded, the Indians would be "driven further and further back into the country, till the whole race is ultimately exterminated, and the territory is incapable of further extension."[30] According to this reasoning, the acquisition and settlement of colonies was no more than a "slight palliative" to a hopeless problem: even if suitable people were willing to emigrate, instead of the dregs of the nation, and even if a callous view were adopted regarding the rights of the natives of the places to be colonized, the normal expansion of the population would soon fill up any territory, leaving the situation more or less as before.

Malthus did not offer any solution to this gloomy state of affairs, except perhaps the hope that the "preventive check" would be used more often. One thing he stressed was the inadvisability of the government's tampering with the natural checks of misery and vice. Legislation providing support for poor men's children would only tend in the long run to make the problem more acute. Malthus wrote of one such attempt: "I entirely acquit Mr. Pitt of any sinister intention in that clause of his poor bill which allows a shilling a week to every laborer for each child he has above three."[31] With these words he exonerated Pitt of displaying anything worse than crass stupidity in wishing to save the lives of starving children.

The conclusions of Malthus were bolstered by numerous examples drawn from the history of many countries. He saw China and Japan being already so intensively cultivated that there did not seem to be any possibility of increasing food production substantially even over many years. How then, he wondered, could the huge population of China be sustained? As an answer he quoted with approval a missionary historian who had written, "Notwithstanding the great sobriety and industry of the inhabitants of China, the prodigious number of them occasions a great deal of misery."[32] Thus the natural check of misery, combined with the vicious practice of infanticide, kept the population of China from exceeding too greatly the limited food supply.

Hung Liang-chi, who based his theory of population growth on personal observation rather than on a reading of world history, came to approximately the same conclusions as Malthus. His views are contained in an essay, *Peace*, written in 1793. As the title of the essay indicates, Hung associated the dangerous growth of the population with the prolonged peace. He began:

There has never been a people that did not like peace, and never a people that did not wish peace to last for a long time. Now that there has been peace for a hundred years, it may be said to be of long duration. If we consider the population, we shall find that it has increased to five times what it was thirty years ago, and ten times what it was sixty years ago. When this inquiry is pushed back one hundred or more years, the increase will be found to be not less than twenty times.[33]

Hung took the case of a prosperous farmer living alone in a large house with one hundred acres of land to cultivate. As his family increases and servants are added to help care for the children, the house will become unbearably crowded, and the produce of the land will support them inadequately. Hung answered the arguments of those who claimed that there were natural checks to population increase such as floods, drought, and epidemics by pointing out that only one or two people in ten ever suffer from these disasters. To those who objected that wise princes could promote the opening of new lands on the borders which would provide additional food, Hung replied that benevolent measures by rulers, however desirable, were only likely to increase the population still more. He concluded:

To sum up, when there has been protracted peace, heaven and earth cannot but produce people, and the substance produced by heaven and earth for the nourishment of man will never equal his numbers. When there has been protracted peace, the princes and ministers naturally cannot keep people from reproducing, and that which they supply for the livelihood of the people cannot meet their needs.[34]

These views were quite exceptional for China, where a large population had always been considered desirable. Another suggestion of Hung's, that the quality of the people may suffer when each family has too many children, seems startlingly modern. But his short essay naturally did not have the epoch-making significance of Malthus's work; it was more in the nature of a wise observation than a manifesto or a proclamation of the shape of things to come. Hung quietly made his point—the paradox between the ideal of peace and the suffering that may come from it—and then moved on.[35]

Honda's chief statement of his views on population was written five years after Hung's essay, but there is nothing to suggest that he was influenced by the Chinese writer. The background of Honda's views was quite different from that of Malthus's or Hung's. Since the beginning of the eighteenth century the population of Japan had been stable, and temporary increases were usually canceled by famines or other disasters. The farming population had probably even decreased during the period. Infanticide was so widely practiced in the north of Japan that it was customary among the farmers to raise only one or two of the children born to them. The farmers also bore the brunt of famine suffering, and their numbers had been much reduced in the period 1770–90. Overpopulation would not appear to have been the serious problem in Honda's Japan that it was threatening to become in China. Rather it was the growth in numbers of unproductive samurai and merchants that had so taxed the resources of the farmers as to force upon them drastic birth-control measures. This Honda understood, and it was his hope that the farming population might be enabled by his plans to increase naturally. Only when he had charted in his mind its possible growth did he realize that someday the territory of Japan would not be able to produce enough food for everyone.

Far from being dismayed by this prospect, as Malthus had been,
Honda saw it as an incentive for overseas expansion and development of an empire.

Honda's point of departure, like Hung's, was in the problems
of an extended peace, but the implications were different for him.

Whenever there has been a period of continued peace, husbands and
wives are fearful lest it become increasingly difficult for them to earn a
living. Aware that if they have many children they will not have any
property to leave them, they confer and decide that rather than rear
children who in later years will have great difficulty in making a decent
living, it is better to take precautions before they are born and not add
another mouth to feed. If they do have a child, they secretly destroy it,
calling the process by the euphemism of "thinning out." This practice is
most prevalent in the thirteen provinces from the Kantō to Ōu. [These
include most of the east and north of Japan.] It is an evil custom that
inevitably arises when there has been a protracted peace, and it is due
also to the lack of any governmental system of guidance.

The state has no more important business than to find a solution to
this problem. If it is neglected, the longer peace continues, the more
the samurai will grow in numbers, and their extravagance will keep
pace. The same will be true of the merchants, and carried along by the
tendency of increase in these two classes, priests, artisans, and idlers will
also multiply in numbers. This will mean, of course, that it will be very
difficult for the farmers to feed them all. Then, when a point is reached
at which there is insufficient food for the samurai, artisans, merchants,
and idlers, there will presumably be nothing better to do than to oppress the farmers, and the farmers will then be in dire straits.

There is a limit to the amount of land that can be farmed. There is
also a limit to the amount of rice that can be grown, a limit to the amount
of annual levies and taxes that can be paid, and a limit to the amount of
rice that will remain when the taxes have been met. There may be an
attempt to make this limited supply of rice meet the needs of all the
people, but the attempt will fail, for the samurai, merchants, artisans,
priests, and idlers are constantly increasing in numbers.[36]

The immediate solution offered by Honda to the problems be-
setting the farmers took the form of state subsidy of children.
Farmers should be granted two sacks of rice a year for each child
until it reaches the age of fifteen, when it can be of use to the nation. Next, various reclamation and development projects (enumerated in the second part of his *Secret Plan*) would bring prosperity to certain depressed regions. Finally, the adoption of his
"four imperative needs" by the government would bring about

general prosperity, and the population would increase at the rate of 19.75 times every thirty-three years. This astounding figure was reached by Honda in a simple enough manner. He began with two newly married couples, the husbands fifteen years of age, the wives thirteen. If they produce a child every two years for thirty-three years, at which point the women can no longer bear children, there will be seventeen boys and girls in each family. These in turn, having married their opposite numbers in the other family, will produce forty-five grandchildren to the original couples by the end of thirty-three years. In this manner a total of seventy-nine children and grandchildren (excluding possible great-grandchildren) will have been born to the original four people, an increase of 19.75 times.*

It is hard to believe that Honda was sincere in giving these figures as the "natural increase." Here, as at certain other points in his work, the propagandist appears to have got the better of the thinker. The same desire to convince that led him to praise Kamchatka as a splendid country, in spite of all he could have read of the land, also induced him to put forward this extravagant figure as the normal birthrate. We may contrast Honda's estimate with Malthus's more conservative claim that the population unchecked would double every twenty-five years, a figure arrived at after careful study of census reports. Honda's theory of population was in comparison no more than an intelligent observation, like that of Hung Liang-chi, but he was not satisfied merely with stating it, as Hung had been. Honda's main thoughts were on the fourth of his "imperative needs," colonization, and he used his distorted population theory merely as a means to this end.

Colonization. There was no subject to which Honda devoted greater attention than colonization, which he termed the "prime duty of the ruler." His chief model in this was England: "Some of the prosperous nations of Europe are themselves small in area but

---

*Honda Toshiaki, *Seiiki Monogatari* in *Honda Toshiaki-shū* (Tokyo, 1935), p. 186. Honda may have been slightly off in his calculations; an ideal combination of male and female offspring would produce fifty grandchildren, resulting in a total of eighty-four children and grandchildren (excluding possible great-grandchildren).

have extensive possessions; such countries are called 'great nations.' Among them is England, a nation about the size of Japan."[37] Lists are given of English colonies in different parts of the
world, and the benefits England receives from them are enumerated. The wonders of England itself are described, the implication
being that there is no reason why Japan cannot follow in her footsteps and attain equal prosperity.

Honda outlined the order to be followed in colonization:

First, ships are dispatched to ascertain the location of the islands to be
taken, and to measure their size. The natural products of the islands are
investigated and the native population estimated. Then, when it is known
about how many provinces the islands will make if they are settled, the
actual work of colonization is begun. If the natives of the islands are
still living in caves, they are taught about houses. Dwellings should be
built for the tribal chiefs. Natives without implements and utensils
should be supplied with them. By helping the natives and giving them
everything they desire, one will inspire a feeling of affection and obedience in them, like the love of children for their parents. This is true
because they are moved by the same feelings that pervade the rest of the
world, even though they are considered barbarians.[38]

The suggestions are followed immediately by a discussion of the
recompense gained by the colonizer in return for his trouble:

The way to compensate for the expenses involved in colonization lies in
taking the natural products of these islands and shipping them to Japan.
Trading marks a beginning of compensation for the expenses. Even barbarians do not expect to ask favors and give nothing in return. The
products they give represent a first form of taxation. Since every island
has wooded areas, there will always be some value in the lumber that can
be taken from it even after a good many years. The value of other
products would be too great to calculate. It is the task of the ruler-father
to direct and educate the natives in such a manner that not a single one
of them spends even one unproductive day. This is a matter that should
not be put off another moment.[39]

Honda's bald program for exploiting the natives would have put
to shame any European contemporary. It is true that he did not
advocate bringing the Word of Shinto to the benighted natives,
but he was quite confident that the blessings of Japanese culture
were sufficiently great to make them forget their enforced servitude.

The first places to be colonized were naturally enough those
closest to Japan. Honda explained:

Japan is as yet unfamiliar with navigation, transport, and foreign trade, and it will not be easy to begin without experience. Japanese should first sail to the Ezo islands, since they are possessions of ours. . . . Trade at these places in Japanese goods will yield steadily increasing profits. Everyone will desire to travel abroad, and this will permit the natural growth of 19.75 times in thirty-three years of which I wrote above.[40]

The Ezo islands, that is Hokkaidō, Saghalien, and the Kuriles, were also well suited as the initial colonization venture because the people were of the same race as the Japanese in spite of their hairiness.* The natives of the Aleutians, including Amchitka, the island where Kōdayū was shipwrecked, were of the same race, and Honda heard that the natives of North America also resembled Japanese. The fact that the Ainu still referred to the Japanese as *kamoedono*—exalted beings—and that there existed a tradition of allegiance to Japan meant that Japan had an advantage over any other country wishing to colonize Ezo. However, if she did not act at once, it would be too late, for the Russians were steadily encroaching on the Ezo domains of Japan. If only Benyowsky's warning had been heeded, this unhappy situation need never have arisen! Every day that passed made the retaking of Ezo more difficult, for the Ainu were gradually being won over to Russian ways.

Honda's worries about the Russification of the natives may have derived from conditions on Etorofu, one of the Kurile Islands where Russian influence was strongest. One traveler had written:

When I went there in 1788 I had one of the natives called over to me, and I asked him what he had learned from the Russians. He said that the Russians had given him holy images and taught him prayers. He had been told that if he believed in them he would prosper in his fishing, would never be shipwrecked, and would not fail to get whatever else he desired. When I inquired about the prayers, the man stood up and, like a Russian, put three fingers together. Pointing at his forehead, chest, and armpits, he three times recited "Ohoppomipomira" and bowed down.†

---

* "Since they are all the descendants of the Emperor Jimmu, they are of the same race as ourselves." This refers to the legend of Jimmu's visit to the Kuriles. Honda believed that in time Ezo could be developed to the "city" level of society. See *Chōkiron* in Honda Toshiaki, *Honda Toshiaki-shū* (Tokyo, 1935), p. 209.

† The words pronounced by the native are apparently "O Gospodi Pomilui," the Russian for "Oh Lord! Have Mercy!" See Kondō Morishige, *Henyō Bunkai Zukō* in *Kondō Seisai Zenshū*, vol. 1, *Kokusho Kankōkai Sōsho* (Tokyo), p. 67.

Kudō Heisuke had earlier warned of just such a tendency. He had written that because of Japanese neglect of the Ezo islands, the natives, who were of the same race as the Kamchadales, already conquered by the Russians, were now obeying Russian orders, and Japanese wishes were no longer consulted.

Honda did not disapprove of the Russian attempts to civilize the Ainu. Had he known of the brutal Russian treatment of the natives, which had sometimes resulted in the annihilation of their villages, he would have been furnished with another argument for Japanese sovereignty over the islands, but as it was he spoke only in the highest terms of their energy, which he contrasted with Japanese sloth. It was compassion for the natives that had induced the Russians to bring them the benefits of civilization, and the Ainu accordingly regarded their conquerors as their parents. Views similar to Honda's were expressed by Habuto Masayasu, the first Magistrate of Hakodate, who wrote in 1803: "According to what I have heard of Russian state policies, countries that are already civilized and where a government exists are never invaded. All the Russians are doing is to educate those natives who at present do not even know the art of cooking their food."[41] Habuto felt it needless to establish military defenses in Ezo as long as Japan made it clear she was bringing civilization to the Ainu.

The desirability of colonizing (or civilizing) Ezo was by no means an undisputed issue. Although advanced writers like Kudō Heisuke, Hayashi Shihei, and Honda Toshiaki favored the immediate assertion of Japanese sovereignty in the north, persons closer to the government continued to voice opposition to any such undertaking. Nakai Chikuzan (1730–1804), one of the leading political thinkers of the time, wrote in 1789 that Japan should confine her activities in Ezo to the establishment of trading posts. Then, if the Russians attacked in strength, the posts could be abandoned with no military disgrace to Japan. He felt that there was no reason to put Japan to the expense and trouble of defending so worthless a place. If the Russians succeeded in capturing Ezo, there would be time enough to decide whether or not to do business with them there. Japan should consider it fortunate that this valueless, scantily populated buffer existed between herself and Russia. Any attempt to colonize Ezo would only lead to the deaths of officials and soldiers, and would destroy Japan's prosperity.[42]

Honda branded such opinions traitorous. He lumped together persons who considered Ezo a foreign country with those who thought that the region's inhabitants, "unlike other human beings, have only one eye, in the middle of their foreheads, which flashes like lightning."[43] But his attempts to discredit Nakai and others of his school counted for little alongside the official patronage of such conservative doctrines by Matsudaira Sadanobu. Other shogunate advisers informed Matsudaira of the military power of the Matsumae clan, and he appears to have been persuaded that no real danger of invasion existed in the face of such strength.

In an attempt to change Matsudaira's views, Honda submitted in 1792 a memorial on the advisability of settling Ezo. He gave five reasons why this should be done: (1) a natural frontier would be established between Japan and Russia, thereby preventing Russians from roaming freely into Japanese territory; (2) a place where criminals might lead useful lives would be provided; (3) the mines would yield valuable metals; (4) the land when cultivated would produce abundant crops that could help Japan in time of famine; and (5) the timber of Ezo could be used to build ships.[44]

The last three of these points need no comment; the first was obviously in answer to Nakai's opinion that Ezo served a useful function as a desolate "no-man's-land" between Japan and Russia. Honda favored a clear-cut frontier; to the conservative officials in power, he pointed out that such a frontier would help to keep out Christians who might otherwise drift into Japan. Honda's second proposal, to use Ezo as a place of exile for criminals, had an interesting background. In 1786 it was suggested to Tanuma Okitsugu that 70,000 eta be forced to migrate to Ezo. When the population of Ezo had increased sufficiently, it would then be feasible to send some of the eta colonists on to Tartary and Manchuria as well as to the remoter Kurile islands. This ambitious plan fell through because of Tanuma's dismissal from office, but Honda may have learned of it.[45]

Honda was aware of the difficulty of finding people willing to serve as colonists in lands whose reputation, in spite of his own efforts, was so unfavorable. At one time he suggested that those farmers from the northern provinces of Japan who visited Ezo every summer be compelled to remain there with their families (which, he believed, they secretly wished to do anyway). Idlers, robbers, and other lawbreakers from parts of Japan where snow falls should be sent to Ezo, there to expiate their sins by leading honest lives as farmers or fishermen, and thus benefiting the country. Persons of similar description from parts of Japan where the snow did not fall should be sent to colonize southern territories like the Bonin Islands.[46]

Honda gave very detailed attention to the problems of colonists in the northern regions, even to prescribing the construction of the houses they were to use, the methods of heating, and the best types of windows and doors. He also listed the steps to be taken in communicating Japanese culture to the natives. Realizing that it would be impossible to convert them overnight to the Japanese way of life, he advocated retaining their good customs and only replacing bad ones with superior Japanese practices. "Japanese customs should be spread very gradually among the natives and the Japanese government also should be established gradually."[47]

The Ezo controversy raged among Japanese scholars for many years with little fruitful result. Men before Honda (as early perhaps as the end of the seventeenth century) and men for many years after him continued to stress the advantages of Ezo, often in exaggerated terms, but the conservatism of the government was too great to be overcome by even the most persuasive of writers. Parties of exploration continued to visit the north, but it was unlikely that any real colonization could take place as long as it was not allowed for Japanese to leave the country, to circulate information about Japan abroad, or to teach the Japanese language to foreigners.*

In the writings of all the advocates of the development of Ezo

---

* Honda's disciple Mogami Tokunai incurred the wrath of the Matsumae clan by teaching an Ainu servant to read and write *katakana*. See below, p. 129.

there was a strong note of urgency: "It will soon be too late; the Russians will beat us to Ezo!" was the cry of many patriots. When Honda learned of the death of Catherine the Great, he felt that the moment had come for Japanese action. The Russian empire would collapse on the death of so incomparably gifted a ruler, and the Japanese could easily extend their possessions up the Kuriles to Kamchatka, to Cape Thadeus beyond, and across to the continent of North America.[48] No show of force would be necessary if only advantage were at once taken of this unique opportunity. "It will soon be too late!"

Nothing happened. The opportunity passed, and the voices most heeded by the government were those that called for maintenance of the status quo. When the Russians sent an embassy in 1804 to ask for trade, the most trusted shogunate counselor advised, "It is the law of our ancestors not to permit trade with nations other than China and Holland."[49] But if the Japanese missed their chance to gain an empire, as Honda believed, they did not suffer the invasion of their territories predicted by many writers since the time of Benyowsky. The benevolent Russian colonial administration, which Honda thought would soon be extended to Hokkaidō found scant favor with the Ainu, who knew it brought only death in the form of gunfire and disease. Those natives who survived the harshness of Russian rule rapidly degenerated, as may be seen even in this account by a Russian apologist:

Although their manner of living be most nasty, and their actions most stupid, yet they think themselves the happiest people in the world, and look upon the Russians who are settled among them with contempt: however this notion begins to change at present; for the old people who are confirmed in their customs, drop off, and the young ones being converted to the Christian religion, adopt the customs of the Russians, and despise the barbarity and superstition of their ancestors.[50]

It may be wondered whether the Japanese would have done better. When Captain Krusenstern contemplated the seizure of Saghalien from Japan, the nominal possessor of the island, he wrote: "The most essential objection would be, that such a capture was made without the approbation of the true possessors of Sachalin, the Ainos; and I honestly confess my doubts whether they would gain by such a change; for they appeared to me to be treated with great humanity by the Japanese."[51]

This tribute would have surprised Honda Toshiaki, who could see only stupidity and inefficiency in Japanese practices as contrasted with the invariably enlightened ways of the West. His attitude has been condemned by modern Japanese critics as showing an unseemly adulation of foreign things, but it was precisely this receptivity on the part of Honda, Shiba, and other advanced men of their time that made it possible for Japan alone among Asian nations to rise to the challenge of the West. Perhaps Honda did go too far in his admiration of Western ways, but only by professing such extreme views could he hope to shake Japan from her long somnolence and reveal to her the possibilities of greatness.

6. Explorers of the North

By the end of the eighteenth century the Japanese were better acquainted with European civilization than the people of any other non-Western country. The Arabs with their proximity to Europe and long history of relations with European states, should have found it easy to learn of the revolution in science that had occurred since the Renaissance, but whether because of apathy or contempt for the infidels, they were less well informed than the Japanese.[1] The Indians and Indonesians resisted colonial rule not by mastering the techniques of their European conquerors, but by staging ill-fated uprisings. The Chinese occasionally made use of the missionaries resident in Peking, particularly when they prepared a new calendar, but on the whole they evinced little interest in Europe. It is paradoxical but true that Japan, despite her geographical isolation and the seclusion policies of her government, alone proved capable of absorbing European civilization.

The receptivity of the Japanese to Western ways was in part the outgrowth of their earlier passion for all things Chinese, a passion that had induced them to adopt and translate much of continental civilization. The Indians, by contrast, were not moved to translate works from other languages until recent times, and the Chinese translated only the Buddhist scriptures, feeling no other need for information from the outside world. The Japanese had turned eagerly to China from the early period of their history, not only translating extensively but seeking to make Chinese civilization a part of themselves. How desperately they craved to be praised by the Chinese as worthy pupils! Many generations of scholars longed to write characters so beautiful that they might be mistaken for those written by a Chinese, to compose poetry in Chinese that could not be faulted for metrics or rhyme, to have their essays on philosophical themes reprinted in China. Even the Shogun Ashikaga Yoshimitsu took a Chinese name, by preference wore Chinese clothes, and was delighted to accept the title "King of Japan" bestowed on him by the Chinese court; and the Confucian scholar Ogyū Sorai once described himself as an "Eastern barbarian." The "Dutch mania" (*rampeki*) that infected many scholars in the eighteenth and nineteenth centuries, a similar phenomenon on a smaller scale, would not have been possible without this background of adulation of a foreign country. Unlike the devotees of China, however, the Dutch scholars were surrounded by suspicion; no Japanese carried away by enthusiasm for Europe would have dared to profess Christianity as the Chinese scholars openly professed Confucianism. Nevertheless, some of the most distinguished men in Japan came to call themselves by Dutch names, wrote poetry and prose to one another in Dutch, and drew carefully detailed landscapes dotted with windmills.

Perhaps the very restrictions imposed on intercourse with foreign countries made some Japanese intellectuals all the more determined to probe the geographical and intellectual boundaries of their world. The bravest seized every opportunity to become friendly with the Dutch traders and doctors, despite the danger of being denounced by a xenophobe. And once they had become friendly with a European, they tried to maintain their contacts, though correspondence with people abroad was strictly forbidden. Letters by thirteen rangaku scholars, including a daimyo, were sent to Isaac Titsingh after he left Japan for Bengal, and correspondence on scientific matters was exchanged with strangers as well as acquaintances. Katsuragawa Hoken, the personal physician of the Shogun, regularly wrote to a German botanist in Indonesia and was even elected a corresponding member of a learned society.[2] Despite the government's interdiction, the Japanese were tireless interrogators of every visitor. According to Captain Golownin, "The curiosity of the Japanese was carried to so great a length, that, at every station at which we halted, we were requested to tell our names, our ages, how many relations we had, where our clothes had been manufactured, &c. Our answers were always set down in writing."[3] Sometimes relations with the Europeans went deeper, as we know from Thunberg's account: "I had the good fortune to gain their love and friendship to such a degree, that they did not only set a high value on my knowledge, but they loved me from the bottom of their hearts, so as greatly to regret my departure."[4]

Relations between the Dutch and the interpreters, the only Japanese officially authorized to talk directly to the foreigners, were not always harmonious. Hendrik Doeff, who lived on Deshima from 1799 to 1817, longer than any other Dutchman, worked with the interpreters for years compiling a Dutch-Japanese dictionary.[5] During the long period when Dutch ships were prevented from traveling to Japan because of the Napoleonic Wars, he depended on their help even for sustenance and clothing; but in his memoirs he wrote more often of "the Argus eyes of the inspectors spying on me from all sides" than of the joys of collaboration.

The interpreters, as officials of the government, may sometimes have been overzealous in their surveillance of the Dutch, but they were by no means hostile. On one occasion they went to considerable trouble to spare Dutch feelings, only to bring disaster on themselves. In 1790 the shogunate issued a decree stating that henceforth the Dutch would be restricted to only one ship a year, halving the quota of silver and copper that might be exported. The interpreters, realizing what a blow this would be to the Dutch merchants, sought to spare them its full particulars, at the same time reporting to the government that the Dutch had unconditionally accepted the changes. The discrepancy was discovered, and the three interpreters responsible were sentenced to five years in prison.[6]

The sharp reduction in the trade quotas was indeed a severe

blow. Doeff, the factory director, wondered why the Japanese even wished to continue commercial relations at all if on such an insignificant scale:

Nobody but the governor and the inhabitants of Nagasaki derives any profit from the trade. Japan has no need of imports from abroad. . . . Such luxury articles as elephant tusks, woollen, silk, and linen fabrics, glass objects, clocks, and other knickknacks the Japanese can well do without. Indeed, as a result of the closure of the country to all foreigners and the prohibition on dealings with them, the Japanese remain unacquainted with many luxuries that we in Europe consider indispensable but which they fortunately do not miss.[7]

The continuation of the Deshima trade, even when it had dwindled to a trickle of luxury goods, may have been allowed by the shogunate merely out of respect for long-standing precedents. But a more important reason for tolerating the Dutch and their wares was undoubtedly the continuing desire to obtain knowledge about the West. The shogunate was aware that isolation alone would not guarantee security from foreign attack. The presence of the Russians in the north and the appearance of other European vessels off the Japanese coast made the government more anxious than ever to learn what was happening in Europe. Even when, at the beginning of the nineteenth century, conditions in Holland made trade impossible, the Dutch on Deshima were useful at least as tutors to the interpreters.

When Dutch independence was restored after the downfall of Napoleon in 1815, the Dutch government for its part decided to make amends for the long failure of the Deshima merchants to inform the world about Japan. A young German physician, Philipp Franz von Siebold (1796–1866), was chosen for the double task of obtaining information about Japan and communicating to the Japanese the new European advances in science. His arrival in Japan in 1823 opened a brief new period of relations between the Japanese and the Dutch, which ended with his expulsion from Japan six years later. In the years after Siebold's departure, Dutch studies again fell under heavy fire. The reactionary rulers in 1839 arrested a group of Dutch scholars suspected of political insubordination; and the opposition of the traditional Chinese schools of medicine to the Dutch-trained physicians was so strong that in 1849 the government forbade the practice of Dutch medical techniques except in surgery or in treatment of the eye.[8] Even among Japanese who recognized the value of Dutch learning, many considered it only in terms of its use in preserving the existing state of things. Others borrowed what they needed from Dutch studies while professing profound contempt for all foreigners.

The men of the generation of Honda Toshiaki were fascinated by the new worlds revealed by Dutch books and objects, but their approach to the West was in some ways superficial. They lacked the linguistic competence and the opportunities to deepen their knowledge. Their successors were to be discoverers on a different level—men who explored the desolate islands to the north, who methodically collated available materials in preparing their accounts of the West, who risked their lives to acquire accurate geographical information. Although they lived in a society that was largely unaware of their achievements and under a government that was ready to use the most despotic means to eliminate any show of insubordination, their knowledge took them beyond the parochial reaches of their predecessors into a world fraternity of knowledge. This chapter will deal chiefly with two scholar-explorers of the new generation.

Mogami Tokunai (1754–1836)

One puzzling aspect of Honda Toshiaki's career is his failure to accompany the shogunate expedition of 1785 to the north. As soon as Honda learned that the expedition was being planned, he spared no efforts to get invited along, in no matter how humble a capacity. He was convinced that the opportunity had at last come to discover whether the development of Ezo he had so eloquently advocated was possible, and if the "science of latitudes" really permitted the geographer to determine the climate of unknown territories. Yet when Honda finally obtained permission to go along (as a foot soldier), he begged to be excused on the grounds of illness and sent his disciple Mogami Tokunai in his place. A letter to a friend indicates that this illness was a pretext, that it had been Honda's intention from the start to send Mogami.[9] Honda must have believed that Mogami was better equipped than he himself was to withstand the arduous journey; in any case, he could hardly have made a better choice. Mogami Tokunai not only was physically able to endure the bitter cold of the Kuriles and Kamchatka as he demonstrated again and again, but possessed the understanding and imagination Honda knew was essential if Japanese preeminence were to be established in the north.

Mogami, like many others of his generation of discoverers, was a farmer's son. In his later years he devoted himself to a study of his genealogy, convinced that he issued from high-ranking samurai stock, but nothing about his poverty-stricken youth suggests grandeur. In 1781, at the age of twenty-six, Mogami left his village in the north of Japan to make his fortune in Edo. He described this period in an autobiographical memoir: "I studied astronomy and geography with Honda Toshiaki, and medicine with Yamada Munetoshi. But I still had not found my vocation. I had word privately at this time that the people of Ezo were ignorant of the art of planting crops and of writing. This was when I first felt I had found a vocation: I would free them from their ignorance."[10] This sudden and unique resolution explains Mogami's consistently sympathetic attitude toward the Ainu, which was to involve him in serious difficulties with the Matsumae clan.[11]

It may be imagined how delighted Mogami was to join the 1785 expedition, even though his function was stated to be merely a carrier of surveyor's poles. The purpose of the expedition was to determine the route by which goods were being smuggled into Ezo from the Asiatic mainland, and to survey the mineral and agricultural resources of the area. Two parties were sent out, one to Saghalien, the other to the Kuriles, with orders to proceed if possible to the islands nearest those held by the Russians. Mogami was in the party sent to the Kuriles, headed by Yamaguchi Tetsugorō and Aoshima Shunzō.

Mogami must have distinguished himself in some way despite his menial status, for he was sent out again early in the following year, this time alone, to make survey charts. After about a month on his own he was sufficiently fluent in the Ainu language to dispense with an interpreter, but he soon picked up an assistant, an Ainu who spoke some Japanese. Noticing the man's intelligence (and perhaps remembering his original resolution), he taught the Ainu to read the Japanese kana, though this was expressly forbidden. This gesture bespeaks Mogami's sympathy for the Ainu at a time when they were generally treated with the utmost harshness by the Japanese. The two men traveled from island to island, as far north as Etorofu and Uruppu.[12] Mogami wrote, "I sailed past the first island [Kunashiri] to reach the second island [Etorofu]. Never before in history had anyone reached that island. I was the first Japanese ever to set foot there. The people of the island were astonished to see me, and surrounded me like a wall to get a look. I was still not familiar with the local pronunciation and could not teach the Great Way."[13]

On Etorofu Mogami heard reports of three Russians who had fled to the island from Uruppu because of a quarrel with their superiors.[14] Mogami wondered if these men might not be spies, sent by the Russian government to survey the islands, or even to prevent him from sailing on to Uruppu. He decided in the end to confront them and to make use of them in his future explorations, whatever their motives might be. His first encounter with them was disarming. As soon as he reached the shore at Sharshamu, the three Russians, led by Simeon Dorofeivitch Ishuyo,[15] came forward to greet him with the utmost deference, removing their caps and shoes and silently bowing. The Ainus spread some matting on the beach for them all to sit on, and Mogami found himself surrounded by foreigners—Russians and Ainus—an unusual predicament for a Japanese in the eighteenth century. Mogami's Ainu companion later reported that although Mogami's face was pale, his clenched teeth revealed his determination not to betray any Japanese weakness.

That night a feast was offered in Mogami's honor. Under the influence of the turbid Ainu liquor, the Ainus and Russians took turns performing songs and dances of their countries, and Mogami, not to be outdone, rendered a Japanese mule-driver's chant. The

13. Mogami Tokunai

next day Mogami invited the Russians to dinner. Overjoyed to taste Japanese rice after months of inadequate nourishment, they were moved to express gratitude and friendship, and Mogami and Ishuyo were soon chatting in broken Ainu about the geography of the Kuriles and Europe. Mogami was impressed by Ishuyo's education, and his suspicions gradually gave way to respect and even affection for the Russian. Ishuyo begged Mogami to take him to Japan, planning to make his way from Nagasaki back to Europe, but Mogami replied that Japanese law did not permit foreigners to enter the country. Finally it was agreed that Mogami would take Ishuyo as far as Akkeshi in Hokkaidō; in return, Ishuyo wrote introductions for Mogami to the Russian officials in Kamchatka. Mogami set sail for Kamchatka with the introductions, but got no farther than the northern tip of Uruppu before storms forced him to return to Etorofu.

In the meantime Mogami's superiors Yamaguchi and Aoshima had at last reached Etorofu, where they spent a month interrogating Ishuyo. Mogami arrived just as Yamaguchi and Aoshima had decided to order the Russians to leave. Embarrassed by this turn of events after he had promised to take Ishuyo to Akkeshi, Mogami remained out of sight when the Russians were informed they must go. But Ishuyo refused to leave without seeing Mogami, declaring in broken Ainu: "I am sure Tokunai is on this island. I want to see Tokunai. I want to talk to him forever."[16] At this, Mogami emerged from his hiding place and with difficulty persuaded Ishuyo to leave for Saghalien in a boat to be provided by the Japanese.

Before his departure Ishuyo invited Mogami to his hut to express his grief at their parting. Seating Mogami in the place of honor, Ishuyo and his assistant knelt on either side of him, each taking one of Mogami's hands in his own and putting his other hand around Mogami's waist in a farewell embrace, much to Mogami's surprise. The two Russians by turns expressed their deep feelings with loud wails of grief. Mogami also choked with tears. In his journal he wrote of Ishuyo that "he was a man of noble, heroic character, far beyond my limited capacities to appreciate."[17]

Mogami was particularly impressed by Ishuyo's gravity, and ascribed his invariably solemn countenance to a Christian avoidance of laughter as the deadliest of sins.[18]

This misapprehension suggests how imperfect the communication between Mogami and Ishuyo must have been, but the chance meeting of these two men is a kind of milestone in Japanese relations with foreigners. Starting in suspicion and fear, their relationship developed in the course of two months into friendship and trust. Mogami returned to Edo in 1787, but soon afterward decided to set out once more for the north. He would search for Ishuyo, and would ask his help in going to Kamchatka and eventually on to Moscow. Ishuyo had given Mogami a laissez-passer before they separated, telling him it would enable him to travel anywhere in Europe. A friend of Mogami's wrote later:

He was sure that as long as he had this document it would be extremely easy to go wherever he pleased. The only problem was to reach Russian territory. Tokunai planned to make a secret journey to the capital of Russia, to travel around the country inspecting conditions, and later to ask the help of the Dutch stationed in Moscow. He would travel with the Dutch around Europe. Then, after sailing round Africa and Asia and visiting all the islands, he planned to sail back to Nagasaki. Such plans tell us what a bold and heroic character Tokunai possessed.[19]

Though Mogami knew it was forbidden for Japanese to go abroad, his boundless curiosity about the world and confidence in his ability to make his way among foreigners, no doubt the result of his friendship with Ishuyo, encouraged him to contemplate so dangerous a journey.

That summer Mogami set out for the north, paying his expenses with money provided by Honda Toshiaki. He reached Matsumae and applied for employment with the clan, but the officials, annoyed with Mogami especially because he had taught an Ainu to read Japanese, not only refused his request but ordered him to leave the island at once. Determined to remain in Ezo, Mogami chose the desperate expedient of shaving his head and becoming the disciple of a Zen priest, but to no avail. He was forced to leave, and was moreover robbed of all his belongings save the clothes on his back. Eventually, through the kindness of a ship's captain, he made his way back to his native village. Far from returning in brocade clothes, the proverbial attire of the local boy who made good in the big city, Mogami returned penniless and in rags. After various efforts to make a living as a woodcutter, a tobacconist, and a medicine peddler, Mogami finally became an arithmetic teacher in the village.[20]

Mogami Tokunai remained in his village until 1789, when word reached him of an Ainu revolt on the island of Kunashiri. The first reports inaccurately stated that Ishuyo had instigated the insurrection, in which seventy or eighty Japanese had been killed. Mogami at once informed Aoshima Shunzō in Edo of what had occurred, and early that summer the shogunate sent Aoshima (disguised as a merchant so as not to arouse the suspicions of the Matsumae clan) to investigate the situation. Aoshima decided to take Mogami along as his guide, so as to interrogate the Ainu freely without recourse to the Matsumae clan's interpreters.

Aoshima Shunzō's report to the shogunate accurately described the unscrupulous trade practices of the Matsumae clan that had inspired the Ainu revolt. But Matsudaira Sadanobu somehow learned that Aoshima while in Hokkaidō had been in close relations with a Matsumae clan official, in apparent contravention of his mission as a spy,[21] and ordered Aoshima's arrest. Mogami, who was living at Aoshima's house at the time, was thrown into prison as an accomplice. Confined to a cell with common criminals, Mogami contracted prison fever, and for some days was in a coma. In a rare fit of despondency, he even contemplated suicide. Eventually it was ascertained that Mogami, far from being in league with the Matsumae clan, was detested by them, and he was released from prison. Still suffering from a contagious disease, he was taken into the home of Honda Toshiaki, where he gradually recovered.[22]

Mogami's report on his activities in the Kuriles, presented through Honda to the authorities, served not only to exonerate him but to gain him an official position as a shogunate retainer.[23] Matsudaira Sadanobu, although reluctant to take any steps toward developing Ezo, decided to permit limited trading between the Japanese and the Ainu, ostensibly as a gesture of compassion for the benighted Ainu. A party of six, headed by Mogami Tokunai, was dispatched to the north.

Mogami recorded in his autobiography that before leaving Honda Toshiaki's house he had asked his teacher the best way to guide the Ainu in the path of civilization. Honda replied, "If you are truly humane, you will enjoy the blessings of Heaven." Mogami's policies toward the Ainu were indeed to be marked by a rare humanity that suggests how deeply he took Honda's words to heart.

Mogami arrived in Matsumae early in 1791, this time as an official representative of the shogunate. The same officials who had treated him so shabbily a few years before were embarrassed, but were powerless to prevent him from moving about their territories. Mogami, aware of the danger that he might be poisoned, took extreme precautions and left Matsumae as quickly as possible for Etorofu, where he hoped to find Ishuyo. By a sad trick of fate, Ishuyo had left Sharushamu just two days earlier, probably because word had reached him of the imminent arrival of a shogunate official. Mogami followed Ishuyo to Uruppu, but never managed to catch up with him.[24]

On Uruppu Mogami, finding crosses erected by the Russians in 1784, decided that the best way to counteract the Christian influences spread by the Russians would be to build Shinto shrines where the Ainu could worship Amaterasu, the Sun Goddess. He wrote, "The natives, being in an uncivilized state, are without religion of their own, and are ready to adopt the religious teachings of any country."[25] Mogami believed that the Ainu, despite being barbarians, were of the same race as the Japanese, and therefore should worship the same gods. Mogami may have been the first Japanese to entertain this belief; Arai Hakuseki had declared that the Ainu were closer to animals than human beings, and the members of the Matsumae clan seemed to be of the same opinion. Mogami wrote, "This year I encountered many Ainu, and I realized what a great mistake it is to think of them as belonging basically to the species of dogs; in fact, they are of the same Japanese stock as ourselves. They have only to adopt the teachings of the Imperial Land for them to become Japanese. I accordingly urged them to worship our divine ancestors, the Sun Goddess, and, delighted to receive this guidance, they worshiped her with the greatest reverence."[26] In 1798, when Mogami accompanied Kondō Morishige to Etorofu, the Japanese party set up a pillar inscribed "Dai Nihon Etorofu" (Etorofu, Great Japan). The names of ten Ainu members of the party were listed below those of the five Japanese, as if to indicate that the two peoples had a communal interest in proclaiming Etorofu to be Japanese.[27]

Mogami's views on the treatment of the Ainu found expression in a directive issued in 1799 by Matsudaira Tadaakira:

The present policy with respect to the Ezo territories is to send our officials there and extend to the Ezo people the benefits of Japanese civilization. We intend to promote education in the hope that the Ezo people will gradually be converted to Japanese customs and become so deeply attached to our ways that even if some foreign power seeks to win their favor with ingratiating tactics, they will not waver in their allegiance. This is the most essential objective. However, if we indiscriminately shower the Ezo people with gifts in the attempt to win them over immediately, their loyalty will be short-lived. The best policy is to continue our efforts to raise their standard of living by means of trade.... It should be remembered that the purpose of this trade is not to obtain profits but to improve the livelihood of the Ezo people.... They should be steadily instructed in the art of agriculture and should learn to sustain themselves on grain.... The Ezo people are by nature stupid, but we have heard they are honest and sincere. The least resort to deceit will cause them to suppose that the Japanese are not to be trusted, and this attitude will impede their acceptance of Japanese rule. They must be treated with the greatest sincerity.... The Ezo people have hitherto been forbidden to use Japanese, but they should henceforth be encouraged to use Japanese exclusively and educated in such a way that they will gradually turn into Japanese. However, Japanese should under no circumstances speak Ainu.... When the Ainu have accepted Imperial rule and, having become familiar with Japanese law, desire to adopt Japanese customs, they should be allowed to shave their foreheads in the Japanese style. They should be given Japanese clothes, and especially loyal persons should have Japanese houses built for them. However, if we attempt to convert these people to Japanese ways too abruptly, our efforts will certainly go against their temperaments and never succeed. We should wait until they themselves desire change.[28]

This enlightened policy, seemingly the fruit of Mogami's recommendations,* was modified by Matsudaira Tadaakira soon after

---

* Mogami did not agree with all the provisions; for example, he saw no reason why Japanese should not be permitted to speak Ainu.

he arrived in Hakodate. No doubt actual contact with the Ainu
made him realize how far they were from discarding their traditional ways. He ordered that the ritual bear festival be discontinued, and forbade tattooing or the piercing of the ears of Ainu
children.[29] Mogami Tokunai was extremely upset by this illiberal
decree, for though he believed the Ainu to be Japanese, he was
convinced that any attempt to force them to abandon their customs overnight in the hope of destroying their identity as Ainu
was doomed to failure. Certain Ainu leaders, knowing Mogami to
be their friend, confided in him their grief and indignation after
Matsudaira Tadaakira had ordered some Ainu youths to shave
their foreheads in the Japanese style. Mogami proved to be right
in predicting failure for these harsh measures: soon afterward
fifty or sixty Ainu fled in their boats from Ezo to Uruppu, preferring to live on the same island with the Russians rather than under
Japanese rule.

Matsudaira Tadaakira's policy was followed by a conservative
reaction. When the shogunate decided in 1802 to establish a
magistracy (*bugyō*) of Matsumae, it issued a directive cautioning
against teaching agriculture to the Ainu or otherwise interfering
with their way of life.[30] Attempts to make Japanese out of the Ainu
were to be discontinued, and even when the Ainu themselves desired instruction in Japanese ways, their requests should not be
lightly granted. The situation thus reverted to what it had been
before Mogami Tokunai's recommendations. The fear of Russian
aggression in the Kuriles had diminished, and the natural disincli-
nation of the authorities to experiment with new policies resulted
in a return to the old attitudes.

The shogunate's position was apparent in its refusal in 1804
even to entertain the request of the Russian Ambassador Rezanov
to open trade relations. Mogami wrote that people all over the
country, on hearing of Rezanov's rebuff, sympathized with the
Russians.[31] Rezanov himself was so angered that he secretly plotted
with two junior Russian naval officers named Khvostov and Davydov to exact revenge, and between 1806 and 1808 the Japanese
settlements in Saghalien and the Kuriles were terrorized by Rus-

sian ships and marines under their command. The shogunate was
naturally alarmed by their attacks but was totally unable to guess
the cause, not connecting them with Rezanov's resentment. Again
the government called on Mogami for advice, granting him an
early promotion.

Mogami urged that strategic places in the islands be fortified
with heavy weapons, but he remained convinced that the best way
to ensure the security of the Japanese possessions was to win the
confidence and respect of the Ainu, who would then resist of their
own free will, sparing the Japanese people the expense of defense
preparations.[32] Mogami's advice seems to have been disregarded.
The reluctance of the shogunate to accept its responsibilities in
the north was plainly revealed in 1821 when it suddenly returned
Ezo to the jurisdiction of the Matsumae clan after thirteen years
of direct rule.

In his late years Mogami continued to enjoy remarkably good
health, despite the hardships he had endured in his travels. One
last event of unusual interest was his meeting with Siebold in Edo.
Siebold's diary entry for April 16, 1826, opens, "Dies sane calculo
candidissimo notandus!" ("A day to be noted as being of the greatest importance.")[33] Siebold was moved to write Latin not only by
his joy at meeting a man who could tell him so much about Ezo,
but also by his fear that if he wrote in Dutch (or German) the
eagle-eyed interpreters might learn that Mogami had lent him
maps of the Kuriles and Kamchatka. During the rest of Siebold's
stay in Edo he met Mogami daily, studying the vocabulary of the
Ainu language and hearing about Mogami's explorations. When
Siebold left Edo for Nagasaki at the end of May, Mogami accompanied him as far as Odawara.

Siebold frequently acknowledged in his books how deeply he
was indebted to Mogami Tokunai, whom he respected above all
other Japanese he had met. Undoubtedly it was some promise to
Mogami that caused Siebold to wait twenty-five years before publishing the prize of his collection of Japanese maps, the chart
Mogami gave him in 1826 showing Saghalien to be an island. We
may wonder why Mogami risked the grave consequences of giving

Siebold this map and other secret information about the Ainu lands. Certainly no thought of personal advantage could have been involved. Only a disinterested desire to promote knowledge—and perhaps also personal affection for Siebold, like the affection he had felt forty years earlier for Ishuyo—could have led Mogami to break the shogunate's law. Nothing about the career of Mogami Tokunai is anything less than admirable, but this gesture bespeaks most eloquently the character of a man whose life was one of discovery.

Mamiya Rinzō (1775–1844)

Mamiya Rinzō was even more celebrated as an explorer than Mogami Tokunai; indeed, his name, first brought to the attention of Western readers by Captain Golownin's account in 1816, gained world renown in 1832 when Siebold named the body of water separating Karafuto from the Asiatic mainland "Mamia Strait," a name still used by the Japanese today.

Mamiya was born in the province of Hitachi in the east of Japan. Like Mogami Tokunai, he believed he was of samurai descent, though his family for generations had tilled the soil. Local tradition had it that Mamiya revealed his unusual intelligence even as a boy, especially by his intuitive grasp of the best way to build irrigation dams.[34] At any rate, his abilities attracted the attention of the geographer Murakami Shimanojō, who was visiting the region, and Murakami took the boy to Edo, probably about 1790. Soon afterward Mamiya was adopted into a samurai family, though he continued to live in Murakami's house and study with him.

Mamiya's first opportunity to make a name for himself occurred in 1799 when he accompanied Murakami to Matsumae, apparently to assist in making a survey of the island. In 1800 he met the great surveyor Inō Tadataka (1745–1818) in Hakodate, a chance encounter that determined Mamiya's life work. A successful sake brewer and firewood dealer, Inō had long dabbled in surveying as a hobby, but in 1795, at the age of fifty, he turned over his business to his heir and went to Edo to study astronomy and surveying with Takahashi Yoshitoki (1764–1804), a man considerably his junior. After five years of constant study Inō felt confident he

could now "make measurements without error."[35] In 1800, with
an official appointment from the shogunate, he embarked on his
great mission of surveying the entire country, a task that would
not be completed until 1821, after his death. Inō went first to
Hakodate, planning to begin the survey in the north; it was there
that he met Mamiya Rinzō, with whom he formed a lifetime relationship of teacher and disciple.

Mamiya remained in Ezo until 1811. His first years there seem
to have been spent surveying and charting the southern Kuriles.
He was on Etorofu in 1807 when the Russian marines led by
Khvostov and Davydov attacked the Japanese settlements, burning and pillaging as they went. Mamiya took an active part in
the defense, urging vigorous countermeasures even as the Japanese
military commander, confident of his forces, discounted the threat
of the Russian landing parties of a mere five or ten men. The ex-
asperated Mamiya threatened to report this complacency to the
shogunate, yet the commander refused even to return the enemy's
fire, alleging a shortage of ammunition. Finally the Japanese fled
to the hills without even putting up a show of resistance. Mamiya
was enraged, but was powerless to fight the Russians unaided; in
the end he also made for the hills. In later years Mamiya remembered with pride his part in the otherwise unimpressive Japanese
defense of Etorofu. Golownin, who met Mamiya in 1811, cynically
described him: "I must here remark, that this was the first Japanese
who ventured, in our presence, to swagger and assume importance
on account of his military skill, and his vapouring made not only
us but even his own countrymen sometimes laugh at him."[36] Perhaps it was also on the basis of reports of the Etorofu incident that
Golownin was moved to make this surprising generalization: "The
Japanese are deficient in only one quality, which we reckon among
the virtues, namely, bravery or courage. If the Japanese are timid,
this is merely in consequence of the peaceful character of their
government, of the long repose which the nation has enjoyed, or
rather of their being unaccustomed to shed blood; but that the
whole people are by nature timid is what I can by no means allow,
whether I may be right or wrong."[37]

As a result of the defeat at Etorofu the magistrate of Matsumae,

Habuto Masayasu, was dismissed from office, charged with the failure of his subordinates to repel the Russian attack. Mamiya Rinzō's actions, however, were favorably noticed, and he was chosen to make a survey of Saghalien in 1808. Apparently he was recommended by the court astronomer Takahashi Kageyasu (1785–1829), the son and successor to Takahashi Yoshitoki.[38] We may further assume that it was Inō Tadataka who first suggested Mamiya for the job to Kageyasu, a brilliant scholar who was at the time engaged in preparing a detailed map of the world, by command of the shogunate. The one area of the globe that remained a mystery to geographers everywhere was Karafuto, as Saghalien was called by the Japanese. European explorers, beginning with Vries in 1642, had sighted the coasts of Karafuto, but had been unable to determine whether it was an island or a peninsula connected to the Asiatic mainland. The Japanese had been exploring the southern part of the island since the early seventeenth century, but their geographers relied on European maps for knowledge of the rest of Karafuto. Hayashi Shihei, writing in 1785, described Karafuto as "a peninsula extending southeast, joined to eastern Tartary." Matsudaira Sadanobu declared in 1792, after examining a translated Dutch map, "Karafuto is connected by land to Manchuria, Santan, and Tartary. The theory that Karafuto is an island is outmoded and untrue." Honda Toshiaki more cautiously stated in *Tales of the West*: "Some say Karafuto is connected by land to Santan at the northwest, others that they are separated by a large river." And Kondō Morishige, following various European authorities, expressed his belief that Karafuto was a peninsula and Saghalien a quite separate island.[39] In the light of such uncertainties it is easy to see why Takahashi Kageyasu was anxious to send a reliable man to Karafuto to ascertain its true geography once and for all.

Takahashi's chief source of information about Karafuto was a map prepared by the English cartographer Aaron Arrowsmith, which incorporated information from the explorations made by La Pérouse in 1787. Takahashi described this map in 1809 as "the newest and most valuable in existence."[40] For one thing, the Arrowsmith map convinced Takahashi that Karafuto and Saghalien were in fact identical. Takahashi at the time did not know that this map was already obsolete: in 1805 Captain Krusenstern, having sailed north from Japan after the failure of the Rezanov mission, carefully surveyed the eastern coast of Karafuto, replacing the guesswork of earlier men with precise findings. But even Krusenstern did not suspect that Karafuto was an island.

Originally it had been planned to send Mogami Tokunai and another high-ranking official to explore Karafuto in 1807, but the expedition was postponed because of the depredations of Khvostov and Davydov. Later its composition was also altered by the decision to send instead two junior persons, an official named Matsuda Denjūrō and a hired assistant, Mamiya Rinzō.[41] Perhaps the shogunate feared the explorers might be captured or killed by the Russians and found it easier to sacrifice younger men.

Mamiya traveled from Matsumae to Sōya, at the northern tip of Hokkaidō, in the spring of 1808. There he met Mogami Tokunai, who had arrived two weeks earlier on a tour of inspection of defenses, and benefited from the advice the older man could give him, the fruit of eight earlier missions to the north. After a month in Sōya, Mamiya and Matsuda were ready to embark on their dangerous journey. Mamiya, no doubt striking a suitably heroic pose, spoke his farewell to a Sōya official: "I swear by my life that I will not return unless successful in my mission. If my mission goes badly, I will remain in Ezo, alone if necessary, and become a part of the barbarian soil or else a barbarian myself. It is unlikely that we shall meet again, but it is the common lot of men that there be beginnings without ends."[42]

After crossing the strait of La Pérouse between Hokkaidō and Karafuto, the two men separated, Matsuda going north along the west coast, Mamiya along the east coast. Mamiya traveled in an Ainu dugout canoe, paddling his way or sometimes dragging the canoe over narrow projections of land. It took him over a month to reach Cape Patience. He attempted to continue farther north, but a powerful current was running against him and the waves made headway impossible. Mamiya turned back to Manui, the narrowest part of Karafuto, crossed over the mountains to the west coast, and eventually caught up with Matsuda at Noteto, about 51°55' N.Lat. The west coast, unlike the sparsely settled east coast, was dotted with Ainu and Giliak villages, and there were signs of civilization: the headman at Nayoro proudly displayed documents written in Manchu and Chinese investing him with the title of chieftain. The Chinese, who apparently first reached the island in the thirteenth century, still claimed sovereignty over the northern part and exacted annual tribute, but their rule by this time was exceedingly tenuous, and the annual tribute was a profitable form of barter as far as the Karafuto natives were concerned. Nevertheless Matsuda and Mamiya were bent on determining the "border" between the Japanese and Chinese domains.

Matsuda, prior to rejoining Mamiya, had gone northward to a point from which he could see the mainland of Santan (the maritime provinces of Siberia) across a narrow strait that seemed to widen out in the distance. The estuary of the Amur River could also be discerned. Matsuda's native guides informed him that if he traveled six days more to the north he would come out on the east coast, and he realized then that Karafuto must be an island. The discovery was Matsuda's, but the credit went largely to Mamiya because he actually explored the region and proved that the reports of the guides were correct.

Mamiya's efforts to persuade Matsuda to continue northward up the coast from Noteto proved unavailing, and the two men turned back a little over two months after landing in Karafuto. A month later they reached Sōya, where Mamiya was informed that he would have to return to Karafuto almost immediately to complete his mission. He rested for only twenty days, most of which he spent preparing official reports. He also sent a letter and a map to Takahashi Kageyasu.

Mamiya spent New Year's Day of the sixth year of Bunka (1809) in a guard's hut in the settlement of Tonnai on the west coast of Karafuto. A month later he set out for the north, but it was not until June that the frozen seas melted sufficiently for him to make his way through the strait that came to bear his name to the tip of

14. Mamiya Rinzō

the island. Mamiya intended to follow the coast round to the eastern shore, but the Ainu, frightened by the dangerous seas, refused to follow him, and he decided instead to cross over to the mainland shore, the coast of Tartary. Luck was with him, for the annual tribute mission of some Ainu and Giliak natives was just about to leave Karafuto for Deren, a Manchu trading station on the Amur. Mamiya joined the mission and discovered Deren to be the source of the Chinese goods that were finding their way into Hokkaidō under the name of "Ezo brocades." The Ainu and Giliak villagers brought the Manchu officials a tribute of furs and returned home with the highly prized brocades.

Mamiya was well received by the Manchu officials and permitted to travel freely in the area. At the end of 1809 he returned to Matsumae, where he spent the following year collaborating with a young official named Murakami Teisuke on two books describing his travels, works of considerable ethnographic interest even today. In 1811 Mamiya at last left the north and returned to Edo. Repeated attacks of frostbite during his eleven years in Ezo had twisted his fingers into claws, and he was physically exhausted. By the middle of the year, however, he seems to have recovered, as we know from an entry in Shiba Kōkan's journal describing a visit by Mamiya.[43] At the time Mamiya was living in the house of Inō Tadataka and studying with him the accurate determination of latitudes by astronomical observation, perhaps with the intent of completing the survey map of Ezo that Inō had started.[44]

That same year, 1811, Captain Golownin and other officers and men of the Russian navy were captured on Etorofu by the Japanese, and carried off trussed like criminals to Matsumae, where they were thrown into prison. The Russians had gone ashore on Etorofu because they desperately needed firewood and water, and the Japanese, taking advantage of the Russians' evidently pacific intentions, seized them as an act of revenge for the wanton attacks of Khvostov and Davydov. For the next two years the captive Russians were subjected to constant interrogations, mainly intended to clarify whether or not they were connected with the attacks on Karafuto and the Kuriles. The Japanese did not confine themselves

to military matters; they extended their questioning to every detail of Russian life, often to the despair of their captives. They
also sought to obtain instruction in the Russian language in return
for which, they hinted, the captives' release might be arranged.
But Captain Golownin refused to cooperate: he had no intention
of becoming a Russian language teacher. He wrote, "We saw
plainly the Japanese were deceiving us, and did not intend to set
us free, because they wished to make use of us as teachers; but that
they had made a great mistake! We were ready to die, but not to
become instructors of the Japanese."[45]

The one pupil the Russians welcomed was Murakami Teisuke,
Mamiya's literary collaborator. Golownin recalled, "Teske shewed
extraordinary capacity even in the very first lessons we gave him.
He had an excellent memory and pronounced the Russian words
with such facility, that we conjectured he had previously learned
the language, and was purposely concealing his knowledge of it,
or, at least, that he was acquainted with some other European
tongues."[46]

Throughout his interrogations Golownin protested that the actions of Khvostov and Davydov had been unauthorized by the Russian government, and that in fact the two officers had subsequently
been imprisoned for their offenses. The magistrate of Matsumae,
Arao Shigeaya, believing his story, recommended that Golownin
be released, but Mamiya was of quite a different opinion. Having
personally suffered the indignity of the Russian attack on Etorofu,
he urged severity. It is not clear how much influence Mamiya's
views exerted, but the advocates of severity prevailed and Golownin's release was delayed.

In the spring of 1812 Mamiya went to Matsumae, charged with
carrying out a land survey of Ezo. He visited Golownin, apparently
to discover if there was anything the Russian could teach him
about astronomy and surveying. Golownin described his visitor:

In the meanwhile we formed an acquaintance with a geometrician and
astronomer named Mamia-Rinso, who had been sent from the Japanese
capital. . . . He visited us every day, and frequently remained with us
from morning until evening, during which time he gave us an account of
his travels, and produced his plans and sketches of the different countries

he had visited.... He had visited all the Kurile Islands, as far as the seventeenth, Sagaleen, and even the land of Mandshuren, and had sailed through the river Amur. He manifested his pride, however, by a constant boasting of the deeds he had performed, and the labours he had endured.[47]

Despite the frequency of Mamiya's visits, the lessons could hardly have been termed a success. He knew no Russian, and Golownin found it exhausting to explain even the simplest principles. Besides, Golownin lacked the proper books and instruments to give instruction. Nevertheless, Mamiya's visits continued. Golownin wrote:

Though Mamia-Rinso was decidedly inimical to us, we were not always engaged in disputes with him; on the contrary, we conversed together in an apparently friendly manner on various subjects, of which the political was the most important. He maintained that the Japanese had well-founded reasons for believing that the Russians entertained evil designs upon them, and that the Dutch had spoken truth in their information respecting several European courts. Teske, however, was not of this opinion. He believed that the Dutch had designedly infused suspicions into the Japanese Government against the Russians and the English.[48]

Mamiya made no effort to understand Golownin's position, and indeed became more and more obdurate in opposing the release of the captives; Golownin considered Mamiya to be his principal adversary. In the end, however, the authorities exonerated Golownin of all part in the Russian attacks on Ezo, and in 1813 he and his party were released. Mamiya's displeasure can be imagined, but Murakami Teisuke and the others who had come to know Golownin were delighted. "The joy of the Japanese was, indeed, unfeigned. We understood from the interpreters, that in consequence of an application from the High Priest of the city, the Bunyo had issued orders that prayers for our safe voyage should be offered up in all the temples for the space of five days."[49]

Mamiya spent most of the years from 1812 to 1822 in Ezo, engaged in the preparation of the land survey. His maps were eagerly sought by Japanese geographers, notably Takahashi Kageyasu and Kondō Morishige. As early as 1809 Takahashi had published a map of Japan and neighboring countries in which he incorporated Mamiya's discoveries of the preceding year.[50] In 1810 Takahashi prepared a large map of the two hemispheres, each about three feet in diameter, but he decided to wait for the results of Mamiya's second expedition before publishing it. The map appeared in 1811, and incorporated Mamiya's findings on the west coast of Karafuto. The areas Mamiya failed to reach—the extreme north of the west coast and the northeast coast, were traced with a dotted line, an indication of how conscientiously Takahashi took his work as a cartographer. It was this conscientiousness that proved his downfall.

Takahashi Kageyasu is a peculiarly tragic figure. A scholar of the highest position—he was the chief court astronomer and commissioner of the shogunate libraries—he enjoyed the esteem of the government, yet he risked his career and even his life for the glory of drawing a reliable map of Karafuto. His knowledge of Dutch was exceptional, and he is considered also to have been the founder of Manchu studies in Japan. His close relations with the Dutch residents in Japan were described by the factory director Doeff:

I made my first acquaintance with him in 1810. He came every day secretly, as a personal friend, and although his visits were at first somewhat tedious, I learned soon to know him better, not only as a capable person, but also as a kind and gentle man, with whom I joined in 1814 in even closer ties of friendship, and who on my departure from Japan in 1817 gave me the clearest proofs of his affection. . . . I was indeed embarrassed to give a Dutch nickname to such a distinguished man, but he himself insisted on it for so long that I finally chose for him the name Johannes Globius.[51]

It was as Globius that Siebold knew Takahashi when they met in Edo in 1826. Takahashi was then forty-one, Siebold thirty. Each of them was anxious not only to learn from the other, but to demonstrate the fruits of his own scholarship to someone who could appreciate their value. Takahashi drew for Siebold "splendid maps of Ezo and Saghalien,"[52] and questioned Siebold in turn about foreign countries. He learned in the meantime from the interpreter Yoshio Chūjirō (1788–1833), who had first arranged their meeting, that Siebold had with him the four volumes of Krusenstern's *Voyage.* He begged Siebold to give him the books, but was refused until he agreed to supply in return various Japanese geographic

15. Philipp Frantz von Siebold

materials, including the survey charts of Japan made by Inō Tadataka. Takahashi knew that giving these maps to Siebold was an offense punishable by death, but in the end he decided to take the risk for the benefits the information in Krusenstern's book would bring Japan. Siebold provided in addition to Krusenstern's *Voyage* a life of Napoleon and maps of the Dutch East Indies; Takahashi sent Inō Tadataka's map of all Japan except Ezo on the scale 1:864,000, and his map of Ezo on the scale 1:432,000, as well as smaller maps of the southern Kuriles and Karafuto.[53] Takahashi personally copied the maps and as he completed them sent them to Siebold by way of interpreters making the journey from Edo to Nagasaki.

Takahashi began his translation of Krusenstern immediately, and by the autumn of 1828 was close to completing the draft. At the same time Siebold, near the end of his tour of duty in Japan, was packing the boxes of books and papers that represented the fruits of his five years' stay. Takahashi did not realize it, but for some months he had been under surveillance by the government police as the result of an incident that had occurred earlier that year. Siebold, who had met Mamiya Rinzō casually during his visit to Edo, decided to correspond with him. He included in a parcel sent to Takahashi a smaller one for Mamiya containing a length of batik cloth[54] and a letter in which he expressed admiration for Mamiya's work, voiced the hope that they might become friends, and asked for pressed botanical specimens from Ezo. Mamiya delivered the parcel, unopened, to the magistrate's office. Takahashi's failure to report the arrival of a present from a foreigner immediately placed him under suspicion. Writing in later years, Siebold expressed his high opinion of Mamiya's work and even published a translation of Mamiya's *Journey to Eastern Tartary (Tōdatsu Kikō)*, but he blamed Mamiya for the subsequent investigation that nearly cost him the loss of all the materials he had gathered.[55]

Given the stringent laws of the time, it may seem surprising that Siebold should have dared to correspond with someone he hardly knew, but no doubt his previous successes in pursuing his academic research had made him suppose that archaic regulations need not trouble him. After all, he had secured permission to establish a school in the city of Nagasaki, outside Deshima, though that too had been forbidden, and he had made many friends and disciples among the intellectuals in both Nagasaki and Edo. Indeed, the readiness with which these friends associated with him, and the frankness of their criticism of the narrow-minded policies of the government, convinced Siebold that as long as he observed the letter of the law he could disregard the intent of the restrictions with impunity. Perhaps he even imagined that the seclusion policy was already no more than an empty formality, and that Japan was about to open normal relations with the rest of the world. If this was his thought, he soon learned how gravely he was mistaken.

On the night of September 17, 1828, a violent typhoon struck the area of Nagasaki. The ship that was to bear Siebold and his belongings to the Indies was lashed by the storm and threatened to capsize. With great effort the Japanese managed to beach the ship and save the cargo. In order to permit repairs to the ship the cargo was later unloaded, and the contents were inspected, following the rule that all goods brought into Japan (though not those exported) had to be verified. Prohibited articles were discovered in the eighty-one boxes of Siebold's effects, including a garment bearing the shogunate crest, weapons and pictures of soldiers, an illustrated edition of *The Tale of Genji*, Japanese shipbuilding tools and pictures, and drawings of Japan.[56]

The authorities reported this find to Edo, where an investigation was immediately undertaken into the source of these forbidden objects. Takahashi, already under suspicion, was an obvious possibility. It was Mamiya Rinzō, if we can believe contemporary gossip, who denounced Takahashi to the authorities. A letter written in 1835 blamed the event on Mamiya's "one-sided loyalty" and "unenlightened loyalty." It goes on to say:

This man at the time was in charge of Ezo affairs, and although he had a high opinion of Western learning, he detested those who dabbled in it for their amusement, saying that he had studied it exclusively for the public good. . . . Sometimes he would visit the houses of people who had studied Dutch learning, and would secretly investigate whether they privately possessed maps and the like. As a result, whenever he appeared they would hide their Dutch books and so on. . . . He constantly used to say that one had no choice but to kill any man who was disloyal to the government. Mr. Takahashi came in contact with his fangs and learned what he meant.[57]

Takahashi Kageyasu was arrested on November 16, 1828. His house was searched, and his books and papers confiscated. On December 7 a fast messenger arrived in Nagasaki from Edo with orders for Siebold to surrender at once all maps of Japan and other objects received from Takahashi. Though the interpreter Yoshio Chūjirō urged Siebold to comply immediately with the order, he refused. On the morning of December 16 thirty policemen descended on the Dutch factory with official letters demanding the maps. On the same day four interpreters were charged with having carried letters between Siebold and Takahashi; they were subsequently imprisoned. Siebold, forewarned by Yoshio that his maps would be seized, spent that afternoon and the whole night making copies. The next morning he handed over to Yoshio the originals after carefully secreting the copies, which he was able to take back to Europe with him when at last he received permission to leave Deshima.[58]

In February 1829, Siebold was handed a list of twenty-three questions on his activities, and was ordered to submit answers in writing to the magistrate. The intent of most of the questions was to force Siebold to reveal who had served as go-betweens in his correspondence with Takahashi, but Siebold steadfastly refused to give this information. A typical question, the third, runs: "In your letter written on Deshima on February 25, 1828, you state that you are sending Sakuzaemon [Takahashi Kageyasu] through the interpreter Gonosuke a separate letter, a *kunstkrim* in a *doos,* and a copy of the *Malay Dictionary* by Roorda van Eysinga. In addition, you mention sending a parcel to Rinzō. What was the nature of the letter sent under separate cover, and what were the contents of the parcel? And whom did you ask to deliver them?"[59] In his answer Siebold explained that *kunstkrim* was a mistake for *kunstkim,* an artificial horizon used in solar measurements, and that a *doos* was a box. He could not remember definitely the content of his other

letter to Takahashi, but suggested a few possibilities. The parcel
sent to Mamiya Rinzō consisted of a cotton towel, sent by way of
greeting, and a postcard asking for pressed botanical specimens.
He concluded, "I cannot remember definitely whom I asked to
take these items."[60]

The investigation dragged on for months, one set of questions
leading to another, and the proceedings were complicated by the
necessity of translating everything into Japanese or Dutch with the
utmost precision. In the meantime twenty-three of Siebold's Deshima associates, including the artist Kawahara Keiga,[61] were arrested. In Edo too the arrests continued. Habu Genseki (1768–
1854), the Shogun's personal physician and a man celebrated for
his skill in treating diseases of the eye, was accused of having given
Siebold his own garment marked with the Shogun's crest. Habu
had given Siebold this present to induce him to disclose the name
of a medicine used in treating a certain ophthalmological disease,
information obviously of value to the country. Nevertheless, Habu
was found guilty of a grave violation of national laws, and in 1830
he was deprived of his status as a samurai.[62] Takahashi himself
died of illness in prison on March 20, 1829. His body was pickled
in brine to preserve it until a sentence could be passed on him.*
A year later he was found guilty, and the verdict stated that if he
were still alive he would be sentenced to death. The head was
struck from Takahashi's pickled corpse. This was the fate of the
most brilliant scholar of his day.

Sentence was passed on Siebold in October 1829. During the long
interval he and his associates had repeatedly been interrogated,
and some of them had been tortured. Siebold was driven to despair
by reports of the sufferings of his friends, for which he held himself
to blame. He punished himself by exposing his body to the bitter

---

* A grisly bit of humor concerning the disposal of Takahashi's corpse may
be found in Ayusawa Shintarō, *Yamamura Saisuke* (Tokyo, 1960), pp. 19–20.
Incredible as it may seem, a long and serious debate took place about whether
Takahashi's body should be preserved in salt or sugar. Those advocating sugar
seemed to be inspired by the pun on *temmondō*, "the art of astronomy," and
temmondō, the name of a plant whose roots were commonly preserved in sugar
as a sweet. A government official finally pronounced in favor of salt.

16. Life on Deshima

winter winds, and when friends remonstrated he answered, "How can I rest peacefully when I have brought such pain and danger to my pupils and friends?"[63] Once, when he had fallen ill, his devoted mistress Sonogi was alarmed to discover him dressed in black and carrying a dagger that he intended to plunge into himself. He was dissuaded only when Sonogi insisted on dying with him. The sentence delivered in October was lighter than Siebold had anticipated: he was ordered to leave the country on the next ship and never to return. His serious crime of accepting forbidden objects and attempting to send them abroad was judged to have been aggravated by his refusal to disclose the truth when interrogated. It was recognized as an extenuating circumstance that he might be ignorant of Japanese law because this was his first visit; nevertheless, he had broken the law and was guilty.

On December 30, 1829, Siebold sailed from Japan, leaving behind Sonogi and his small daughter Iné. He returned to Europe, where his writings about Japan and things Japanese earned him an honored place among natural scientists. The Japanese government pardoned his crimes in 1858 with the signing of the commercial treaty between Japan and the Netherlands. Siebold made a second visit to Japan between 1859 and 1862 and was warmly welcomed by his friends of thirty years before, but the memory of the tragic events surrounding his departure must have shadowed the familiar landscapes.

Mamiya Rinzō, whom Siebold believed to be the cause of his persecution, was praised by patriots for his uncompromising loyalty, but was despised by most intellectuals, even those who had been close to him, for what they saw as his betrayal of Takahashi and Siebold.[64] Mamiya undoubtedly was convinced he had acted as a loyal subject. He could feel no compassion for anyone who broke the law, regardless of his motives. The dogged determination that had carried Mamiya forward on lonely missions was not matched by a flexibility that might admit more than one proper course of action.

In 1829 he became a government informer, serving under secret orders and charged with investigating suspicious activities in dif-

ferent parts of the country. His first mission may have been to Nagasaki, where he was apparently sent to investigate illegal trading
with the Dutch. A Japanese friend of Jan Overmeer Fisscher (who
served on Deshima from 1820 to 1829) encountered Mamiya entering a shop to buy a contraband article for the Dutch and fled in
terror, knowing Mamiya to be a spy.[65] Mamiya's most renowned
success, however, was in Satsuma, a domain normally forbidden to
agents of the shogunate, where he spent three years learning the
trade of paperhanger in order to gain admission to the castle. On
other missions he often disguised himself as a beggar or an outcast.

Mamiya in later years mingled with government spies and super-
patriots. Watanabe Kazan (1793–1841), who was to die a prisoner
after being denounced by an informer for anti-shogunate views,
wrote in 1831, "Mamiya Rinzō was in my service. He was a most
efficient spy, but he had an extremely peculiar disposition, and he
was so headstrong that it was difficult to control him."[66] Tokugawa
Nariaki, the violently xenophobic daimyo of Mito, invited Mamiya to his domain, where he became intimate with such nationalistic scholars as Fujita Tōko. He was reported at the end of his life
to be receiving a regular monthly stipend from the Mito clan.

It is hard to escape a feeling of revulsion at the thought of
Mamiya Rinzō, the conqueror of the north, ending his life as a
paid informer. Yet this does not diminish his contribution to geographical knowledge, not only in Japan but throughout the world.
Perhaps his greatest tribute came from a rival. In 1834, when Siebold showed Captain Krusenstern a chart based on Mamiya's
discoveries twenty-five years earlier, with the strait separating Saghalien from the mainland, the captain exclaimed, "Les Japonais
m'ont vaincu!"[67]

7. Hirata Atsutane and Western Learning

Most of the men who took up the study of Dutch learning had been trained in the type of neo-Confucianism that, whatever its developments in nineteenth-century Japan, had originally sprung from a scientific interest in an "investigation of things."[1] The attraction of Western ways to such men is understandable; what is surprising is that scholars of Western learning also included zealots of the Shinto persuasion. Among these the most extreme example and the most interesting was Hirata Atsutane (1776–1843). Hirata had received Confucian training as a boy, although, if we can believe family gossip,[2] he was so deficient in his studies as to be the despair of his father and the laughingstock of his village. When he ran away from home at the age of nineteen to escape his humiliating condition and win celebrity in the capital, he was ready to adopt any new ideas that promised to bring him success. In a later and less strictly controlled society he would probably have joined or founded a new political party.

After several years of a hand-to-mouth existence about which we know very little, Hirata was adopted by a samurai whose name he took in place of his original surname, Ōwada. His new station enabled him to devote his time to study. During his days of hardship Hirata had read the Chinese Taoist philosopher Chuang Tzu with great admiration, and his interest in Taoism (which was rather unusual at the time in Japan) remained with him until the end of his career, markedly coloring many of his beliefs. Not until about 1801 did Hirata begin the study of Shinto that was to become the chief pursuit of his life. Unfortunately, the great master of Shinto, Motoori Norinaga (1730–1801), died before Hirata could enroll in his school. Nevertheless Hirata in later years invariably styled himself a pupil of Motoori's, on the ground that Motoori once appeared to him in a dream and accepted him formally as a pupil, reciting two poems to celebrate the occasion.[3]

It is not clear just when Hirata's interest in Western learning was awakened. Already in his first major work, *New Discussion of the Gods* (*Kishin Shinron,* 1805), Hirata shows some knowledge of European inventions. In a long description he relates how "several years before" (probably about the time that he was first studying Shinto) he had taken part in the demonstration of an electrostatic machine at a friend's house. After the *erekiteru,* as it was called, had produced a flash like lightning, Hirata's friend turned to him and said, "Exactly the same principles govern thunder and lightning in the sky. How foolish people are to be terrified by thunder simply out of ignorance of these principles! What is there to be afraid of?" Hirata answered:

This is indeed a very cleverly contrived machine, but it is quite a different matter whether or not real thunder and lightning operate on the same principles. Even supposing they do, is it not true that although we can make the machine produce lightning it cannot produce it by itself? The machine is made by men and will do men's bidding. There is thus nothing to fear from it. But the real lightning rages and twists through the clouds of its own will, breaking through, whenever and wherever it chooses, to split trees or to smash boulders. You may imagine that it is without dislikes or emotions, but there have been numerous instances from ancient times of wicked things and people destroyed by lightning. . . . How can the principles governing so unpredictable and so awe-inspiring a thing be understood by means of a machine devised by man's meager wisdom? I can by no means accept so shallow a conjecture. If you really desire to understand such matters, forget for a while the petty ways of human learning and study with a sincere heart the ancient things.[4]

From these remarks we can see the difference in attitude toward Western learning between Hirata and a true rangaku scholar.

Hirata's friend thought that man had at last been enabled by scientific knowledge to free himself from superstitious fear. Hirata, by contrast, though he accepted Dutch learning and even insisted on its importance, denied that it could explain the nature of lightning or any of the other mysteries of the universe with which he was passionately concerned. He studied Western learning not for its own sake, but mainly as a means of disproving Chinese and Buddhist beliefs, and thus directly or indirectly lending support to Shinto doctrines. As he expressed it, "The only reason to study foreign books is for the potential benefits they contain for Japan."[5]

Hirata's Scientific Borrowings from the West

Almost any argument of Hirata's, however couched and however heavily dependent on foreign testimony, is apt to end with an assertion that Japanese are quite unlike and far superior to "Chinese, Indians, Russians, Dutch, Siamese, Cambodians, or any other people."[6] Hirata's conclusions are usually foregone and not very original. That Japan was the Land of the Gods, the Japanese the descendants of gods, and Japan superior to all other nations because of its unbroken line of emperors—favorite theses of Hirata's —had all been stated in similar terms by Kitabatake Chikafusa (1292–1354) many years before. The interest of Hirata's writings lies in the methods by which he arrived at these conclusions. Unlike Kitabatake, Hirata emphasized the learning of the Way of the Gods as well as its superior spiritual content. He made light of the accomplishments of the Confucian scholars, who were familiar with only a few classics and prided themselves on even slight proficiency in writing Chinese prose and poetry. In comparison, the Buddhists were well educated, for they were obliged to read the Tripitaka (or at least parts of it) in addition to the Confucian classics. But, said Hirata, Japanese learning is by far the most extensive of all because it encompasses both Confucian and Buddhist learning. "It is just like the great sea into which flow and mix the waters of many rivers." Hirata concluded, "Thus we see that a man who wishes to attain the pure and correct Way of Japan must know all these kinds of learning. Foreign though they are, they can help Japan if Japanese study them and select their good points. It is thus quite proper to speak of Chinese learning, and even of Indian and Dutch learning, as Japanese learning."[7]

Hirata's views on the importance of foreign learning were not shared by most of the Shinto scholars of his day. He was bitterly attacked for his advocacy of Western theories of astronomy and medicine. His opponents declared that scholars of the ancient Japanese learning should not permit their ears to be defiled by meretricious, rationalistic theories about the earth's rotation, but should preserve the simplicity of the men of old.[8] Hirata replied that scholars should not attempt to imitate the innocence of the men of old, however admirable it was, but must seek the truth. One critic, attacking the statement in one of Hirata's works that the moon when viewed through a telescope has a surface like the earth's, asserted, "There may indeed be objects on the moon that look like countries, but we should not believe in things that are not mentioned in the ancient classics." Hirata sarcastically rejoined, "If you refuse to believe in things that are not mentioned in the ancient classics, you cannot very well believe what we now know about man's internal organs, for they are not mentioned in the classics. But will you deny that they exist?"[9]

Hirata insisted that the Japanese adopt the worthwhile parts of Western learning. Only beginners unsure of themselves or self-satisfied people like the Chinese would refuse to profit from its many excellences.[10] Of course, not all of Western science should be accepted; certain tenets, such as the theory that each fixed star is itself a sun, must be rejected as groundless lies.[11] "The reason those barbarians spew forth such shallow falsehoods . . . is because they were born in filthy, remote countries, far from the Divine Land, and have had no opportunity to hear the ancient words from the divine mouth of Musubi no kami.[12] In this manner Hirata disposed of a theory that tended to depreciate the unique importance of the sun and the Sun Goddess.

By and large, however, Hirata was prepared to accept Western science except where he saw it as clashing irreconcilably with Shinto doctrine. The uses to which he put his Western learning were varied. Hirata was a practicing physician as well as a theologian; in treating his patients, he may have used European medical techniques learned from books.* He was most enthusiastic about Western medicine: "It goes without saying how accomplished they are in astronomy and geography; people have also been amazed by the precision of their machines. They are particularly skilled in medicine and the preparation of drugs. It has doubtless been the will of the gods that European medical books have been brought here in ever-increasing numbers and have attracted wide attention."[13] At one point he even said of a certain medical opinion that "since it is held by the Europeans, there should be no objection to giving it full credence."[14] Unlike Chinese physicians, who resorted to guesswork, the Europeans based their theories on actual observation, invariably dissecting the corpse of anyone who had died of an unusual malady; European medical information had been greatly enriched by the dissection of "many hundreds of bodies during the past 1500 years."[15] Hirata disapproved, however, of Japanese dissecting human beings: "It smells of the barbarian and is not proper for Japanese." People who failed to understand fully the anatomical diagrams in works translated from the Dutch were advised to dissect animals, preferably monkeys, because their organs were just like men's.[16]

Hirata admitted that the study of medicine in Japan had lagged behind the advances made abroad, but he had a ready excuse for this seeming deficiency: the medical arts failed to develop in ancient Japan because they were unnecessary. Japan had never suffered from serious diseases before engaging in relations with China and other nations whose endemic noxiousness was the cause of countless maladies.[17] To cure what were essentially foreign diseases it was quite proper to resort to foreign medicines. They had, of course, to be employed with great care; an inexperi-

---

* Though Hirata may have used some Western techniques, he was also heavily dependent on magic and spells. He taught his pupils, for example, that to revive a man who had swooned it was effective to summon him by shouting his name into the family well, which was considered to be the shortest way to the afterworld. See Watanabe Kinzō, *Hirata Atsutane Kenkyū* (Tokyo, 1942), pp. 219–21.

enced doctor with some of the powerful Dutch drugs might be like a "monkey with a sword."

The contention that the backwardness of medicine in Japan resulted naturally from the salubrity of the country is typical of Hirata's answers to criticism of ancient Japan and the Way. For example, the Confucian scholar Dazai Jun (1680–1747) had asserted that the lack of native Japanese words for benevolence, righteousness, rites, music, filial piety, and chastity proved that in ancient times Japan lacked the teachings of a Way. Hirata retorted, "Since the men of old in Japan always behaved in the proper way, there was no need for any special Way to be taught."[18] The reason the sages in China had been compelled to devise laws of marriage was that previously the Chinese had coupled like beasts, but since in Japan from remotest antiquity the conduct of man and wife had been perfectly decorous, regulations or special terms governing behavior were superfluous.[19] "If there is truth, teachings are unnecessary," proclaimed Hirata, no doubt under Taoist influence.[20]

Western science not only filled such gaps in Japanese learning as had been occasioned by the perfect health and morals of the fortunate ancients, but served to verify the truth of the classics.[21] For example, the introduction of the heliocentric Copernican theory confirmed the importance of the Sun Goddess, and even the use of a solar calendar was proof of the justice of the homage paid to that great deity. Hirata advised people not to think of the rotation of the earth as a foreign idea, for it was in accord with facts clearly stated in the classics and may indeed have been transmitted to the West from the Divine Land by way of India.[22] Vehement nationalistic arguments alternated with candid admissions of the superiority of Western notions of astronomy and geography, which Hirata considered "the most precise and most easily intelligible."[23] He praised Nishikawa Joken (1648–1724) of Nagasaki for having introduced European learning to Japan, saying, "Before him people knew nothing whatsoever about astronomy, geography, or the ways of foreign countries."[24]

Hirata's knowledge of Western astronomy, though not profound, was unusual for his time. He was familiar with the Japanese popularizers of Dutch science and was quite capable, say, of stating the sun's diameter or the relative sizes of the planets Mars and Jupiter.[25] But Hirata was interested in Western astronomy less for its own sake than as a means of bolstering his theses, and he was almost equally prepared to entertain completely unscientific astronomical information if it seemed of use. Thus he was led to interrogate at great length Torakichi and (several years later) Katsugorō, the two "divine boys";[26] the former claimed to have dwelt for years among the devils of the afterworld, and the latter to have been born a second time. Hirata recorded quite seriously the details of Torakichi's alleged visit to the "Island of Women," situated about 1,000 miles to the east of Japan, and to other fabulous lands.[27] When he asked Torakichi if it were true, as reported in Western books of astronomy, that the surface of the moon was composed of seas and mountains like the earth, the boy laughed and said, "Your information is false because you got it out of books. I don't know about books, but only what I saw when I was near the moon. My teacher had also told me that there were mountains, just as you say, but when I got quite close to the moon I could plainly see two or three big holes through which the stars were visible behind. There is no doubt that the holes exist."[28]

Hirata was always particularly interested in the moon because of its important place in his theology. Some Shinto scholars claimed that the moon was still the world of the dead, but Hirata believed that the moon, which at one time had been part of the earth and thus easily accessible to the dead, had ceased to serve as an afterworld once the two bodies had separated.[29] When he heard that the Europeans had invented a powerful telescope through which it was possible to see men and horses on the moon, he was disturbed and immediately wrote for more detailed information, including copies of drawings that had been made of the men on the moon.[30]

If Hirata's interest in Western astronomy stemmed from a desire to prove his theological views, his knowledge of Western geography was a means of demonstrating that Japan was the most happily endowed country in the world. To those (notably the Confucianists) who thought of Japan as a small, second-rate country, Hirata declared, "No matter how small a superior country may be, it remains superior, and no matter how big an inferior country may be, it remains inferior. When we examine maps of the world we find many huge countries like Russia and America, parts of which have no vegetation or human population. Can we call such countries superior?"[31] Japan, unlike those dreary wastelands, was blessed in being situated between 30 and 40 degrees of latitude, thus enjoying a perfect balance of seasons.[32] An abundance of produce of every variety enabled Japan to be quite self-sufficient and independent of the vagaries of foreign trade. How much better off Japan was than Holland, a cold country with few natural resources, which had no choice but to engage in trade with more fortunate lands in order to survive! The fact that other nations were beseeching Japan to trade with them was proof of the special favor of the gods, a favor that was indeed recognized throughout the world.[33]

Why was it that Japan was so much more fortunate than other countries? Hirata found the answer in the circumstances of Japan's creation. Unlike the rest of the world, which was formed of coagulated brine and mud, Japan was procreated by the divinities Izanagi and Izanami.[34] Moreover, the special geographic position of Japan could be proved by testimony in Western books; there is mention, for example, of a great flood that all but wiped out mankind.[35] Only Noah and a few others survived the deluge in Europe. Although the date of the flood corresponds to a period during the Age of the Gods, there is not the slightest mention of such a disaster in the Japanese chronicles; it followed, according to Hirata, that Japan must be situated higher than the continent of Europe. If the flood was not so calamitous in China as in Europe, and if Korea escaped it altogether (as the silence in the Korean records indicated), it was undoubtedly because of the relative proximity of these two countries to the Divine Land. Hirata concluded, "Is it not fair to say that the Imperial Land stands at the summit of the world?"[36]

Hirata's use of Western scientific material was in accordance with what he considered to be the true nature of European learning. He declared:

The rangaku scholars misunderstand the true meaning of their studies. They style themselves "scientists" and claim that there is nothing they cannot deduce from scientific principles. In so saying they run contrary to the spirit of the learning of the Europeans, who term anything they have not been able to discover after an exhaustive study of natural principles "the work of God," and who devoutly worship their God. It must be that the rangaku scholars, in spite of their denunciations of the extreme inadequacy of Chinese learning, have still not been able to liberate themselves from Chinese thought. As I mentioned in the *New Discussion of the Gods,* the Chinese in ancient times were not atheistic, but with the later vogue of superficial ideas it became customary to disbelieve the old legends of the Heavenly Sovereign (*t'ien-ti*) and the stories of the afterworld. This attitude was introduced to Japan and propagated here. The present-day rangaku scholars began their studies in childhood with Chinese texts, and the shallow ideas that they first imbibed have apparently become a stumbling block in the path of their knowledge. For them to denounce the narrowness of Chinese learning without examining their own behavior is like someone who has fled fifty steps laughing at someone else who has fled a hundred. How greatly they contradict the true meaning of Dutch studies![37]

Hirata was thus, according to his own interpretation of the word, a true rangaku scholar. He attempted to combine a mastery of medicine, astronomy, and other sciences with a devoutly pious respect for the gods, who control the unknowable. He was not content, however, with the fields of learning of the ordinary rangaku scholar; he utilized his acquaintance with Western theology in his exegesis of the sacred texts of Shinto.

Hirata's Theological Borrowings from the West

Hirata's first impressions of Western religion are found in his *New Discussion of the Gods,* a work largely devoted to attacks on Confucianist atheism. Hirata greatly esteemed Confucius (even going so far as to praise him for possessing "Japanese spirit" though a Chinese)[38] but had nothing but hatred and contempt for his self-styled followers. In a rebuttal of the Confucianist belief that the sun is the essence of the *yang* (male, positive) principle, Hirata wrote with admiration of the Dutch, who, though they were vilified in China with such names as "red barbarians," recognized how awe-inspiring and exalted a diety the Sun Goddess was. He had read that the Dutch worshiped this goddess every day at dawn and dusk, leading him to comment, "Is that not an amiable practice?"[39]

This curious misapprehension on Hirata's part was soon to be replaced by a much more accurate impression of the religious beliefs of the Dutch and other Europeans. He somehow obtained copies of at least three Christian works written in Chinese by Jesuit priests: *The Ten Chapters of an Eccentric* (1608) and *The True Meaning of Christianity* (1603) by Matteo Ricci, and *Seven Conquests* (1614) by Didacus de Pantoja.[40] All three works had been banned in 1686 by the Japanese government, and severe punishments were prescribed for anyone caught with them. In 1827, for example, a rangaku scholar was crucified for owning prohibited Christian books.[41] Nevertheless, as we know from various sources, some copies circulated clandestinely.[42] Hirata had connections with the scholars of Mito, a center of historical research where there was a collection of Christian books and objects, and may have borrowed the books he read from them. In any case, his *Outer Chapters of Our Doctrine (Honkyō Gaihen, 1806)* could not have been written without a knowledge of these three Christian books, and he may have read others.

The *Outer Chapters* was not printed during Hirata's lifetime; the manuscript was in fact marked by him "not to be seen by other people."[43] He apparently devoted most of his attention to the first part of the work, which is mainly a Japanese paraphrase of Ricci's *Ten Chapters.* Hirata considerably modified the expression, if not the ideas, of the Christian text. Where, for example, Ricci has a Confucian scholar state, "We consider man the noblest of all the creatures of heaven and earth," Hirata has "a certain person" say, "Not only in our [Japanese] Ancient Way, but even in the teachings of China, man is considered chief of all creatures." In answer to the question whether man should really be considered better off than the beasts, Ricci replies, "God set man in this world to test his heart and to determine the degree of his virtuous actions.

The present world is thus our temporary lodging and not our eternal home." Hirata renders Ricci's statement as: "This present world is not the real world. The reason the gods created man in this world was to purify his heart and to determine and test the degree of his virtuous actions; for this reason they caused him to lodge here temporarily."[44] In contrast to such examples of paraphrase in the first part of the *Outer Chapters,* in the second part Hirata copied almost word for word passages from the *Seven Conquests.* His changes in Pantoja's text were limited to the occasional substitution of a non-Christian word for the Supreme Being.[45]

It is hard to know what to make of the *Outer Chapters.*[46] If Hirata was sincere when writing the book, he must have felt that the Shinto and Christian doctrines were interchangeable, for wherever Ricci or Pantoja states an opinion, Hirata echoes it exactly and claims that it is Shinto doctrine. In later works Hirata was often to cite items of Christian and other foreign religious beliefs and declare them to be distortions of Shinto truths (as, for instance, the story of Adam and Eve, which somewhat resembles that of Izanagi and Izanami),[47] but in the *Outer Chapters* he made no significant changes in Christian doctrines. We thus find him quoting the New Testament as though it were a Shinto classic.

The test of the importance of the *Outer Chapters* in Hirata's work must be how great an influence its Christian ideology exerted on his subsequent writings. There are some reasonably certain examples of survivals of *Outer Chapters* ideas. Hirata's conception of an afterworld, for example, appears to have been evolved under Christian guidance. One must, however, be cautious in ascribing his views to Christian influence, for in general outline, at least, Christian and Buddhist ideas of a paradise where virtuous men are rewarded and a hell where wicked men are punished much resemble one another, and it is difficult to know which religion influenced Hirata. That some outside influence was present is clear —pure Shinto lacked a tradition of a paradise and a hell. Motoori had interpreted the ancient texts as saying that the souls of the dead all went to *yomi,* a gloomy afterworld. This view was repugnant to Hirata, for unlike Motoori he had no residual Buddhist trust in the saving help of Amida Buddha underlying his comfortless Shinto creed. He had to seek consolation in Shinto itself, and was led to proclaim under foreign influence his concept of a desirable, pleasant afterworld for those who merited it.[48] This for Hirata became the "real world" of which the visible world was only the transitory image.

The idea of hell appears to have developed more slowly in Hirata's theology. In his early writings he rejected as so much Buddhist cant the belief in punishment after death for sins done on earth, but he was later persuaded to accept the idea because of the numerous "authentic" stories of hell in Japanese and Chinese sources.[49] He was always more interested, however, in the Shinto paradise, possibly because he was convinced that he was destined to go there. In a long lyric section that is a pastiche of ancient phraseology, Hirata related how after his death, wherever his mortal body might be interred, his soul would go to Mount Yamamuro, the residence of Motoori's spirit. He intended to take his recently deceased wife along, although she was only a woman, because she had greatly encouraged his studies of Shinto. There, on the holy mountain, the three of them would enjoy together the lovely cherry blossoms of spring, the blue mountains of summer, the red leaves and the moon of autumn, and the winter's snow. But if any wicked barbarians were to aim their darts against the Divine Land, Hirata would ask leave of Motoori to join the Divine Army of the gods in Japan's defense. He would descend to the battlefield with an "eight-span spear" in his right hand, a bow of *mayumi* wood in his left, a quiver on his back, and at his side an "eight-grasp broadsword." Together with the gods he would rout the barbarians, twisting off their loathsome heads. Once the victory was achieved he would return to Mount Yamamuro and report to Motoori. "Ah, how happy I shall be!" exclaimed Hirata.[50]

Hirata attempted to prove the validity of his conception of the afterworld with quotations from the Shinto scriptures, particularly the *Kojiki* and the *Nihon Shoki,* but in fact those works bear very little or no relation to his theories. The Christian teachings to which Hirata subscribed in the *Outer Chapters* may have ex-

ercised a conscious influence on his thought, or perhaps in spite
of himself he allowed the validity of some Buddhist doctrines. He
naturally did not admit that there was any foreign influence in his
work, insisting always that it was purely Shinto.

It would seem that the main obstacle to a more extensive adoption of Christian doctrines by Hirata (apart, of course, from the
official prohibition of the religion in Japan) was their superficial
resemblance to the doctrines of Buddhism.[51] If in the *Outer Chapters* Hirata dutifully copied Ricci in stating that sexual desire is
the basest of the appetites (also the Buddhist view),[52] his later
writings are for the most part filled with glorifications of sexual
passion. The gods, he declared, provided mankind with sexual
organs, and gave the example for their use. To attempt to put
an end to lust is as foolish as to attempt to draw up the tides of the
ocean. The sexual organs are the gift of the gods that we should
value most and be most grateful for.[53]

Hirata's kind words for sex were not entirely by way of reaction
to Buddhism, nor apparently did they stem from an unusually
amorous nature,[54] as might be imagined. It should not be forgotten
that he was committed to revering as a sacred text the *Kojiki,* a
work distinguished by the number of passages that translators
prefer to render into the decent obscurity of Latin. Hirata could
not ignore this aspect of the "divine classics"; he chose instead
to exalt sex, sometimes for its own sweet sake but more commonly
because it represented the beginning of creation. Fertility and
creation became central themes in Hirata's theology. In place of
the more usual Shinto conception of many gods, all of approximately equal powers, Hirata exalted almost to the degree of mono-
theism the Creator-God (Musubi no kami) in his two aspects.[55] The
other gods and all men were created by Musubi no kami, and the
whole of the material world as well.

To corroborate this thesis Hirata was forced by the paucity of
native material to turn to foreign learning. He referred to the
ancient Chinese legends of Shang Ti, who ruled the world from
Heaven and who had created man and given him the virtues he
possessed.[56] Unfortunately, complained Hirata, the modern Chi-

nese were a frivolous lot and treated the legends humorously as if they were pure fable. Brahma in India was merely a distorted version of Musubi no kami;[57] the distance between Japan and India was responsible for a corruption of the authentic tradition. The same god under different names was also worshiped by the Europeans and even by the darkskinned natives of Ceylon and Java.[58] All other religions were secondary, for the wonderful creative powers of Musubi no kami had produced Buddha and Confucius no less than cats and spoons.[59] The sexual desire that he had implanted in men as a means of promoting fertility and creation should under no circumstances be suppressed.[60]

It may be wondered how deeply Hirata was indebted to the West for his concept of the Creator-God. He refers several times to the Dutch God, sometimes using ideographs given the sound *gotto* and meaning "the Creator."[61] We know that Hirata was familiar with a Japanese account of parts of Genesis (he mentions the Creation, Adam and Eve, Noah, and the Tower of Babel), and it would not be surprising if he had adopted the conception of God the Creator from the same book of the Bible, where it is more conspicuous than in other Christian writings. Such a conception of godhead suited Hirata admirably; it was clearly neither Buddhist nor Confucian (the idea of a Creator is particularly alien to Buddhism) and could be accommodated easily within the nebulous framework of Shinto beliefs. Hirata reduced the importance of the Central Ruling God (Ame-no-minaka-nushi no kami) and even of the Sun Goddess (Amaterasu ōmikami) in order to lend unique dignity to his Creator-God. If we cannot be sure of the origins of Hirata's theory of the afterworld, it seems quite likely at least that the Creator-God was a genuine contribution of the West to his theology.

Hirata's Opinion of Europeans

Hirata's professed admiration for Western science and his favorable view of certain Christian doctrines might lead one to suppose that he held the Dutch and other Europeans in high esteem. He apparently felt, however, that to admire foreigners was to denigrate Japan's national prestige and to obscure the incomparable qualities of the Japanese. Though prepared to admit that the Dutch were skilled in the sciences and in craftsmanship, and that they were far superior to the mendacious and unclean Chinese, he nevertheless sought to discredit them in the most scurrilous terms:

As everybody knows who has seen one, the Dutch are taller than other people and have fair complexions, big noses, and white stars in their eyes. By nature they are lighthearted and often laugh. They are seldom angry, a fact that does not accord with their appearance and is a seeming sign of weakness. They shave their beards, cut their nails, and are not dirty like the Chinese. Their clothing is extremely beautiful and ornamented with gold and silver. Their eyes are really just like those of a dog. They are long from the waist downwards, and the slenderness of their legs also makes them resemble animals. When they urinate they lift one leg, the way dogs do. Moreover, apparently because the backs of their feet do not reach to the ground, they fasten wooden heels to their shoes, which makes them look all the more like dogs. This may explain also why a Dutchman's penis appears to be cut short at the end, just like a dog's.[62] Though this may sound like a joke, it is quite true, not only of Dutchmen but of Russians. Kōdayū, a ship's captain from Shirako in Ise, who some years ago visited Russia,[63] recorded in the account of his travels that when he saw Russians in a bathhouse, the end was cut short, just like a dog's. . . . This may be the reason the Dutch are as lascivious as dogs and spend their entire nights at erotic practices. . . . Because they are thus addicted to sexual excesses and to drink, none of them lives very long. For a Dutchman to reach fifty is as rare as for a Japanese to live to be a hundred. However, the Dutch are a nation given to a deep study of things and to fundamental investigations of every description. That is why they are certainly the most skilled people in the world in fine works of all sorts, and excel in medicine as well as in astronomy and geography.[64]

Hirata's crude attempt to represent the Dutch as animals is all the more astonishing when one considers that Ōtsuki Gentaku (1757–1827) twenty-five years before had answered absurd contentions like Hirata's almost point for point in dialogue form:

There is a rumor that Dutchmen are short-lived. Is it true?
I cannot imagine where such a report originated. The length of human life is bestowed by Heaven and does not appear to differ in any way from one country to another. . . . The life-span of the Dutch, like that of the Japanese, is not the same for all. Some men live to be a hundred; others die at a mere ten or twenty years of age.

People say that the Dutch are born without heels, or that their eyes are like animals', or that they are giants. Is it true?

Where, I wonder, do such false reports originate? Is it because their eyes differ somewhat in shape from ours that the Dutch are slandered as being animal-like? Perhaps because of the difference in continents, Europeans do differ somewhat from us Asians in appearance. But there is no difference whatever in the organs they possess or in their functions. If one goes to Nagasaki, one sees that the dark people from India [Javanese servants of the Dutch] also have eyes of a rather different shape. There are differences too among Chinese, Koreans, and Ryukyuans. Even among Japanese there are recognizable differences in the appearance of the eyes of people from different parts of the country. In each instance the eyes may differ a little in appearance, but the use made of them is always identical. If Japanese differ, how much more likely is it that people living over 20,000 miles away on a different continent should differ! Although we are all products of the same Creator,[65] it is only to be expected that there should be regional differences in looks. As for the heels, they are the base on which the entire body rests—how could anyone get along without them? It is a subject unworthy of discussion. And as for the Dutch being giants, to judge by the height of the three men I have seen in Edo, it is the same way it is with age I mentioned—some are tall and some short. . . . Moreover, stories to the effect that when Dutchmen urinate they lift one leg like dogs, or that they have many erotic arts, or that they use all kinds of aphrodisiacs are all base canards undeserving of consideration.[66]

Why did Hirata take up arguments that had already been thus discredited and that his training in Western learning should have caused him to reject? Presumably he was fearful that the rangaku scholars would become as deferential toward the Dutch as the Confucian scholars were to the Chinese;[67] only by appealing to the lowest prejudices of the Japanese, he seems to have felt, could he forestall their uncritical admiration for Western ways. In a similar manner he attempted in his *Jests on Emerging from Meditation (Shutsujō Shōgo,* 1811) to ridicule the person of the Buddha, often by means of scurrilous details artfully selected from the Buddhist canon.[68] But whereas Hirata could denounce everything to do with Buddhism, he was committed to a respect for Western science (and secretly, it would seem, for Western religion), and was thus forced to regard the Dutch as animals with surprisingly developed skills.[69] This grudging concession at least established the Dutch and other Europeans next after the Japanese in the hierarchy of world peoples. Then followed the Chinese, and finally the Indians and the dark Indonesians.⁷⁰ According to Hirata, the Indonesians not only exhibited remarkable baseness but also emitted so foul an odor that their land produced cloves and other fragrant spices by way of mitigation.

It was proper, in Hirata's view, for Japanese to study Dutch learning, but they must not forget the vile nation from which it sprang. Some people were so insensate, however, as to use in their speech the "ludicrous, impure, and rather dirty" language of the Dutch as if they had trouble expressing themselves in Japanese.⁷¹ Hirata was particularly infuriated that physicians, puffed up with their knowledge of the otherwise useful foreign medicine, had acquired the habit of referring to diseases and their remedies by Dutch names. He described a conversation between two doctors, one of whom frequently used Dutch words that he was forced to explain afterward in Japanese. "He seemed to think that the other man was an ignoramus beneath his contempt; in fact, the man who talked Dutch was the ignoramus."⁷² To imitate the language of the Dutch was as senseless as to imitate the gibbering of the apes.

Hirata's conclusion may seem strange or amusing to a Western reader, but he was quite in earnest. It was, in fact, his advocacy of a combination of Japanese bigotry and Western science that colored the Japanese attitude toward the West during much of the nineteenth century and afterward. The earlier rangaku scholars had found something approaching the brotherhood of man through their Dutch studies, and many had turned to the West not only for mechanical knowledge but for a way of life. With Hirata and his disciples, the supposed natural claims of the Japanese to superiority over all other mortals came to be the object and justification of all recourse to Western learning. This combination was to be of great importance in the Meiji Restoration of 1868; it was also to play its part in the tragic events of more recent years.

Appendix

Excerpts from the Writings of Honda Toshiaki

In an effort to convey the thought of Honda Toshiaki more fully and directly than can be done by the brief passages cited in Chapters 4 and 5, I have translated parts of the first half of *A Secret Plan of Government (Keisei Hisaku)* and of the second volume of the *Tales of the West (Seiiki Monogatari)*. The *Secret Plan*, undoubtedly his most important work, would naturally be included in any collection of Honda's writings, but its second half, concerned chiefly with minor matters ("lesser needs" as Honda himself termed them), is no longer of much interest today and has therefore been omitted.

The *Tales of the West,* a work of much looser construction, could not have been given in full, or even after simple abridging. Parts of its are so confused that few readers would care to wade through them. The second volume, however, is of considerable interest, containing as it does Honda's best piece of descriptive writing, his account of a journey through the famine-stricken northern provinces of Japan.

If Honda's thoughts, even in this doctored version, appear somewhat illogical and unconvincing by Western standards, it must be remembered that he had no heritage of Greek logic to fall back on, and that in his attempts to break away from the well-worn paths of Confucian doctrines he was very much a pioneer.

A Secret Plan of Government

Can it be that anyone born in Japan would fail to think of what is beneficial to his country or would rejoice in Japan's misfortunes and begrudge her good fortune? Rather it should be in the nature of every person born in Japan to share in the joy of his country's good fortune and the desire to promote it, as well as in the sorrow over her ill fortune and the desire to prevent it. . . .

The chief object of [governmental policy] should be how to keep from hindering the natural increase in numbers of the four classes of society. Toward this end, the four imperative needs should be made the prime consideration of the government. . . . The four imperative needs are so called because they represent the four things that are most urgently required at present: gunpowder, metals, shipping, and colonization. . . . [Honda's discussion of the first two "needs" has been omitted.]

Shipping. By shipping I mean the trade and transport of the products of the whole country by means of government-owned ships, and the relief of the hunger and cold of all people by supplying each region with what it needs. Shipping and foreign trade are the responsibility of the ruler and should not be left to the merchants. If shipping is left entirely in the hands of merchants, they act as their greed and evil purposes dictate, thereby disturbing commodity prices throughout the country. Prices then fluctuate enormously, and the farmers find it difficult to survive. If this situation is remedied by using government-owned ships for transport and trade, the prices of commodities will be stabilized naturally and the farmers will be relieved.

As long as there are no government-owned ships and the merchants have complete control over transport and trade, the economic conditions of the samurai and farmers grow steadily worse. In years when the harvest is bad and people die of starvation, the farmers perish in greater numbers than people of any other class. With fields abandoned, food production reduced, and the nation short of food, the people grow restive, and numerous criminals have to be punished. In this way citizens are lost to the state. Since its citizens are a country's most important possession, it cannot afford to lose even one, and it is therefore most unfortunate that any should be sentenced to death. It is entirely the fault of the ruler if the life of even a single subject is lost.

All the troubles, disasters, and crimes of the common people are a product of their unhappiness and anger over fluctuations in commodity prices; such fluctuations are caused by the inadequacy of sea transport, which in turn is caused by the fact that the ruler controls no ships, and there is no government service. It cannot be estimated how greatly the prerogatives of the ruler are impaired by this condition. Shipping and trade are now the business of merchants. Under this system no distinction is made between the interests of the merchants and the duties of the ruler. By developing the techniques of shipping it would become possible to equalize prices throughout the country, thus helping both the samurai and the farmers. There would be a steady increase in food production, which in turn would make the nation prosperous.

It is obviously impossible to feed the thousands of people living in a great city with only the food that can be brought in by coolie labor or on the backs of beasts; unless food is transported in ships, the population will go hungry. But when shipping is controlled by merchants, as is the case at present, it will lead in the end to disaster; this must be changed. Let me give an idea of the disasters that this condition has engendered. At present, when a most thorough search for bandits and robbers is supposed to be in progress, the inquiries are getting nowhere; about a quarter of the rice being transported to Edo for the samurai is robbed on the way by the captain and crew of the rice ships. Afterwards false affidavits are lodged, and the matter is brought to a close. The affidavits state that the ship encountered a storm at sea and was damaged, that the cargo was jettisoned in order to lighten the ship, and that the crew barely managed to scrape through the storm with their lives. These affidavits are presented to officials who to themselves conjecture that the statements are false, but who have no way of establishing the truth because there are no officials aboard private vessels, no government supervisors, and no loading inspectors. Since the officials have made it their practice not to press matters beyond the affidavits, the above condition prevails to the present day.

An extreme case of this malpractice is to be found at Tonoura in Sado.[1] The people there have a saying, "This is no year to make any commitments—shipwrecks have been few and far between." They will then postpone until the following year giving away a bride already promised or taking into their household a son-in-law as previously arranged, saying, "Next year if things are better we will go through with the marriage as we had planned." This is what they actually do. Whenever there has been a severe storm and ships at sea are tossed about, they climb to the top of the hill on the shore of Tonoura Bay and light bonfires there in the middle of the night. A ship captain seeing the bonfire may take it for the all-night beacon of a harbor or anchorage. The people on shore wait for the ship to be guided inshore by the light of the fire. Then, as soon as it runs aground they rush forward in great numbers with whatever implements they happen to have; far from attempting to save the lives of the shipwrecked crew, they throw everyone aboard the ship into the sea. If any of the crew attempt to get ashore, they are beaten back into the water until they are all drowned. After this the people of Sado gather together and divide up the ship's cargo. Finally they set fire to the ship to remove the evidence.

This type of occurrence is not restricted to Tonoura, but happens at all out-of-the-way bays throughout the country. It represents the greatest peril to ships at sea, a first beginning of piracy that has arisen from a grave defect in the government of the nation. Some daimyo have now ceased to pay their retainers their basic stipends. These men have had half their property confiscated by the daimyo as well, and hate them so much that they find it impossible to contain their ever-accumulating resentment. They finally leave their clan and become bandits. They wander law-

---

[1] Sado is an island in the Japan Sea off the northwest coast of Honshu.

lessly over the entire country, plotting with the natives who live on the shore and thus entering a career of piracy. As they become ever more entrenched in their banditry there is a growing tendency to revert to olden times.[2]

It is because of the danger of such occurrences that in Europe a king governs his subjects with solicitude. It is considered to be the appointed duty of a king to save his people from hunger and cold by shipping and trading. This is the reason there are no bandits in Europe. A similar approach would be especially applicable to Japan, which is a maritime nation. It is obvious that transport and trade are essential functions of the government.

Ships that are at present engaged in transport do not leave coastal waters and put out to sea. They always have to skirt along the shore, and can navigate only by using as landmarks mountains or islands within sight. Sometimes, inevitably, they are blown out to sea by a storm and lose their way. Then, when they are so far away from their familiar landmarks that they can no longer see them, they drift about with no knowledge of their location. This is because the captains are ignorant of astronomy and mathematics, and because they do not possess the rules of navigation. Countless ships are lost in this way every year. Not only does this represent an enormous annual waste of produce, but valuable subjects also perish. If the methods of navigation were developed, the loss at sea of rice and other food products would be reduced, thus effecting a great saving. This would not only increase the wealth of the nation, but would help stabilize the prices of rice and other produce throughout Japan. The people, finding that they are treated equally irrespective of occupation and seeing that the methods of government are fair, would no longer harbor any resentment, but would raise their voices in unison to pray for the prosperity of the rulers. By saving the lives of those subjects who would otherwise be lost at sea every year, we would also be able to make up for our past shame, and would keep foreign nations from learning about weak spots in the institutions of Japan from Japanese sailors

---

[2] A reference to the *bahan*, Japanese pirates who were at their strongest in the fifteenth and sixteenth centuries.

shipwrecked on their shores. Because of these and numerous other
benefits to be derived from shipping, I have termed it the third
imperative need.

Colonization.[3] If the islands near Japan were colonized, they
would be highly desirable places. By such colonization numerous
possessions—some sixty or more—would be created, which not only
would serve as military outposts for Japan, but would produce in
abundance metals, grain, fruit, and various other products, thus
greatly adding to Japan's strength. I presume that run-of-the-mill
officials must think of colonization as achievable only at the expense of the ruler, and that the authorities are not in the least
inclined to spend any government money on developing farmland.
This is the way mediocre minds always react.

The order to be followed in colonizing territories is as follows.
First, ships are dispatched to ascertain the location of the islands
to be taken, and to measure their extent. The natural products of
the islands are investigated, and the native population estimated.
Then, when it is known about how many provinces the islands
would make if colonized, the actual work is begun. If the natives
are still living in caves, they are taught about houses. A house
should be built for the tribal chief. Natives without implements
or utensils should be supplied with them. By helping the natives
and giving them everything they desire, we will inspire a feeling
of affection and obedience in them, like the love of children for
their parents. This is true because they are moved by the same
feelings that pervade the rest of the world, barbarians though they
may be considered.

The way to compensate for the expenses involved in colonization is to take the natural products of the islands and ship them
to Japan. Trading marks a beginning of compensation for those
expenses. Even barbarians do not expect to ask favors and give
nothing in return. The products they offer represent the beginning
of taxation. Since every island has wooded areas, there will always
be some value in the lumber that can be taken from the islands,

---

[3] Although this section in the original is placed at the conclusion of the
entire volume, it most properly belongs at this point.

even after a great many years. The value of other products besides lumber would be too great to calculate. It is the task of the ruler-father to direct and educate the natives so that not one of them will spend even one unprofitable day. This matter should not be put off for another moment; it is a vital state duty.

At this point we must discuss the foundation of colonization—the sciences of astronomy and mathematics. In Japan these sciences are not as yet fully known, and there are few men who understand their significance. Even in China the principles of astronomy and mathematics have roughly been understood since the arrival of a number of Europeans late in the seventeenth century.[4] If, in connection with colonization projects, ships cross the seas without reference to the principles of astronomy and mathematics, there is no way to tell how much easier sea travel is than land travel. The name of the book in which the natural laws behind these principles are contained is *Schatkamer*,[5] a European work. One may learn from the latitude of a particular island what its climate is like throughout the year, and without actually visiting an island, one can predict in this way whether it will prove fertile. This may be done with certainty; false tales need not be believed.

The key to colonization is to establish a system[6] with long-range objectives about future profit and loss. By encouraging the good customs of the natives and eliminating the bad ones, it is possible to have them maintain human dignity. They should never be permitted to forget the generosity of the Japanese ruler. This is how colonization should be set about, but Japan persists in her bad habit of imitating old Chinese ways. Very few of the government authorities possess any real knowledge of astronomy or mathematics, and it is because of their ignorance that whenever

4 Honda is a century out: late sixteenth century would be more accurate.

5 Possibly this is the *Schatkamer of te Konst der Stuur-Leiden* by Klaas de Vries, a navigator's handbook frequently reissued in Holland. The book was best known in Japan before the country was opened. See Ayusawa and Ōkubo, *Sakoku Jidai Nihonjin no Kaigai Chishiki* (Tokyo, 1953). It has been suggested (*ibid.*, p. 86) that *Schatkamer* is the same book translated by Motoki Ryōei, a Nagasaki interpreter, in 1781 with the title *Oranda Kaikyōsho*.

6 *Seido*, here translated "system," is a difficult word; it means more or less "that which can be established by means of laws."

there is talk of colonizing the northern territories, as occasionally
happens, the project is never carried through. It is Japan's misfortune that her officials are misled by foolish tales about these
great countries, which are actually far superior to Japan, and
consequently do not take advantage of great opportunities for
profitable ventures. This is a matter of especial regret because
there have been Russian officials in the islands inhabited by the
Ainu since about 1765.[7] They have displayed such diligence in
their colonization efforts that eighteen or nineteen Kurile islands
and the great land of Kamchatka have already been occupied.
Forts are said to have been built at various places, and a central
administration established (the staff of which is regularly changed)
that rules the natives with benevolence. I have heard that the natives trust the Russians as they would their own parents.

In Japan, on the other hand, this system is not as yet followed.
It is forbidden to carry from the country seeds for the five cereals
or edged tools for use in building houses. It is forbidden to teach
Japanese to any natives. These lamentable prohibitions are sup-
plemented by a host of others, all designed to keep barbarians forever in their present condition. Since the Russians systematically
send their own subjects out to live among the natives, it is only
to be expected that the Ainu look up to the Russian officials as gods
and worship them.

There is a story that I would like to relate at this point. There
was a European named Baron Moritz Aladar von Benyowsky,[8] who
was defeated and taken prisoner with his force of fifty men after
an engagement with the Russians. His life was spared, but he was
sent into exile at Kamchatka. In return for having his life spared,
he was made to help in the colonization of the eastern Ezo islands,
but he waited only for an opportunity to escape. He managed to
gain control of a government vessel and attempted then to sail
back to his native country in Europe. After navigating in the
waters east of Japan, he anchored at Awa, where he requested fuel
and water. In response to his appeal to the kindness of the daimyo

[7] See above, p. 38.
[8] See above, Chapter 3.

of that province, he was presented with several hundred sacks of rice, and then he set sail from Awa. Later he again called at a Japanese port, anchoring this time at Ōshima in Satsuma.

When he visited Japanese waters for a second time, he desired to express his gratitude for the kind treatment he had been accorded at Awa. He addressed a letter in European script to the Dutch factory director in Nagasaki in which, intending to demonstrate his good wishes toward Japan, he described the plans of the Russian emperor. This incident took place in 1771. The Nagasaki magistrate of the time, a certain Natsume,[9] discussed the document with his subordinates and various other people in order to determine its truth. It was a very difficult communication to handle, and it finally was left to disappear.

If one examines present conditions in the Ezo islands, one will observe that they are exactly as Benyowsky described them in his letter. All the islands are now Russian possessions. Until about 1765 dried salmon and fish oil used to be obtained every year from Kamchatka. Sealskins, *kajika*,[10] and fish oil were sent from the eastern Ezo islands and placed on sale at Matsumae.[11] The island of Ezo alone used to yield over 20,000 deerskins annually, but it should be noted that not a single deerskin is coming to Japan at present; they are all collected by the Russians. Weeping over this situation will not bring back our territories to us; we must save at least the island of Ezo. Since this is a place that will prove very valuable to us, we must act at once and not be careless. If we abandon it, it will be just like attempting to keep out bandits without a fence. Nothing could be more dangerous.

The island of Ezo has a circumference of somewhat less than a thousand *ri*.[12] It lies between 40° and 43° N. Lat. and enjoys a climate comparable to that of Shun-t'ien-fu in China.[13] Since the

9 Natsume Izumi-no-kami Nobumasa, in office 1770–74.

10 A large fish (*Cottus pollux*) used for food and medicinal purposes.

11 Matsumae was the name of the clan that ruled over the island now called Hokkaidō. In Honda's time the island itself was sometimes called Matsumae, but more frequently Ezo. By "Matsumae," Honda here meant the town at the southern end of the island (modern Fukuyama), which was the seat of the clan.

12 One *ri* equals about 2.5 miles, but Honda's figures are not to be trusted.

13 Shun-t'ien-fu was an administrative area that included Peking.

southern tip of Kamchatka is located at 51° N. Lat., it follows that all the Kuriles lie between 40° and 50°. It is clear from their latitudes that they must be fertile lands, where all varieties of grain and fruit will grow. By way of proof, the capital city of Holland, one of the chief European countries, is located at 53° 23' N. Lat. Because it is possible to determine from the latitude of a place its climate and fertility, the first step in colonization is thus achieved.

The harbor of Okhotsk is now being developed into one of the key points of the East. I have been informed that a central administrative staff is sent there for regular terms of office from Russia to look after the area. Ships are sent out for purposes of trade from Okhotsk to the Kurile islands and to North and South America, supplying whatever is needed in each place. The king[14] rules the natives benevolently and is most generous to them in the capacity of father and mother to the people. Okhotsk is located around 55° N. Lat., and is thus an extremely cold place. Every year from April to September government-owned ships ply to and from Okhotsk in great numbers, but during the winter months the snows lie deep and no ships can arrive or depart. During this time there is no work to be done. Okhotsk lies northwest of Kunashiri and Etorofu, and due north of Karafuto[15] at a distance of about four hundred ri across the water.

Since no Japanese ever go abroad, and since most Japanese are ignorant of astronomy and mathematics, we shall be unable to win profits as great as those Russia obtains unless we undergo a complete awakening, so besotted is the nation by the foolish tales constantly spread by suspicious and ignorant people. This is a grave misfortune for Japan. I imagine it is because Japan has not been civilized even half as long as the nations of Europe that there are as yet very few men who are versed in the processes of government. It is to be expected that henceforth there will be people who do possess this ability as more and more people gain familiarity with the sciences.

There is a large island called Karafuto in western Ezo, located

[14] Presumably the Russian official in charge at Okhotsk.
[15] Karafuto was the name used by the Japanese for Saghalien.

67 ri northwest of Sōya on the western coast of Matsumae. Japanese merchants have been crossing over to this island for about 150 years to trade with the natives, and have built little houses called *unjōya* for this purpose.[16] They decide on the number of years they intend to trade at the place, and it is calculated how much has to be paid to the house of Matsumae for the privilege. Whoever pays the tax becomes the local administrator and appoints the three groups of people who work there: the managers, the interpreters, and the guards. These people build houses on the island and engage in beneficial trade with the natives. This situation holds true for both eastern and western Ezo.

To the northwest of Karafuto is the country of Santan.[17] Beyond Santan to the northwest is Manchuria, which in ancient times was known as Tartary. The territory to the west of this country extends as far as Europe. Thus, however far removed Europe may be, it is connected to Santan by a continuous landmass; this in turn makes Karafuto an important frontier. It is important because of the seemingly irresistible conquest of half the world by Russia in recent years, which has resulted from the Russian policy of making colonization the prime function of the state. A start should therefore be made from the trading stations that are on Karafuto now. They should gradually be improved and other stations added. Japanese will then come in steadily increasing numbers.

It is surprising that the trading stations were built so long ago. It would seem to show that even the merchants of the period after the civil wars were bolder than the samurai of today. Did they first cross over to Matsumae in the footsteps of Yoshitsune (who later went on to Tartary)?[18] There are even historical remains of the Emperor Jimmu in the Ezo islands.[19] No place in the world is of greater historical significance to Japan than this region, yet for the past ten years Russian officials have been stationed there.

[16] *Unjōya* was also the name given to the trading stations in Ezo.

[17] By Santan, Honda meant the region of the Siberian maritime provinces.

[18] There was a legend that Minamoto no Yoshitsune (1159–89) escaped to the island of Ezo, from which he made his way to Mongolia and established himself as Genghis Khan.

[19] Another legend.

キス

取オツミ矢
ヘツトセフス
キミスルを以
スヲルる鉢ガ
ガ実ナ

17. Life among the Hairy Ainu

Some years ago a complaint was directed to the Matsumae clan about the activities of the Russians in the area of the trading stations, and officials were accordingly dispatched to investigate. They were told by the Russians: "We were cast ashore on this island two or three years ago. Our ship was wrecked, and we have been unable to return to our country. If you would be so kind as to take us back to Japan and send us on to Nagasaki, it will be the best place from which to return, since there are Europeans there. Grant us this favor and save our lives." Thus they pleaded to the accompaniment of tears.[20]

On first hearing their story, one might think that these were unfortunate men deserving of help, but they were Europeans, whose nature it is to be very cunning. One should never take what a European says for the simple truth. To give an idea how skilled they are in deception, let me relate the story of a Russian named Simeon Dorofeivitch Ishuyo,[21] who spent eight years in the islands from Etorofu to Kunashiri. Officials were sent from Matsumae who ordered him on several occasions to return to his country, but Ishuyo replied each time, "I fled here because I was convicted of a crime in Russia, and I cannot return. Even now, if I were caught by a Russian official I would be executed. It is only natural in such circumstances that I have no desire to go back to my country. Rather than be driven from here, I would prefer that you cut off my head." In so saying, he stuck out his head and did not withdraw it an inch.

The officials were at a loss what to do. They delayed deciding his case from day to day, but in May of the same year that Kōdayū, the sailor from Shirako-machi in Ise,[22] was returned to Japan, a Russian envoy came for Ishuyo and they went back to Russia together. The story that he was a criminal and therefore could not return was thus so much deception and cunning.

This Ishuyo showed in his daily behavior that he was no or-

[20] This apparently refers to the mission of 1786 described in Satō Genrokuro's *Ezo Shūi* in Ōtomo, *Hokumon Sōsho*, I (Tokyo, 1943). See above, p. 38.

[21] Conjectural reading of a Russian name. See above, p. 130.

[22] Ise is southwest of modern Tokyo. For a discussion of Kōdayū, see Chapter 3. The year mentioned by Honda was presumably 1792.

dinary man. He is reported to have been not only courageous but learned and accomplished. I imagine that he was a Russian spy who had been selected for his heroism, conspicuous even in Russia, to keep watch on the government and people of Japan. Since such persons as Ishuyo exist, it seems highly improbable that the Russians at present on Karafuto just happen to have been shipwrecked there. I believe that Benyowsky's warning meant that the Russians would resort to every variety of stratagem rather than withdraw. There are grounds for suspicion already in the religious teachings being given to the natives of Etorofu and Kunashiri by Russian officials. Crosses over ten feet high have been erected in front of the thrones of the tribal chiefs and are worshiped morning and night. (The cross is called *kurusu*.) There are also three types of images—paintings, wooden statues, and metal statues—in twelve aspects. They are called *teusu*.[23] I imagine that they are connected with the heretical sect that was proscribed at the end of the sixteenth century.[24] It is especially noteworthy that the tribal chiefs of Etorofu and Kunashiri have been taken by ship to Okhotsk, where they have met high Russian officials and been given lavish presents. Many similar instances could be cited. For Japan such incidents at present constitute a minor disgrace, but I need not go into what may happen if things continue in this manner.

It is clear that when the Ezo islands are colonized they will yield several times as much produce as Japan does today. Although there are other islands to the east and west that should also be Japanese possessions, I shall not discuss them for the moment. At this crucial time when the Ezo islands are being seized by Russia, we are faced with an emergency within an emergency. When, as now, Japan does not have any system for colonizing her island possessions, there is no way of telling whether they will be seized by foreign countries or remain safe. This is not the moment for neglect; such actions by foreign powers may lead to the destruction of our national defense. With the establishment of a system of

---

[23] I.e. *deus*. Pictures of the Russian icons discovered are included in Satō's *Ezo Shūi*.

[24] Christianity—not prohibited, however, until 1636.

colonization, a knowledge of navigation will naturally develop among Japanese, but if navigation, shipping, and trade continue to be considered the occupation of merchants, the natives of our island possessions are doomed to an eternal want of civilization. The fact that the Ainu are living in a state of barbarity has been regarded by Russia as affording a fine opportunity for devoting her energies to the colonization of the islands, a timely undertaking. The lack of a colonization system has kept Japanese rule from the island, and has meant that the natives are unaware of the goodness of the ruler of Japan. Because of this ignorance they have been quick to become subject to Russia.

So important is colonization that I have termed it the fourth imperative need.

When a country or province, or the whole country itself, is governed in accordance with these needs, every part of Japan, even the wastelands and mountainous regions, can be turned into cultivated fields. Villages will spring up about them, and as this trend increases in strength, there will finally be an overflowing to island possessions. Mines will be developed and all varieties of crops will be produced in increasing quantities each year. There will be no such thing as insufficiency in the country.

It is a good policy to rule the country in such a way as to permit the natural increase of the population. The ruler encourages this increase and is greatly pleased by it. By not helping that which is bad and by commending that which is good, he will avoid crippling the natural population growth. His enterprises will all meet with success, and the nation will be rich and strong. This new development will accord with Japan's reputation as a country of great military prowess and will so impress nearby countries that they will accept Japanese suzerainty.

The cultivation of a national spirit to complement the martial strength of the country is called "paternalism."[25] The method employed is valid in all situations. Governing a province, a county, or the whole country amounts to the same thing as governing

25 *Buiku*, literally, to "instruct soothingly" or "govern clemently."

the household of one of the common people. This spirit is found in the sentiment, possessed by rich and poor alike, of being "master in one's house."

The four imperative needs thus elaborated are such important duties of the state that they should not be neglected for an instant; it is the height of the inexpedient that they have not as yet been adopted. If one were to attempt seriously to trace their origins, one would have to go back over eight hundred years to the times when the country was divided by internal strife. In those days men were so intent on devoting all of their energies to military activity that they naturally did not have time to learn the art of government.[26]

.   .   .

Not until Tokugawa Ieyasu used his power to control the strong and give succor to the weak did the warfare that had lasted for three hundred years without a halt suddenly abate. Arrows were left in their quivers and spears in their racks. If now, in such a time of peace, the country were ruled in accordance with the four imperative needs, the prices of all commodities would be stabilized, and the discontent of the people would thus be cut off at the root. This is the true method of establishing a permanent foundation for the nation, so that the people will become honest in their hearts and cultivate orderly ways even if they are not governed. It must have been because he realized how difficult it would be to preserve the empire for all ages to come if the people were not honest in their hearts that Ieyasu, in his testament,[27] exhorted shoguns who would succeed him to abstain from any irregularities in government, and to rule on a basis of benevolence and honesty. It was his counsel that the shoguns should serve as models to the people, and by their honesty train the people in the ways of humanity and justice. He taught that the shogun should not compel

[26] I have omitted at this point a long and essentially irrelevant retelling of the main events of Japanese history.

[27] Translated in James Murdoch, *A History of Japan* (London, 1925–26), III, 796–894.

obedience merely by the use of force, but by his acts of benevolence should keep the nation at peace.

Ieyasu had the great lords of the empire leave their families behind in Edo, where they themselves had to be in attendance every other year.[28] In that way he could learn of the government of the domains. This is an example of the profound insight of Ieyasu. He taught the daimyo that the duties of a governor consisted in the careful attempt to guide the people of their domains in such a way as both to bring about the prosperity of the land and to encourage the literary and military arts.

However, in recent days there has been the spectacle of lords confiscating the allocated property of their retainers on the pretext of paying back debts to the merchants. The debts do not then decrease, but usually seem rather to grow larger. One daimyo with an income of 60,000 *koku*[29] so increased his borrowings that he could not make good his debts, and there was a public suit. The court judgment in the case was said to have been over 1,180,000 *ryō*.[30] Even if repayment had been attempted on the basis of his income of 60,000 koku, the debt would not have been completely settled for fifty or sixty years, so long a time that it is difficult to imagine the day would actually come.

All the daimyo are not in this position, but there is not one who has not borrowed from the merchants. Is this not a sad state of affairs? The merchant, watching this spectacle, must feel like a fisherman who sees a fish swim into his net. Officials of the daimyo harass the farmers for money, which they claim they need to repay the daimyo's debts, but the debts do not diminish. Instead, the daimyo go on contracting new ones year after year. The officials are blamed for this situation, and are dismissed as incompetent. New officials then harass and afflict the farmers in much the same way as the old ones, and so it goes on. However talented the officials may be, they become disgusted and abandon the effort. Some pre-

28 This was the *sankin kōtai* system. See above, p. 101.

29 A *koku* is about five bushels; the incomes of daimyo were calculated in terms of the number of *koku* of rice they received a year.

30 A *ryō* was a weight of gold. It was worth about fifty dollars in terms of the amount of rice it would purchase today.

tend sickness and remain in their homes; others are indiscreet and die young.

No matter how hard the daimyo and his officials rack their brains, they do not seem to be able to reduce the debts. The lords are "sunk in a pool of debts," as it is popularly said, a pool from which their children and grandchildren will be unable to escape. Everything will be as the merchants wish it. The daimyo turn over their domains to the merchants, receiving in return an allowance with which to pay their public and private expenses. Such daimyo give no thought at all to Heaven,[31] to fulfilling their duties as samurai, or to the proper way of looking after the farmers.

Many fields have turned into wasteland since the famine of 1783, when thousands of farmers starved to death. Wherever one goes from the Kantō to Ōu, one hears people say, "There used to be a village here. . . . The land over there was once part of such-and-such a county, but now there is no village and no revenue comes from the land." This condition prevails especially in Ōu, in which province alone five counties have reverted to wasteland. During the three years of bad crops and famine that followed 1783, over two million people in the province of Ōu alone starved to death. When so many farmers starved, reducing still further their already insufficient numbers, the amount of uncultivated land greatly increased. If the wicked practice of infanticide, now so prevalent, is not stopped, the farming population will dwindle until it tends to die out altogether. Generous protective and relief measures must be put into effect immediately if this evil practice is to be stamped out.

A wise ruler could end this practice in short order and create an atmosphere favorable to the prosperity of the nation by establishing a system based on generosity and compassion. When a woman of one of the lower classes becomes pregnant, a government agent should be sent to investigate the situation. The mother of the child should then be given two sacks of rice each year from the month the child is born until he is ten years old. The practice

---

[31] That is, to the punishment they will receive from Heaven for their improper conduct.

of infanticide would soon stop. Thus by spending a mere twenty sacks of rice over a period of ten years, the country would at the same time gain a good farmer and atone for the misery caused in the past.

Though I say "misery," there are no words capable of expressing the feeling that everyone must have when he thinks of people killing with their own hands the children they have brought into the world. Dumb animals and birds all experience love and compassion for their young. How can it be that man kills his children? The Confucian scholars of ancient and modern times have talked a great deal about benevolence and compassion, but they possess neither in their hearts. Officials and authorities talk about benevolent government, but they have no understanding of what that means. Whose fault is it that the farmers are dying of starvation and that good fields are turning into wasteland? The fault lies entirely with the ruler. I am at a loss to describe the disloyalty and faithlessness of such actions. The rage that overpowers me when I consider how slow in coming is the punishment sent by Heaven is a sincere expression of my thoughts on the matter.

I have traveled three times through the provinces of the country examining conditions. Since I am a poor person, I have at times been forced to sleep in fields or in the mountains. I have experienced all kinds of physical hardships and want. I have noted the conditions of farm roads in the provinces, roads so poor that produce was left to rot on the ground for want of a way to transport it. I have described such things as the location of mines, the activities of robbers in different places, and the secret disposal at some remote port of goods that were being shipped from one harbor to another and that had been stolen from the owner under the pretense of a shipwreck. These records I leave to future men of goodwill. I have sought to give to the nation what I have come to understand about the significance of the four imperative needs in the humble hope that my plan will relieve the suffering of the farmers and help to bring about the disappearance of infanticide. I am hesitant about leaving behind these crude writings when there are so many learned and brilliant persons in the world today, but if it is true, as the proverb says, that a three-year-old child can show the way over a dangerous crossing, persons who condescend to read these lines carefully may derive profit from them.

Of all the countries of Europe, Africa, Asia, and America, the one with the longest history is Egypt, which lies on the eastern shores of Africa. Over six thousand years ago Egypt was civilized. The Egyptians knew the art of writing, had a calendar at that remote date, and had a system of time notation that was in use throughout the country.

There later appeared a man named Christ in a country called Judea at the northwest end of Asia; he established the Catholic religion, which spread northward to Europe. In India, to the east, Sakyamuni appeared, and in China there were the sage-rulers Yao, Shun, Yu, T'ang, Wen, and Wu. All these men were teachers. Although what they taught differed, their doctrines amounted in each instance to an explanation of the way countries should be ruled and kept at peace. The particulars differed from country to country, but in all cases their meaning could be reduced to the principle of encouraging virtue and punishing vice.

Every country has a system of writing with which it transmits the teachings of its sages. Our country adopted Chinese writing and philosophy. Thus there are persons who enjoy a reputation for wide scholarship when all they know is the origin and history of one country, China. China became civilized three thousand years ago, and was thus over three thousand years slower than Egypt. Because of this difference in antiquity there are many faults in Chinese state policies that time has not as yet corrected.

The great number and inconvenience of Chinese characters make them useless in dealings with foreign countries. There are now barely three countries besides China where they may be understood: Korea, the Ryukyus, and Japan. And even in these countries it is considered a difficult task to gain a thorough knowledge of them. The European alphabet has twenty-five letters, each of which may be written in eight different forms.[32] With these letters

---

[32] By this Honda meant capital, lower-case, italic, etc.

one can describe anything in the world. Nothing could be simpler. If one tried to memorize all the hundreds of thousands of Chinese characters and devoted one's life's energies to the task, how many could one actually learn? One would be sure to forget a great many. Even supposing that some man could learn them all, the best he could do would be to copy in Japan all the old Chinese stories. Rather than attempt to help the nation in this way, it would be simpler to turn to profit those resources with which Japan is naturally endowed.

There is a country called Italy at the southern end of Europe, lying between 35° and 36° N. Lat. The good laws of Judea, which is separated from the southern tip of Italy by the Mediterranean Sea, appear to have been transmitted there. Thus it was that an enlightened ruler established a benevolent rule in Italy that was cheerfully obeyed by the people. He was considered so wise a man that he was given the title of Emperor of Europe, and for many generations afterward all Europe was under one sovereign. However, there came a foolish emperor whose regime was disordered. The subject countries then rebelled, and now all the countries formerly under one emperor are independent.

The capitals of France, Spain, England, and Holland have become thriving places. There are reasons for their prosperity that I shall attempt to explain by using the example of one of them. France long ago became the first country to manufacture cannon, and she also invented the method of making gunpowder for military use.[33] This gave her supremacy over the neighboring countries. She afterward used her inventions against those countries that were at war, thus compelling them to cease fighting. This was the great achievement of France. No matter how well equipped a nation was, even if it possessed mighty fortresses of steel, when French cannons were brought to bear or French privateers[34] attacked, not only would its fortresses fall, but very few of its people

---

[33] There is a confusion here between *furanki*, an old name for firearms, and *Furansu*, the name for France. See Paul Pelliot, "Le Hôja et le Sayyid Husain," *T'oung Pao*, XXXVIII (1938), 204–5.

[34] *Dokujinsen*, literally, "solitary fast ships."

would be left to tell the tale. For fear of loss of human life France has not yet transmitted her inventions to other countries.

Europe was first with all other important inventions as well. Because astronomy, calendar making, and mathematics are considered the ruler's business, the European kings are well versed in celestial and terrestrial principles, and instruct the common people in them. Thus even among the lower classes one finds men who show great ability in their particular fields. The Europeans as a result have been able to establish industries with which the rest of the world is unfamiliar. It is for this reason that all the treasures of the world are said to be attracted to Europe. There is nowhere the Europeans' ships do not go in order to obtain the different products and treasures of the world. They trade their own rare products, superior implements, and unusual inventions for the precious metals and valuable goods of others, which they bring back to enrich their own countries. Their prosperity makes them strong, and it is because of their strength that they are never invaded or pillaged, whereas for their part they have invaded countless non-European countries. Spain has conquered many of the best parts of North and South America, and has moved her capital there.[35] Portugal, England, and France also have possessions in the Americas. The islands of the eastern oceans, such as Java, Sumatra, Borneo, and Luzon, are all European possessions. In those countries that have not as yet submitted to the Europeans, they have set up trading stations where they trade with the local rulers, seeking only to obtain the greatest possible profits. Even countries that have not yielded to European might are devoting all their energies to producing things for Europe. The real objectives of the European nations are thus achieved anyway.

There is no place in the world to compare with Europe. It may be wondered in what way this supremacy was achieved. In the first place, the European nations have behind them a history of five to six thousand years. In this period they have delved deep into the beauties of the arts, have divined the foundations of government, and have established a system based on a thorough ex-

---

[35] Possibly Honda, hearing of the Viceroy of Peru and his court, imagined that the Spanish capital had been moved from Madrid to Lima.

amination of the factors that naturally make a nation prosperous. Because of their proficiency in mathematics, they have excelled also in astronomy, calendar making, and surveying. They have elaborated laws of navigation such that there is nothing simpler for them than to sail the oceans of the world.

There is no positive evidence on when European ships first reached the nations of the Far East, but it would appear from the descriptions in the "Foreign Events" section of the *Ming History* that they first came to China during the Wan-li era.[36] It cannot have been so very long, in any case, since they first came. As far as our country's history is concerned, it was not until the opening years of the seventeenth century that Dutch ships came regularly every year for trade. It is by such trade that the European nations have become so wealthy.

Nothing can compare in size with the great bell of Moscow or the copper lantern of France.[37] Nor is there elsewhere in the world anything to compare with their practice of building houses of stone. These are a product of their achievements in sailing over the world. To complete any great undertaking—for example, a major public works project or a powerful fortress—with the resources of one country alone is very difficult, and results in the exhaustion of the people; but when the resources of foreign countries are added, there is no undertaking, however great, that cannot be accomplished. This is true in particular of those nations of Europe celebrated for their strength and prosperity. Because they are cold northern countries, they could not afford any large-scale expenditures if they had only the resources of their own country to depend on. In spite of this example, however, the Japanese do not look elsewhere than to China for good or beautiful things, so tainted are the customs and temperament of Japan by Chinese teachings. Japanese are therefore unaware of such things as the four imperative needs, since they do not figure in the teachings of the Chinese sages.

China is a mountainous country that extends as far as Europe

[36] Covering the years 1573–1620.
[37] A confusion for Pharos? The lantern of Pharos was one of the wonders of the world.

and Africa. It is bounded by the ocean to the south, but water communication within the country is not feasible. Since it is impossible to feed the huge population of cities when transport can be effected only by human or animal strength, there are no big cities in China away from the coast.[38] China is therefore a much less favored country than Japan, which is surrounded by water, and this factor shows in the deficiencies and faults of Chinese state policies. China does not merit being used as a model. Since Japan is a maritime nation, shipping and trade should be the chief concerns of the ruler. Ships should be sent to all countries to obtain products needed for national consumption and to bring precious metals to Japan. A maritime nation is equipped with the means to increase her national strength.

By contrast, a nation that attempts to get along on its own resources will grow steadily weaker. The nation's weakness will affect the farmers, and there will be a tendency for the number of farmers to decrease over the years. It becomes a grave national problem when this crisis is reached. To put the matter more bluntly, the policies followed by the various ruling families until now have determined that the lower classes must lead a hand-to-mouth existence. The best part of the harvests of the farmers who live on the domains of the empire is wrenched away from them. The lords spend all they take within the same year, and if they then do not have enough, they oppress the farmers all the more cruelly in an effort to obtain additional funds. This goes on year after year. It is no wonder that when, on top of the grave afflictions that have exhausted the farmers in recent times, there have come bad harvests and famines in the years since 1783, farmers from the Kantō to Ōu have starved to death, and good fields that could produce millions of koku of rice have been turned into wasteland. Is it not true that the people living on a daimyo's domains are imperial subjects left in his care? Is there any reason why even a single one of their precious lives should be left to the caprices of a lord? Is not caring for them the function of a governor and the concern of the ruler?

[38] A curious error on Honda's part; perhaps here again his desire to propagandize overcame his better knowledge.

During the first twenty years of a man's life he is supported by the efforts of his parents, consuming huge quantities of food without producing any himself. If then he reaches manhood and is at long last able to be of service to his country, it is the worst possible loss for him to be left to die by his lord. Man, unlike other creatures, becomes of service to his country only after twenty years of life have gone by, and thus every single subject is precious.

Is it not true that if the ruler fails to cherish his people, he is remiss in his duties, and that the fate of the nation is determined by his actions? The ruler who is lax in looking after the people's needs will fall naturally into profligacy and idleness, and his extravagances will mount without limit. In extreme cases he may go so far as to destroy his house and ruin his province, but even if this does not occur, the gods will surely punish him for his wickedness. He will sink into a pool of debts from which his children and grandchildren will not be able to escape, and in this manner his domains will pass into the hands of the merchants. He will be trapped and forced by this means to pay his debts. There is no point in my expanding further on the fact that samurai, who enjoy hereditary stipends, are falling into the traps of the stipendless merchants. The samurai pretend that this is actually not so bad, but it represents a terrible state of affairs. The tribute paid by the farmers of the domains, the product of their tears of blood and their hardships of a year, is seized before it reaches their lords and delivered directly into the hands of the merchants. The ruling class does not even dream that these offerings are made only after great exertions and tears of blood.

It is a great shame that such conditions prevail, but it is said that "even the thoughts of an ant may reach up to Heaven." Though their conditions differ, the highest and the lowest alike are human beings, and the rulers ought to think about those who are less fortunate than themselves. Soon all the gold and silver currency will pass into the hands of the merchants, and only merchants will be deserving of the epithets "rich" and "mighty." Their power will thus grow until they stand first among the four classes. When I investigated the incomes of present-day merchants, I discovered that fifteen-sixteenths of the total income of Japan goes to the merchants, with only one-sixteenth left for the samurai. As proof of this statement, I cite the following case. When there are good rice harvests at Yonezawa in Dewa or in Semboku-gun in Akita[39] the price is five or six *mon*[40] for one *shō*. The rice is sold to merchants who ship it to Edo, where the price is about 100 mon, regardless of the original cost. At this rate, if one bought 10,000 ryō's worth of rice in Dewa, sent it to Edo and sold it there, one's capital would be increased to 160,000 ryō. If the 160,000 ryō in turn were used as capital, the return in Edo would be 2,560,000 ryō. With only two exchanges of trade it is possible to make enormous profits.

It may be claimed that of this sum part must go for shipping expenses and pack-horse charges, but the fact remains that one gets back sixteen times what one has paid for the rice. It is thus apparent that fifteen-sixteenths of the nation's income goes to the merchants.[41] In terms of the production of an individual farmer, out of thirty days a month he works twenty-eight for the merchants and two for the samurai; or, out of 360 days in a year, he works 337½ for the merchants and 22½ for the samurai. Clearly, then, unless the samurai store grain it is impossible for them to offer any relief to the farmers in years of famine. This may be why they can do no more than look on when the farmers are dying of starvation. And all this because the right system has not been established. It is a most lamentable state of affairs that the farmers have to shoulder the weight of this error and die of starvation as inevitably as "water collecting in a hollow."

The price of rice determines that of other cereals and also affects foodstuff prices as a whole; as it fluctuates so will the others. One can thus judge its importance. Since the market price of rice concerns the ruler, it should not be left for merchants to determine, but should be controlled by the government authorities. The present attitude is that since trade involves buying and selling, and

---

39 Dewa and Akita were provinces in northern Honshu.
40 A *mon* was a copper coin. A *shō* was about 3.2 pints.
41 Honda's figures here go quite astray; again, his desire to make a point leads him to make unreasonable statements.

since buying and selling is the merchants' profession, involving a contest with the people for profits, the samurai are absolutely resolved not to engage in trade. This is an unintelligent and ill-informed attitude.

Japan is a long, narrow country that stretches over ten degrees of latitude from its northeastern extreme to its southwest corner, a distance of about 550 ri. Even in bad years, when the crops failed to ripen in one place, there has never been a case when the drought extended to every part of the nation. It is therefore the parental duty of the ruler toward the people to relieve their hunger by shipping grain from provinces with rich harvests to those with poor ones, thus ministering to their wants. This is imperative. There is a difference between this duty of the ruler and what the merchants do to make a living. The merchants buy up produce at a low price at the place where it is harvested and then store it. They wait for a drought or for other natural disasters to harm the crops and cause the price of rice to go up. They then sell the grain at the place where it was originally purchased at a price several times what they paid. In this way they struggle with the people in their greed for high profits. Gentlemen would never do this.

In the summer of 1787 the price of one hundred 35-shō sacks of rice climbed from 250 ryō to 300 ryō in the capital. There was a plot to make the prices go even higher. It was announced that the stocks of rice in the city had been exhausted. This was really not true; there was a perfectly adequate supply, but the merchants planned the announcement in order to get even bigger profits. In view of the disrgaceful motives that inspire merchants, it is impossible to live in security unless some plan is devised to deal with them once and for all. Trading stations should therefore be established at important inland ports and seaports throughout Japan. Rice and other grain offered for sale should be bought during the year at the natural market price, as determined by the quality of the harvest, and stored at the station. A survey should be made of crop conditions in all parts of the nation, and the information obtained should be quickly circulated by couriers in boats. Every year each county should estimate the amount of food it will need, and leave that amount in the appropriate station. The remainder should be transported on station ships to provinces that have had bad crops distributed there to relieve hunger. In all provinces, including the capital, the normal price paid to the farmers during the previous year should be used as the price standard. If the price does not go up or down more than ten to twenty percent from this level, the station should not buy or sell; if it rises above the limit, the station should sell. Buying and selling would thus maintain prices within ten to twenty percent of the average price paid to farmers during the previous year. The stations could then keep the highest price of rice fixed according to the price in the capital. It is inevitable that there should be some discrepancies, since shipping costs to places nearer or farther away will differ, but the prices would be roughly the same, and the people would be greatly helped. This plan would give the farmers a new lease on life.

Then, even if no formal regulations are made on the subject, the evil practice of infanticide would stop. Within twenty years not only would there be a better race increasing in numbers, but the abandoned fields would gradually be cultivated again and return to their original fertile state. This plan will permit millions of koku of additional income to be raised without persecuting the farmers. When a policy truly designed to bring peace and prosperity to the country is adopted, the people will show honest obedience, and they will share in the fifteen-sixteenths of the national income the merchants now take. Then in two or three years provinces now so impoverished that infanticide is the general rule will be put on their feet, and the farmers will be rehabilitated.

Even during the short period that Hideyoshi[42] was in power, he managed to distribute 465,000 ryō (767,250 ryō in current exchange) among the lords of the empire in the fourth moon of 1588. If he had lived to old age, he would probably have made even China a tributary nation of Japan, but unhappily he died in his sixty-third year on September 18, 1598. Because the country

---

[42] Toyotomi Hideyoshi (1536–98), one of the great men of modern Japan.

was at war at the time, he gave the money to the lords; if peace had prevailed, he would have given it to the farmers for their relief.

Unless the ruler is possessed of great genius, the country will be poorly governed. Examples of this adage may be found throughout the ancient and modern histories of both Japan and China. The present times are the first since Minamoto Yoritomo[43] founded the military order that the samurai have been in such a sorry state. This situation must be changed at once, and the old order of samurai, farmers, artisans, merchants, and idlers restored. Trading stations should be established steadily throughout the country, as I have suggested, and extensive trading carried out. The wants of one section should be supplied with what another possesses by transporting the produce in government-owned ships. This would both help the people and bring money into the government treasuries. If the ruler should become very wealthy without courting wealth and without seeking profit, proving himself thus worthy of the name "richest in the land," he would preserve his authority and his fortune. This would be a most felicitous and extraordinary thing, and would lay the cornerstone for ten thousand years of prosperity.[44]

. . .

By means of the plans outlined in the account of the four imperative needs and the three great sources of worry, the present corrupt and jejune society could be restored to its former prosperity and strength. The ancient glories of the warrior-nation of Japan would be revived. Colonization projects would gradually be commenced and would meet with great success. A capital city would be built in eastern Ezo for northern Japan. The central capital would be at Edo, and the southern one at Osaka. The capital of the entire nation would alternate among these three locations. Then, under enlightened government, Japan could certainly be made the richest and strongest country in the world. This is because Japan, unlike other nations, has ample deposits of gold, silver, lead, and iron.

[43] Minamoto Yoritomo (1147–99), founder of the Kamakura Shogunate.
[44] Several pages about the three sources of worry—fire, rice shortages, and night robbery—are omitted here.

Everything depends entirely on the course of action adopted. If it is a good one, the outstanding men of the country will come forward to serve the ruler and demonstrate their loyalty. The precious metals of the country will gravitate toward the ruler and circulate as he chooses. The people will all seek to be perfectly loyal to the ruler, and will direct their faithful attentions toward him. Everyone will sincerely desire to support the program. Since there will be no opposition to the government, there will be few criminals. When the country is ruled by force against the will of the people, many in their hearts oppose this compulsion and become criminals. All these blessings depend on finding men who are talented and able, and who are versed in the laws of Heaven, earth, and man. If the rulers lack the appropriate talents, the people will not have faith in their decrees.

The above secret program may seem like outspoken criticism of the government because it gets at the very roots of contemporary practices and openly discusses their merits and demerits. This is a point on which I feel very fearful. Yet if my fears had caused me to write with deference and reverence, the principles I have presented might have appeared less weighty. I have accordingly recorded my thoughts plainly, even at the risk of speaking in a manner unbefitting my status.

Tales of the West

This book is one that describes Japan, China, and the West as they actually are. Thus, it will probably arouse much controversy, but I have not hedged on that account. If one hedges too much, the rights and wrongs become confounded and cannot easily be told apart. I have therefore not taken into consideration what dangers may be involved, and, in the interests of my country and the people, I have come out directly to call right what is right and wrong what is wrong, leaving out all roundabout expressions and falsifications. What I have said may sound like slander or abuse, and I realize that as an inferior criticizing my superiors I must inevitably incur censure. It has been customary since olden times to describe as wise those people who are cautious in such matters and keep to the approved way; such people have won the world's

acclaim. Those who have not so acted have all met with misfortunes and perished, thanks to the severity of government regulations.

Since this book, in which vital matters are discussed, has not
been written in the approved spirit, I too may be unable to escape
misfortune. But even if the book falls into the hands of people
who may be my enemies, if its contents are carefully read and examined to determine whether it was written for personal profit
or for the benefit of the nation, they will find that it was conceived
in goodwill, and whatever merits it may have will also become apparent. To write with such goodwill is what is to be expected of
every person born in Japan. I have come to grips with the natural
principles insofar as my limited intelligence has permitted, and
I have described without ornamentation the general features of
Japan, China, and the West, mixing the three together. I have
entitled the work *Tales of the West.* Although the book actually
treats the three regions, the facts about China and Japan are
known to everyone, and I have therefore mentioned only the West
in the title.

This is to serve as preface.[45]

September 1798

· · ·

The Dutch have been coming to Japan for over a hundred and
fifty years. During this time their writings for the people of their
country must have included many amusing descriptions of Japanese religious and popular observances. I shall relate a few of the
things I have heard. When the Dutch go into temples and see
peculiarly shaped images like those of Aizen, the Guardian King,
or Kōjin, the Hearth God, or Shōten, with three eyes, six or seven
arms sticking out of their backs, and their whole bodies colored
vermilion and green, or like Fudō, with fire flaming from his back,
they think that these must all be false gods, and that the Japanese
people believe only in empty idols. Japan harbors an exceptionally
great number of foolish customs, but among them the one of

[45] Volume One of *The Tales of the West* is omitted. What follows is an
abridged version of Volume Two.

having the common people pray to such things must count as the most absurd. However, since this practice is of many years' standing, I suppose nothing can be done about it now.

Among the factory directors who have come to Japan was one named Kaempfer. He remained in Nagasaki for three years and studied Japanese history with the interpreters. After he had sailed home, he wrote a book about events in Japan from the Age of the Gods to the present. Later, when Natsume, Lord of Izumi, was governor of Nagasaki, a factory director named Arend Willem Feith visited Edo twice. He was especially familiar with Japanese institutions and wrote a book called *Amoenitatum*. When I examined this book, the first thing I saw was an account of the imperial palace giving a detailed description of various ceremonies observed, of the appearance of the lords assembled in the palace on the occasion of a performance of *nō* and *kyōgen*, and of various minor matters as well.[46]

In certain of their books of miscellaneous essays resembling our *Tsurezure-gusa*,[47] the Dutch include illustrations of everything from people and beautiful scenery down to implements. These pictures, which are copperplate engravings of the type used in Holland, are even more beautiful than the real things. Since there have been a number of Japanese in times past who have left Japan for good and never returned, the Westerners have been able to learn everything about our country from them.

Someone asked me, "Are there formal, running-hand, and cursive forms to the European letters?" I answered, "In Europe they do not use characters such as we have in China or Japan. They have only twenty-five letters, and these have eight forms that differ from one another in much the same way as the formal, running-hand, and cursive scripts do. These twenty-five letters suffice for writing anything. In Japan there is a particular character used

---

[46] This work was actually by Kaempfer, not Feith, and does not contain any account of the imperial palace. Probably a triple confusion, involving Kaempfer's *History of Japan* (Glasgow, 1906).

[47] A book of short essays by Kenkō Hōshi (1283–1350), translated into English by Donald Keene under the title *Essays in Idleness* (New York, 1967).

for every single thing, in imitation of Chinese usage, which means that there is an inconveniently large number of characters. For example, *ten* in Japanese is written with one character, while in Dutch it is *hemel,* four letters.[48] *Chi* in Japanese is another character, while *aard* has four letters. It might seem simpler to use one character than four letters, but if a man were to attempt to memorize the tens of thousands of Chinese characters, he might not succeed even if he devoted his life's energies to it. This would certainly be a great waste of time. Even supposing there were someone who could memorize them all, I doubt whether it would be of any service to the nation. It must have been because the Europeans realized this fact that they adopted a simpler method. Since the chief function of writing is considered to be the recording of facts and opinions, it would be far more expedient to do so with our Japanese kana instead of attempting to memorize all the thousands of Chinese characters.

A person may acquire the reputation of being a great Confucian scholar and yet not be really familiar with the affairs of even one country. However, I understand that in the West a man who has a reputation for wide learning will know the languages of over thirty foreign countries, and will be perfectly acquainted with their conditions and products as well. This must be because, having few letters to learn, Westerners can devote all their energies to the study of more important things.

In Europe a large goose quill is used for writing. The Europeans sharpen the end to a point and fill the opening with ink. They start writing from the top left, and write across to the top right. The sentences are written underneath one another in layers. Most of the world uses this kind of writing. Chinese characters are used only in Korea, the Ryukyus and Japan (to the east of China), in the various provinces of Manchuria (to the north), and in eastern India. European letters are used in the countries of Europe and America, along the southern and western coasts of Africa, from the islands south of eastern India to the islands south of China, in

---

[48] Either Honda could not count the number of letters in *hemel* (heaven), or there has been a misprint in the text.

the islands south of Japan, in the eastern Ezo islands, in the area of Kamchatka, and as far as the continent of North America. All of these places use twenty-five letters in writing. Although each country has a different language, all of them may be recorded with the twenty-five letters. The alphabet resembles the Japanese kana, but the latter has twice as many symbols as there are letters. One might expect that any sound could be recorded exactly by means of the kana, but this is not so. The kana cannot represent even the forty-three tables of sound changes listed in the *Mirror of Sounds*,[49] and these are still not all the possible sounds.

If a careful study is made of their system of writing and ours, it will become apparent which is correct and which false. The failings in our way of life cause people to spend most of their time in idle and elegant pursuits, the number of which constantly increases. They are forgetful of themselves, and when they reach old age it is too late for them to repent. It was fortunate for the Westerners that they foresaw this eventuality and took steps to avoid a system of writing so profitless to the nation.

"Why is it that European painting differs from Japanese and Chinese painting?" someone asked. I replied, "European paintings are executed in great detail, with a view to making them resemble exactly the objects portrayed, so that they may be of some use. There are rules of painting to achieve this effect. They observe the division of sunlight into light and shade, and also what are called the rules of perspective. For example, if one wishes to depict a person's nose from the front, there is no way in Japanese painting to represent the central line of the nose. In the European style of painting, shading is used on the sides of the nose, and one may thereby perceive the height of the nose. Again, if one wishes to draw a sphere, there is no way to make the center appear to stand out in Japanese painting, but the Europeans shade the edges to permit one to see the height of the center. In Japan this is called *ukie*. Since it is the custom in Europe to consider above all whether something is of use to the nation, there is an academy that exam-

---

[49] *Inkyō* (in Chinese, *Yün-ching*), a late T'ang work on phonetics.

ines all books before they are printed so that no books of a frivolous
or indecent nature will be published."

In Europe and Africa are the huge edifices known as the Seven
Wonders, considered the most remarkable sights of the world. The
pyramids of Egypt and the tower of Babylon were both built for
worshiping God. The latter, constructed of stone and ornamented
with sculptures, was round in shape, and of a splendor difficult to
describe. A spiral staircase ascended to the summit, at which point
the tower was very broad, with balconies on every side from which
the mountains and oceans could be seen. There one was truly above
the clouds. These two wonders were both located in countries at
the eastern end of Africa.

There was also the Colossus of Rhodes, which stood astride the
mouth of the harbor of that island. It is said that large ships with
full sail could pass between its legs. It was built because ships
traveling to and from the island at night were apt to run aground
on the concealed rocks in the Mediterranean some six or seven
miles around the harbor mouth. The Lord of Rhodes, deploring
this situation, decided to erect an all-night beacon in the form of
a human figure built with two bodies, holding aloft beacons on
both sides. It was so constructed that ships had no trouble sailing
through. Some years ago, when war broke out in that country, the
Colossus was destroyed, and it is no longer standing. Its remains
are nevertheless very considerable, and people from many countries come to view them. The destruction of the Colossus demonstrates that even in Europe the failure to obtain natural good government has resulted in disorder of the kind that prevailed in
Japan up to the end of the sixteenth century.

The wonders that still exist at present are the Great Bell of
Muscovy and the Stone Bridge of London. When Kōdayū returned to Japan a few years ago after seeing the Great Bell, he
said that it looked like a small mountain. In the capital city of
London there is a broad river called the Thames. A stone bridge
spans its width of about three ri, and at both ends there are markets
and temples. Large ships with sails raised can pass under the
bridge. The construction of the stone embankment along the river

and of the bridge itself is so magnificent that one doubts it was
accomplished by human labor. When it comes to grand edifices,
no country in the world can compare with England.

There is also no country comparable to England in the manufacture of very fine things. Among the articles imported into Japan
by the Dutch, there have been none more precious than the
watches. Some of them are so exquisite that hairs are split to make
them. London is thought to produce the finest such workmanship
in the world. Next comes Paris in France, and then Amsterdam
in Holland. In these three capitals live people virtually without
peer in the world, who are the handsomest of men. The houses in
their towns and cities, even in the outskirts, are built of stone.
They are from two to five stories high and surpassingly beautiful.
Why is it that the people of these three cities, who are human
beings like everyone else, have attained such excellence? It is because many centuries have elapsed since they were civilized and
because their political institutions are founded on the principles
of natural government. Their nations are thus so prosperous that
even among the commoners one finds many wealthy persons. That
is why the Europeans do not begrudge expenses but insist that
even the smallest parts of their implements be made with the
highest degree of skill.

Since the merit system is practiced in Europe, talented and
capable people all flock to these three capitals, and it is because
of their efforts that these cities stand unique in the world. It would
seem that the inhabitants of these cities must have some special
cleverness, but the secret of their supremacy is inseparable from
the above considerations. Their prosperity is probably entirely
due to the excellence of their political system and the great number of years of experience they have had. This is not an isolated
instance, and the excellence of their whole society cannot be conjectured from Japanese and Chinese equivalents.

There are books entitled *Buys, Chomel, Kunstkabinett,* etc.,[50]
in which are listed in detail methods of making unusual devices.

[50] Buys' *Dictionary* and Chomel's *Encyclopaedia* have been mentioned. I am
not sure what *Kunstkabinett* refers to.

These are most helpful books that seem to lead one by the hand. Although parts of the explanations are difficult to understand, there is an attempt to make them as clear as possible by means of the illustrations. We are really fortunate to possess such books. In contrast to Westerners, however, Japanese keep good things for themselves and are reluctant to pass them on to others. It is a shameful state of affairs when people think only how they can profit themselves.

I have been told that in the Edo Observatory is kept a map of the world about seven feet wide and ten feet long; it is a copper-plate engraving colored in gold, silver, red, and green. The precision and splendor of this map are said to surpass all description. It is extremely difficult to make an engraving of so great a size. Sometime during the 1650's several hundred copies of this map were made. Each of them was rolled up and placed in a box sealed with cloth and pitch, and the boxes were then thrown into the Atlantic and Pacific oceans as presents for the world. I have heard this story and imagine that the maps were thus distributed because it was desired to teach the world that the various nations were located as shown on the map. From this one example we can appreciate how lofty the Westerners' national spirit is. One of these maps floated ashore in Satsuma and has been kept there by the daimyo as his secret possession. The map in the Observatory was obtained as a present from Holland when Yoshimune was shogun.

Some years ago a Roman was taken prisoner when he landed on Yaku Island off Kyushu.[51] He was brought to Edo, where in accordance with a shogunate order the scholar Hakuseki interrogated him with the aid of this map. The Roman was greatly surprised that there was a copy of this map in Japan, and said that copies were rare even in his own country. The Roman, able to converse in Japanese, had arrived here with his head shaved in the Japanese manner, bringing with him about 1,000 ryō in gold and silver coins, both old coins and coins of Kan'ei mintage.[52]

---

[51] The career of this "Roman" combines facts from the experiences of Giovanni Batista Sidotti (1668–1715) and Giuseppe Chiara (1606–85).

[52] The Kan'ei era was 1624–43.

He had been selected by the Emperor of Rome to sail to Japan and to give instruction in the Catholic religion as well as in the principles of natural government. He was not to prepare the people for a conquest of the country as the Portuguese had done, but to transmit the benevolent and merciful institutions of the Roman emperor. He stated that he had come to Japan knowing all along that there was a severe prohibition in this country against Christianity, but he declared repeatedly and at great length how different his intent was from that of the Portuguese. His explanations were never accepted by the shogunate, probably because the troubles with the Portuguese were still recent. He lived in Japan for more than forty years, and finally died of illness when over eighty without having succeeded in his plans. He was buried in the Muryō-in in Koishigawa.

When he was on the point of death he said, "Now that I have attained so great an age, my death may come today or tomorrow. I should like now to transmit to the Tairōsama[53] the greatest thing in the world, in return for the kindness I have received for so many years. The thing of which I speak is a system of laws that will keep the country free from disturbances for all time to come, even if no precautionary measures are taken. It is because Japan has not yet learned the true method of government that the spirit of bloodshed still prevails, and that one must always take precautions here. It was my desire to inform the Tairōsama of this system, but to the end he has not wished to hear me. This is the source of the greatest regret to me."

The spirit of bloodshed has still not vanished, and that is why it is so difficult for the people to feel a sense of security. In the midst of peace the farmers are gradually being impoverished, a situation that will in the end lead to unrest within the country. But a way exists to remedy this condition. When this way is taught and understood, all classes of society in Japan will greatly rejoice. Furthermore, whoever puts it into effect will leave a name for all generations to come as a great leader. The benevolent and merciful

53 An honorific title for a high shogunate adviser. The office was vacant at the time that Chiara supposedly made his request (1685).

system of the Emperor of Rome should naturally be introduced. If this happens, the two nations will be friendly, ships will go back and forth between them, and considerable profits will accrue to both countries. Since the two nations lie at corresponding degrees of latitude, it is likely that their products and people are similar. It is indeed a pity that there should be this antagonism because of a difference in religion.

The bloodthirsty spirit of war vanishes when the world's religious teachings are good, and this spirit flares up when they are bad. There is thus nothing more valuable or loftier in the world than religious teachings. This great Roman leader changed his name while in Japan and called himself Okamoto Sanemon, in accordance with a shogunate order.[54] It was unfortunate and unkind that this person, who could have helped the nation, was cruelly neglected during the forty years he lived in Japan.

. . .

I have a story to relate at this point. In the summer of 1783 Mount Asama in Shinano[55] erupted, and ashes fell in such quantities on the surrounding provinces that farming became impossible. Famine conditions already existed when in 1786 a volcano erupted on Ōshima in Izu,[56] and all summer long the sky was overcast. In the middle of the seventh moon, there were great falls of hail and floods in twelve provinces from the Kantō to Ōu, the Etsus,[57] and Shinano, and a grave famine resulted. In Edo the price of one hundred 35-shō sacks of rice rose from about 250 gold ryō to 300 ryō. The retail price of polished rice rose in the towns to 100 mon for three-tenths of a shō. When the stocks of rice on sale were finally exhausted, grave disorders broke out among the common people, who were hard pressed to survive, but the situation abated when the government gave the people relief.

---

[54] Chiara went by this name after he was apostasized. See Anesaki Masaharu, "Kirishitan Kyōshi no Nihon Sennyū," *Shigaku Zasshi*, XL (1929), 739–41.

[55] A province in central Honshu.

[56] Ōshima is one of the islands of the Izu Shichitō.

[57] Echigo, Echizen, and Etchū were three provinces on the Japan Sea coast of Honshu.

When I passed through the domain of Aizu in Ōu during the tenth moon of that year on business, foodstuffs were scarce and expensive. One seldom saw any of the local people going about, and there were empty houses everywhere. I arrived at a place called Harajuku at dusk, and I looked around from place to place, thinking that there would surely be an inn in the town where I could spend the night. At last, when it must have been about eight o'clock, I saw a light, and smoke rising from a large house. I thought then that I would ask to spend the night there, but when I knocked at the door there was no reply. Wondering what kind of house this might be, I went inside. I called out what I had come for, and then an old woman appeared and said, "Your request is a very moderate one, but we have no food, no bedding, nothing at all. If you are willing to accept these conditions, you may do as you please here." She went within and made no sign of looking after me.

There was now no alternative to spending the night in this house, and so, without food, bedding, or light, my servant and I lay down in the utter darkness of what I imagined to be a drawing room. I could not sleep on account of the pangs of my empty stomach. As I turned over the situation in my mind, I felt that there was something mysterious about the place, and I got up and went farther back into the house toward the kitchen, thinking that I would have a look into what was going on in the house.

When I reached the kitchen and looked about, I could see six or seven emaciated figures, who might have been either men or women, huddled about the edges of an oblong brazier. I went up to them, thinking I might ask for some hot water to relieve my thirst, and then I saw that they were all women. They might have been young, but in appearance they were aged, and their features were like those of monkeys. I cannot describe the grief and pity I felt on seeing their emaciated state.

Barely able to hold back my tears, I asked them how they had come to this unfortunate condition, but no one answered me. When I had asked a second and a third time, one of them, a girl of fourteen or fifteen, answered, "Don't you know? This is not our house. We are people from the mountain villages fifteen miles around here. We have had a famine ever since the ashes began to fall. At first we got along eating things we were never meant to eat, but in time we became thin and more and more of us died. Now there is no one left in the villages. I could not bring myself even to tell you what we have gone through in these three years of suffering—it has been too sad, too cruel for my words. The men, perhaps because they have always worked so hard, are weak in the face of death. I have no words to tell you the sorrow of seeing them die. We women, unfortunate creatures that we are, have been left behind, but we too are dying away, and now all that is left is the whitened bones of our parents, children, and kin." She wept as she said these words. I too was so filled with tears that I could not speak.

Then I said, "This is indeed most pitiful. Has it been so with all you ladies?"

"We seven women come from seven different places, all who were left living in those villages, gathered together, living from one day to the next, uncertain of the morrow, spending our days in hunger; thus are we seven. This year we had planted a little rice, but, as in other years, it did not ripen. We cut it when it withered still green. There were no ripe ears, but only blasted ones like straw, which we parch on the fire and pound in mortars. We make it into a kind of flour paste and round it into dumplings, which we boil in salt water. A bowl or two of this we eat a day, and with this food, more fit for horses than for human beings, we are barely able to prolong our lives from one day to the next. But it is not likely we will be able to last through this winter until the spring when the flowers bloom."

When I heard these words said in tears, I could not control my grief. "I think I may have a plan," I said to the seven women. "We shall be returning presently to Edo. If I escorted all of you there, you could somehow make a living in Edo. If you are willing, I shall do whatever I can to help you on the way."

They answered me, "Thank you for your kindness, but we are all sinners who have escaped death when we should have died with our parents, husbands, and brothers. Our duty was to die with them, and however much we regret it now, it will always be true that they died before us. Why, then, should we now go to Edo or wherever it may be? To die here is the proper thing for us, even if it must be of starvation." They refused my offer with these words. However much I tried to coax them, they refused, which moved me greatly.

I felt that there was nothing I could do, and so I took out what little money I had and gave it to them, saying, "This is only a little money, but please buy something with it for yourselves."

They answered me, "It must seem very strange for us to refuse when your wish comes from such deep compassion, but here, even if one has money, it is of no use. There is nothing at all being sold. Up until last year there was a little to be had, although at high prices, and the money would have been of use. This year the money is useless, since everyone for fifteen miles around is dead, and there would be no one to buy, even if there were something to sell. A traveler has nothing to depend on save his money. Please keep it for your own needs." These words they said and would not talk further on it. So stubborn were these good people that I could do nothing for them, and I withdrew, wringing my hands.

The next morning my servant and I got up, muttering to ourselves because we had had no means of filling our empty stomachs. We set off in the direction of Sendai.[58] On the way I noticed that almost all the houses in the villages were empty, and if rarely we met a villager, it would be a woman with an emaciated face and feeble eyes, looking as if she might collapse at any moment. We did not come across a single man. They say that in the time of starvation, it is the men who die first, and I thought that the statement must be true.

Next we passed through villages in the domain of Sendai. If all those mountain villages had been put together, they would have made over five counties in which everyone was dead and only empty houses stood. We headed from there toward the interior,

[58] Sendai is a port northeast of Tokyo.

which was still an area of great famine. It was the same in the domains of Sōma, Iwaki, Nambu, and Tsugaru, and in the area of Semboku County.[59] Alongside the roads were many whitened human bones. I reflected that I had never heard of such a thing happening in former ages.

I stopped at a certain inn. While I was there the woman of the house told me, "There is a strange woman living in this village. She had a boy who was two this year, who already could say a few words and was just at his loveliest. She had always been poor, and with the famine of the past few years she had nothing at all left to eat this year. There was no food left on sale, and she was in a desperate plight. Her little boy wanted to suck her breast, but she no longer had any milk to give. She said, 'If I abandon him, he is weak and will die. I have no way to keep him alive. If I die and he is left behind, he will be eaten by wolves. It is better that he die before me. Since he originally came from my belly, he should go back again into my belly.' She took the boy by the head and twisted it off. Then she ate him, bones and all. I have heard in stories of olden times that when there was a great famine people would eat one another, but now such stories must be told of the present."

In another village where I stopped, there was a family cat in the inn. Some of the village people came and said, "Please let us have your cat." They seized it, and then produced 700 mon as "compensation" for it. They said, "It will save you the bother of feeding the cat," but the owner would not agree to the arrangement. While they were arguing over it, I excused myself and went out. It is impossible for me to describe how these wretched people looked. I recall that at the time I thought how lucky I was to live in the capital. This reflection served as a warning; I realized after seeing these things that if I valued my life I should return to Edo at once. A woman of the town said to me, "Things are still worse farther on. Instead of continuing on this dangerous journey, you should return at once to Edo and look to living out your full span of life." I then changed my plans and hurried back to Edo. This is how I managed to save my life.

[59] All places in northern Honshu.

In the two provinces of Ōu alone, the number of persons who died of hunger is said to have reached two million during the years 1783–86. This figure must be true. I was astonished when I saw the amount of wasteland in both provinces. If these facts were made known to the Europeans, would they not despise us? They would say that it is because people who live in wooden houses are stupid and of feeble intelligence that so many citizens have been lost.[60]

.   .   .

The greater part of the precious metals mined in the various Japanese deposits during the past three hundred years has been exported to foreign countries, and the little that now remains here has passed into the hands of the merchants.[61] As an example of this tendency, consider the money obtained from the sale of unrefined sugar produced in the domains of the Lord of Satsuma. The value of the amount sold in Edo every year is from 280,000 to 300,000 ryō of gold. With such a sum pouring into Satsuma each year, it is natural that some of it also overflows into the Ryukyus. There the market price is one gold ryō coin for about 4,700 mon of Kan'ei copper cash.[62] The unscrupulous Nagasaki merchants therefore secretly load copper cash aboard ships, and send it off to the Ryukyus where great profits can be made by trading it for gold coins. Of course there have been prohibitions on such smuggling activities for many years, so if by some chance these merchants are caught, they are punished with death. But with full knowledge of the hazards they perform their risky business in the hope of profit. It is bad enough that they break the laws, violate the borders, and disobey the government, but they are also deficient in their loyalty to Japan. The ships of the Lord of Satsuma

[60] Honda elsewhere gives corroborative evidence for this opinion: A Dutchman said, "Children who are born in wooden houses have the nature of plants and trees. They are bound to be slow-witted and undistinguished. Children born in houses of stone are like metal; they have keen intelligences and are gifted. Having traveled all over the world and been a student of human nature, I have found this always to be so." (*Seiiki Monogatari*, pp. 160–61.)

[61] A short digression on the sorrows of the farmer is omitted.

[62] Copper coins (*sen*) issued 1624–43.

are said to load merchandise for China in the Ryukyus and then sail for trade to ports in the area of Cha-p'u and Chekiang.[63] A great deal of gold coin, among other things, must be carried off in this way.

It is a most unfortunate situation when no measures are taken to prevent this sapping of our nation's strength. The situation shows no sign of improving; eventually all the gold and silver will have been exported, leaving none in Japan. It will then be recounted as a tale of days gone by that once there was something called gold coin, which was used as money. If that happens, far from building our houses of stone, we may eventually find wood so scarce in Japan that it is not possible to build houses of it. Then people may begin to show a fondness for the old cave dwellings.

Here is a suggestion. In former days, the nation was torn by wars that lasted for many years, and the administration of the government was not unified. Finally, in the late sixteenth century, peace was established, but the ways of the period of warfare were still retained. That is why many provisional laws, which were designed as temporary expedients, continue to be used in governing the country. They have been left just as they were, without any attempt being made to determine their value in later years. They must now be changed, or the farmers will become exhausted and incapable of survival. I believe that a solution exists for the problems of our times, one that is simpler than any other to introduce, and one that will bear fruit. Wise rulers, however, are rare. When, for want of a wise ruler, everything is left entirely to the wisdom of aged counselors, there may be inferior persons in office before projects can be seen through. Over and over in the course of history one reads of persons of considerable talent who devoted themselves to their country's welfare, only to have things turn against them before they could accomplish anything, and who thus spent their lives pointlessly; this is the highest good fortune that such persons can hope for! One does not read of more fortunate officials. Therefore, the sovereign and his ministers must work together.

[63] Cha-p'u (Ningpo) was the major seaport of the province of Chekiang, on China's central coast.

They must acquire a good knowledge of conditions and strive to take suitable steps to improve them. The people should be informed that whatever is done for them by anyone is a result of the sovereign's great generosity. The ministers should not assert their own preferences in even the smallest respect, but should show perfect obedience in all matters, taking care not to deviate from the way of good subjects. Thus, by having whatever good things happen each day attributed to the ruler, the people's confidence will be directed toward the government, and all plans may then succeed. This is a general outline of the way to begin the task.

Some of the prosperous nations of Europe are themselves small in area but have extensive possessions. Such countries are called "great nations." Among them is England, a country about the size of Japan, which extends only from 50° to 60° N. Lat. and is no more than ten degrees broad from east to west. It is a far colder country than Japan. The great country called Kamchatka, in Japan's eastern Ezo territories, is also situated between 51° and 70° N. Lat., and thus has a climate similar to England's. Japanese, even some learned philosophers, say that the interior of Matsumae is too cold for growing cereals there, and that no one could live in such a place. Some go so far as to claim that Ezo is a foreign country, declaring that the inhabitants, unlike other human beings, have only one eye, in the middle of their foreheads, and that it flashes like lightning! They say moreover that if ships make port there, they never return to Japan, and that the extreme severity of the winters would freeze anyone to death. There are quite a few of these people who are very worthy men, who understand the principles of things and teach others about them, and who even after an uncomprehending reading of a book feel qualified to give instruction on it. This is the situation that prevails today; is it not scandalous? It arises because such men are ignorant of the sciences of astronomy, geography, and navigation. A person who is ignorant of these sciences has no possible way of knowing about the basic principles of colonization.

Matsumae is located at 40° N. Lat. Since its climate is similar to that of Shun-t'ien-fu, the capital of China, the same great variety of cereals and fruit will grow in both places. When this territory, which is somewhat less than 1,000 ri in circumference, has been settled, it will yield as much produce as now grows in all of Japan put together, and when this produce is brought into Japan, there will be double the present amount of food. Ezo would be of great help in creating abundance within Japan; it must not be neglected. If we abandon Ezo, it will fall to foreign countries. The proper attention can keep it Japanese. If this care is given, the development of Ezo will eventually be accomplished. This development will be in keeping with the basic policies of national defense. A natural frontier between Japan and foreign nations will be formed, affording protection to the nation.[64]

It is hard to estimate the extent of the disasters that may some-day occur if we persist in our negligence. Since it is a national obligation to attempt to increase the size of the country, even if this involves invading other countries, it makes me speechless with despair when I realize that we have permitted all our possessions to be snatched away by another country.

How may Japan become the greatest nation in the world? She should profit by the arts of civilization that she has learned during the 1,500 years that have elapsed since the time of the Emperor Jimmu. She should move her main capital to the country of Kamchatka. (It is located at 51° N. Lat., the same as London, so the climates must be similar.) She should build a great stronghold on Karafuto. She should trade with Santan and Manchuria, giving what they need in return for what they have to offer. The large ginseng roots are a product of the neighboring regions of Chien-chou and Chiang-ning-fu;[65] thus it will be possible to obtain as much of this product as desired at low prices to meet the nation's needs. Gold and silver will not be necessary in carrying on this trade; instead there will be a barter exchange of goods, the amount to be determined by how much is needed. The lower classes will

[64] At this point is given again the story of the Russians in Ezo and of Benyowsky's warning. We omit it here.

[65] Places in Manchuria. Ginseng is a root widely used in East Asia for medicinal purposes.

feel that they have been helped, and great profits will accrue to the government. Such an arrangement will prove highly advantageous for all concerned. It will be "getting good things with both hands," as the proverb goes.

The people of Santan have had the custom of sailing two or three boats a year to Sōya, a place at the western end of the island of Ezo, by way of the southern coast of Karafuto. There they trade with the natives such articles as ceremonial coats (popularly called "Ezo brocade," the court costume of Manchuria), green stones (known as "insect nests"), and various luxury items, all of which have come to be commonly used among the Ainu natives. Japan, on the other hand, sends the Ainu such things as pans and iron-ware, receiving in return the skins of sea and land animals. If routes were opened to facilitate this trade, Karafuto would soon be very prosperous. It is a larger country than Japan, and will probably develop into an even better place. In Japan one can as yet obtain no detailed information about Karafuto. Some say that it is connected in the northwest to Santan; others say that a broad river divides them.[66] Its area is probably twice that of Japan, but its exact size is not certain. However, there is positive evidence that it is a very large country. Karafuto must also possess many gold and silver deposits, for it is located a bare two days' sailing northwest of Sado.

To a person ignorant of navigation Karafuto must seem like a very distant place, but to one who is versed in the science it is much closer than Nagasaki. The development of Karafuto is an urgent matter, especially because it concerns our frontiers. As the proverb says, "Finders, keepers." What sensible person would fail to give this matter his consideration? We must not let Karafuto slip through our fingers. The existing trading stations should be made the starting point for continued developments. Karafuto will eventually become a land of great cities, and there will naturally also be great strongholds there.

Once great cities spring up in Karafuto and Kamchatka, the momentum will carry on to the islands to the south, and the grow-

---

[66] It was Mamiya Rinzō who first explored the strait. See above, Chapter 6.

ing prosperity of each of these places will raise the prestige of Edo to great heights. This, in turn, will naturally result in the acquisition of the American islands, which manifestly belong by right to Japan.

There are two of these islands lying in a northeasterly direction from Hitachi.[67] Together they are probably about half the size of Japan, and they have a large native population. East-northeast of these two places are a great many other islands, one of which is Amchitka, where the vessel *Shinshō Maru* was wrecked. The captain of the ship, Daikokuya Kōdayū, a native of Shirako-machi in Ise,[68] was rescued along with his crew by a Russian official making a tour of the region. Kōdayū was returned to Japan by way of Russia, and has now been pensioned by the government. Since he actually saw what he reported, what he says may be taken as certain.

According to Kōdayū, there is a large river between Karafuto and Santan that flows into the northern sea, and there is an island at the mouth of the river about as big as Shikoku and Kyūshū combined. This island is called Saghalien.[69] From there it is about 5,000 *chō*[70] due north to the port of Okhotsk, from where Kōdayū sailed back to Japan. Okhotsk, in Russian territory, is a key point in the transport of all commodities to the islands to the east. The crews of the Japanese ships that have been wrecked in this area since the Enkyō era[71] have all been given funds by the Russian government, and now live in Siberia, Russia, and Okhotsk. It is a fact that they have all married women of these countries and have had children by them.[72] Although the *Shinshō Maru* was the fourteenth ship to be wrecked in the region, the only sailors to have been re-

---

[67] Hitachi is northeast of Tokyo. The identification of these islands is not clear.

[68] See above, Chapter 3.

[69] Honda was apparently unaware that Karafuto and Saghalien were the same island.

[70] One *chō* equals about 119 yards.

[71] Covering the years 1744–47.

[72] The 1786 expedition came across Feodor, the half-caste son of Tokubei, a castaway. Feodor told them that all the earlier castaways had married Russian women and were supported by the Russian government. See Satō Genrokurō, *Ezo Shūi*, in Ōtomo, *Hokumon Sōsho*, I (Tokyo, 1943).

turned to Japan were Kōdayū and Isokichi. There has been a
report of four other shipwrecks in Kamchatka since the *Shinshō
Maru*'s, and it is said, though this report is not verified, that the
crews of these vessels have been helped by the government of Kamchatka and are living there.[73]

Each of the chieftains of the twenty eastern Ezo islands sends
native boats laden with the special products of his island to Okhotsk by way of offering tribute. Since there are always Russian
officials resident in Okhotsk, the chieftains offer their presents
when they appear for an audience. Gifts from the Emperor of
Russia are then bestowed on them. It will probably be a difficult
matter to change the customs of the natives who have been thus
befriended by Russia, but it is a tradition among them, transmitted from the days of their distant ancestors, that their islands
belong to Japan, and the practice of respectfully addressing the
Japanese as *kamoedono*[74] has not died out to this day. Before this
practice disappears, Japanese vessels should begin sailing and trading there throughout the year. Then a benevolent rule can ensure that the natives are supplied with what they need, and that
their surplus products are carried off in trade. When such beneficial trade is established, it will be very easy to get the natives
to submit to us. It has been barely twenty-five years that the Russians have been in the Ezo islands. If, then, a Japanese policy is
put into effect now, before all the old natives are dead, and if
talented officials are sent there who will get the old natives to tell
the others about days gone by and keep the old gratitude to Japan
alive, before many years have elapsed the inhabitants of Ezo will
yield to and obey Japan.

There is a reason why this is true. Russia, first of all, is a distant
country, accessible only over land; it is thus impossible to transport things back and forth with the requisite ease. If the Russians
were to use ships for transport, they would have to sail from their
own country, pass through the North Sea and the Straits of Dover,
double round the Cape of Good Hope, and then head for eastern
Ezo.

[73] A description of several unidentifiable islands is deleted here.
[74] *Kamoe* is an Ainu word derived from the Japanese *kami*, "exalted being."

Russia may have some more immediate plan than the vague and general one I have indicated, but she would probably not go so far as to attempt to take the eastern Ezo islands if the attempt involved her in a war. But even if Russia seeks only to relieve the suffering of the natives of the area around Okhotsk, the transport of products from the distant home country is blocked by many mountains. It would seem that good use might be made of the great rivers within that country's roughly 5,000 miles of land, but there are numerous obstacles in the form of narrows and ravines. That must be why the Russians decided that the best way to foster the development of the eastern Ezo islands was by trading with Japan. The fact that Kōdayū was accorded high rank and sent back all the way from Russia at great expense shows more clearly than words how thoroughgoing their policy is, and how carefully they cultivate the role of parents toward all people. But however intelligently they act, they have found it impossible, because of Japanese laws, to carry out their plans satisfactorily. This has probably been fortunate for Japan.

It may be that to further her plans in this connection Russia has selected officials and sent them to Japan as crew members of Dutch ships.[75] They may even have come to Edo, visited the castle, and examined conditions there. On returning to their country they may have reported that if, when transport facilities are improved in Ezo, it is established as the frontier, there will be no disputes in the future about the border between Japan and Russia, and that it would be most practical to foster the development of eastern Ezo by using Japan's abundant resources. This was apparently the plan underlying the desire to return Kōdayū, but things have not gone in accordance with their plans. The Russians were informed that they might visit Nagasaki and trade there, and they obtained documents of authorization before they returned home, but they have yet to visit Nagasaki. This is presumably because their plans have been upset.

Since, as I have written, the nature of their country is such that

---

[75] One of Honda's alarmist rumors, probably derived from Kudō Heisuke. See Kudō, "Aka Ezo Fūsetsu Kō," in Ōtomo, *Hokumon Sōsho*, I (Tokyo, 1943), 216.

transport is most difficult, the Russians have not been able to do as much for the natives of Ezo as they had wished. Now, while this remains true, is the time to take the islands back. If we plan secretly, we can make the Ezo islands Japanese, as they used to be. If these plans are put into effect, there will unquestionably come to be two supremely prosperous and powerful countries in the world: Japan in the East and England in the West.

England is located between 50° and 60° N. Lat., lying to the northwest of France, from which country it is separated by a channel barely six ri wide. To the west of England is the Atlantic Ocean; to the south are Portugal, France, Germany, etc.; and to the east are the territories of Russia. To the north, lands of night succeed frozen seas, and civilization there comes to an end. England is an island, a land of great cold, which produces little food. Perhaps by diligent study one may be able to discover in general how it was possible for this wretched island without a single redeeming feature to become so splendid a nation. With this information we would have the means to make Kamchatka into a great country as well.

Kamchatka lies between 51° and 70° N. Lat. and is thus in a location similar to England's. Since its climate, produce, and people must also be comparable, it should become as fine a country as England. It has been by the system of education that the clever and the stupid have been divided; by virtue of the natural law that the wise make use of the foolish, England is a master nation with island and continental possessions. The proper behavior for rulers and subjects is followed, which is the way of virtue on earth.

Notes

Notes

Complete authors' names, titles, and publication data are given in the Bibliography, pp. 245–50.

Chapter 1

1. See Boxer, *Jan Compagnie*, p. 4. This work contains valuable information on the early period of the Dutch factory, only briefly treated here.

2. Vondel, III, 628–29.   3. Kaempfer, III, 87–88.

4. *Ibid.*, pp. 93–94.   5. Vixseboxse, p. 67.

6. Ch'en Fu-kuang, p. 488. This was Spafari's mission of 1676.

7. *History of the Internal Affairs of the United Provinces*, p. 24.

8. Playfair, p. 68.

9. C. Snouck Hurgronje, quoted in Du Perron, p. 13.

10. Feenstra Kuiper, p. 40.

11. O. Z. van Haren, quoted in Du Perron, p. 198.

12. Thunberg, III, 64.

13. Krusenstern, I, 252.

14. Itazawa, "Rangaku no Igi," pp. 460–61.

15. *Ibid.*, p. 466.

16. See Sugita, pp. 38–39.

17. See Sakanishi. The fullest account of the banned books is in Nakamura.

18. Nakamura, p. 203.

19. The work was the *Li-suan Ch'üan-shu (Rekisan Zensho)*, a collection by Mei Wen-t'ing (1633–1721) compiled from various Western works. This was a pre-Copernican study, but the Japanese were impressed

by even so outdated a book. See Shimmura, *Zoku Namban Kōki,* p. 120.

20. *Tokugawa Jikki,* XLVI, 292.

21. It has often been stated since Ōtsuki's *Rangaku Kaitei* (1783) that Aoki actually visited Nagasaki, but Shimmura shows convincingly that this was not the case.

Chapter 2

1. *Tokugawa Kinrei-kō,* VI, 572.
2. Hirazawa, pp. 2–3.
3. Ōtsuki Gentaku, *Ransetsu Benwaku,* p. 494. See also pp. 170–71 for a more extended translation.
4. Honda, *Seiiki Monogatari,* in *Honda Toshiaki-shū,* pp. 126–27.
5. Quoted in Muraoka, "Shisei no Tetsujin," p. 32.
6. Shiba, *Kōkan Saiyū Nikki,* p. 92.
7. Imamura and Namura, *Oranda Mondō* (1724), pp. 3–7.
8. Ōtsuki Gentaku, *Rangaku Kaitei,* p. 221.
9. Amenomori, p. 11.
10. Morishima, p. 454.
11. Shiba, *Kōkan Saiyū Nikki,* pp. 100–106.
12. Shimmura, *Zoku Namban Kōki,* pp. 2–5.
13. Itazawa, *Rangaku no Hattatsu,* p. 30.
14. Sugita, p. 46.
15. Kulmus's work was more properly called *Tabulae Anatomicae,* but here as elsewhere Sugita's memory apparently betrayed him. The other book he was offered, the *Anatomia Nova* of the Danish scholar Caspar Bartholin (1585–1629), entered his collection somewhat later. Sugita consulted both works and various other textbooks of anatomy in making his translation of *Tafel Anatomia* known as *Kaitai Shinsho.* For the background of this translation, see Ogawa, pp. 7–98.
16. Sugita, p. 52.
17. *Ibid.,* pp. 51–52.
18. This work, called in Japanese *Oranda-Banashi,* was written by Gotō Rishun (1702–71).
19. Thunberg, III, 256.
20. *Ibid.,* p. 201.
21. Ōtsuki Gentaku, *Rangaku Kaitei.*
22. *Ibid.,* p. 226.
23. *Ibid.*
24. The preface by Kuchiki Ryūkyō (1750–1802) is of special interest because the author was the daimyo of Fukuchiyama as well as an important patron of Dutch learning. Kuchiki himself published in 1789 a massive geography of the West called *Taisei Yochi Zusetsu.*

25. Ōtsuki Gentaku, *Rangaku Kaitei*, p. 226.

26. Itazawa, *Rangaku no Hattatsu*, p. 53.

27. Sugita, p. 86.

Chapter 3

1. Benyowsky, I, 398.

2. Kropf (p. 324) quoted this account by Stepanov, a man who sailed with Benyowsky from Kamchatka.

3. Copies of Benyowsky's six letters are preserved in document 40/11488 in the Rijksarchief at The Hague. Document 11710 (part of the Deshima *Dagregister*) contains the account of the Dutch reaction to the letters. I have quoted from these two documents. Kondō Morishige (in *Henyō Bunkai Zukō*, p. 70) gave a translation of the warning letter that is approximately correct in outline, but considerably altered from the original.

4. Hirazawa, p. 8.

5. Shimmura, *Zoku Namban Kōki*, pp. 29–33.

6. Kudō, p. 217. See also Kōno, "Aka Ezo Fūsetsu-kō," p. 605.

7. Kudō, p. 218. For a discussion of the influence of Kudō Heisuke on the writings of Honda Toshiaki, see Ōtomo, I, 42–49.

8. Satō, p. 304.

9. Hayashi Shihei, *Kaikoku Heidan*, p. 261 (biographical notes by Muraoka Tsunetsugu). The surname Hayashi is pronounced "Rin" by some writers, i.e. Rin Shihei.

10. *Ibid.*, p. 7.   11. *Ibid.*, p. 9.

12. *Ibid.*, p. 9.   13. *Ibid.*, p. 45.

14. *Ibid.*, p. 19.   15. *Ibid.*, p. 11.

16. *Ibid.*, pp. 24–25.   17. *Ibid.*, p. 18.

18. *Ibid.*, p. 242.   19. Boxer, "Rin Shihei," p. 53.

20. Hayashi Shihei, *Kaikoku Heidan*, pp. 11–12.

21. Komiyama, pp. 125–26. In the original, "*Kono kōbe, tobu ka to-banu ka? Ake no haru.*" Since Hayashi was arrested at the end of the year, it was the "eve of spring"; in the lunar calendar, spring begins with the first day of the first moon.

22. This famous poem is known in two versions. The one quoted is "*Chichi haha mo naku, tsuma naku ko naku, hangi naku, zeni mo nake-reba, mata omoshiro mo nashi.*" The other version substitutes for the last three words "*shinitaku mo nashi,*" or "I don't want to die either."

23. Sansom (p. 226) states that another reason for Hayashi's arrest was his crime in having "confided his views to certain Court nobles who were known to be hostile to the shogun's government."

24. Kaempfer, II, 1.

25. See Matsudaira. pp. 167–69, for his views on sea defense.

26. Scherer's memoir is printed in full in Lefèvre-Pontalis, pp. 440–43.

27. *Tokugawa Kinrei-kō*, VI, 568–69.

28. Honda, *Chōki-ron*, in *Honda Toshiaki-shū*, pp. 211–12.

29. *Tokugawa Kinrei-kō*, VI, 594–98.

30. Strahlenberg, p. 462.

31. Barthold, p. 229.

32. Harima, "Rokoku ni okeru Nihongo Gakkō," pp. 791ff. Harima's account is the most complete. Cf. Lensen, "Early Russo-Japanese Relations," p. 9.

33. Katsuragawa, pp. 259–60.   34. Broughton, p. v.

35. Krusenstern, II, 67–68.   36. Golder, pp. 220–21.

37. Lesseps, I, 211–15.

38. The voyage is described in Hayashi Fukusai, *Tsūkō Ichiran*, VIII, 134ff.

39. Krusenstern, II, 219.

40. Katsuragawa, p. 254. Shinzō was given the name of Nicolai Kolotygin and was so known to Klaproth, who consulted him in 1805 about problems of translation. See Klaproth, p. ii.

41. A full account of Laxman's part in the return of Kōdayū and the text of Catherine's edict may be found in Lagus, pp. 227–35. A Japanese translation of the edict is in Harima, "Rokoku Saisho."

42. Matsudaira (pp. 164–67) contains his account of the incident.

43. Kaempfer (III, 341–60) contains the "Japan Diary" of the 1674 English ship.

44. Inobe, "Matsudaira Sadanobu," p. 1367.

45. *Ibid.*, p. 1369.

46. A translation of Adam Laxman's diary may be found in Harima, "Rokoku Saisho."

47. Ramming, *Russland-Berichte*, pp. 37–39. The shogun's questions were apparently based on an account by the factory director Hemmij, translated by Katsuragawa as *Roshiya-shi*, in *Nihon Bunko*, vol. V (Tokyo, 1891). See also Kamei, pp. 143–48.

48. Katsuragawa's book was entitled *Hokusa Bunryaku*.

49. Kamei, pp. 149–52.

50. Shiba, *Shumparō Hikki*, p. 472.

Chapter 4

1. See Morishima, p. 454. Boxer (*Jan Compagnie*, p. 171) quotes an account by Hayashi Shihei fixing the foundation of Holland at A.D. 6. The only Japanese who fully understood the Christian dating was apparently Miura Baien, who visited Nagasaki in 1778. See Miura, p. 1064.

2. Shiba, *Shumparō Hikki*, p. 461.

3. *Ibid.*, p. 403. For an account of Hiraga's career, see Irita, "Gennai Sensei no Kotodomo" in *Hiraga Gennai Zenshū*, vol. 2. Shiba Kōkan's picturesque account may have been an embroidery on the truth; it seems more likely Hiraga received the book as a present.

4. Ishii, pp. 8–9. See also Okamura, pp. 167ff, for a letter by Hiraga boasting of the skill of his pupil Ōdano.

5. Ishii, p. 9. See also Shiba, *Seiyō Gadan*, p. 366. Shiba declared that all painting was artisans' work; the brush was a tool for making pictures.

6. Honda, *Seiiki Monogatari* in *Honda Toshiaki-shū*, p. 155.

7. Ishii, p. 6.

8. Shiba, *Shumparō Hikki*, pp. 401–2.

9. *Ibid.*, p. 421.

10. *Ibid.*, p. 405.

11. *Ibid.*, pp. 406–7.

12. Letter to Tachihara in *Honda Toshiaki-shū*, p. 381.

13. *Nieuw en Volkomen Woordenboek van Konsten en Weetenschappen.*

14. Shiba, *Seiyō Gadan*, p. 369.

15. For a full account of Aōdō Denzen, see Nishimura, pp. 408–73. Aōdō's real name was Nagata Zenkichi (1748–1822). Nishimura is inclined to discount the generally accepted story that Matsudaira Sadanobu sent Aōdō to Nagasaki. Okamura (pp. 207–23) believes that Aōdō learned the art of engraving from books available in Edo, and especially from the etchings of Johan Elias Ridinger (1698–1767).

16. *Groot Schilderboek.* Shiba, *Seiyō Gadan*, p. 367.

17. Morishima, p. 479.

18. Ishii, p. 16. The founder of the group was Araki Genyū, who attempted to blend Chinese and Western techniques. His son, Araki (or Ishizaki) Yūshi, possessed greater talent and was known for his oil paintings on glass.

19. Arai, p. 814.

20. Gotō, pp. 436–37.

21. Morishima, p. 474.

22. Honda, *Seiiki Monogatari* in *Honda Toshiaki-shū*, p. 140.

23. Shiba, *Oranda Tensetsu*, p. 2a. See also Amenomori, p. 69, for a defense of the desirability of each country having its own phonetic system of writing.

24. Honda, *Seiiki Monogatari* in *Honda Toshiaki-shū*, p. 155.

25. Golownin, *Narrative of My Captivity*, I, 111.

26. For a discussion of early translations of European poetry, see Okamura, pp. 114–38. The subject is treated in detail by Chiba.

27. Honda, *Seiiki Monogatari* in *Honda Toshiaki-shū*, p. 156. Oka-

mura, p. 104, states that the first Dutch poem translated into Japanese was a drinking song translated by Aoki Konyō in 1745. In the early part of the nineteenth century Japanese scholars, now more proficient with Dutch, showed greater interest in translating poetry. The amateur theatricals staged by the Dutch on Deshima in 1820 were also described at considerable length by Ōta.

28. Shiba, *Tenchi Ridan,* p. 30. Among the fables Shiba translated were "The Fox and the Crow" and "The Wolf and the Crane."

29. Hirazawa, pp. 58–60.

30. This translation was made by Kuroda Kikuro (1827–92). It was not published until after the Meiji Restoration. A somewhat later translation by Yokoyama Yoshikiyo (1826–79) was published earlier, in 1857, with illustrations in the Western manner. See Shimmura, *Shimmura Izuru Senshū,* I, 516–18, 546–49.

31. Feenstra Kuiper, *Japan en de Buitenwereld,* p. 253.

32. Matsudaira, p. 177.

33. Kaempfer, III, 301–36. Kaempfer's conclusion was that it was more advantageous for Japan to remain "shut up."

34. Honda, *Seiiki Monogatari* in *Honda Toshiaki-shū,* p. 152.

35. Itazawa, "Rangaku to Jugaku," pp. 657–58.

36. Maeno, p. 1. The engravings were the work of Stradanus (1523–1605), possibly part of the series *Venationes ferarum, avium, piscium pugnae.* They were Flemish rather than French pictures: Maeno mistook the name of the publisher, "Galle," for "Gallic." The date of the engravings makes it likely that they had been in the possession of the shogunate for many years.

37. Golownin, *Narrative,* II, 116–17.

38. Broughton, p. 101. Could this Japanese have been Isokichi, Kōdayū's companion?

39. Itazawa, *Rangaku no Hattatsu,* p. 82.

40. Kondō, *Kōsho Koji,* pp. 242–59.

41. Kumazawa, p. 325.

42. Shiba, *Shumparō Hikki,* pp. 422–23.

43. *Ibid.,* p. 474.   44. *Ibid.,* p. 453.
45. *Ibid.,* p. 397.   46. Shiba, *Tenchi Ridan,* p. 87.
47. *Ibid.,* p. 120.   48. See Ōnishi.

49. Shiba, *Dokushō Bōgen,* quoted in Muraoka, *Zoku Nihon Shisō-shi Kenkyū,* p. 253. See also Arisaka, "Shiba Kōkan."

50. *Ibid.*

51. Quoted in Muraoka, "Shisei no Tetsujin," p. 18.

52. Honda, *Seiiki Monogatari* in *Honda Toshiaki-shū,* p. 129.

53. *Ibid.,* p. 132.

54. *Ibid.,* p. 182.

55. *Ibid.*, p. 136. See also Satō Genrokurō, *Ezo Shūi*, p. 306, for a sympathetic description of the basic doctrines of Christianity. Satō learned about the Virgin Birth, the Crucifixion, etc., from Russian traders.

56. Honda, *Seiiki Monogatari* in *Honda Toshiaki-shū*, p. 158. The facts ascribed to this priest belong to the careers of two actual priests, the Italians Sidotti and Chiara.

57. *Ibid.*, p. 159.

58. Muraoka, *Nihon Shisō-shi Kenkyū*, p. 332.

59. Miura, p. 1073.

60. Quoted in Muraoka, "Shisei no Tetsujin," p. 46.

61. Honda, *Seiiki Monogatari* in *Honda Toshiaki-shū*, pp. 130–31.

62. Sansom, p. 234.

63. Golownin, *Narrative*, II, 118. See also Shiba, *Tenchi Ridan*, p. 38.

64. Hirazawa, p. 88.

Chapter 5

1. "Honda Sensei Gyōjō-ki," in *Honda Toshiaki-shū*, pp. 399–404.

2. Honda, *Ezo Kaihatsu ni Kansuru Jōsho* in *Honda Toshiaki-shū*, p. 321.

3. See Uno, in *Honda Toshiaki-shū*, p. 400.

4. In *Honda Toshiaki-shū*, pp. 359–95. With two later exceptions only, the letters here given date from the years 1799 to 1801.

5. Honjō, Introduction to *Honda Toshiaki-shū*, p. 10.

6. Uno, in *Honda Toshiaki-shū*, p. 402. There is nothing in Honda's writings to indicate that he himself had visited Kamchatka in 1784, and there is much to make one think he had not. However, since Uno's statement was made while Honda was still alive, it cannot summarily be rejected.

7. *Ibid.*

8. See Honjō, *Kinsei no Keizai Shisō*, pp. 219–23. The 1888 edition of *Seiiki Monogatari* has become extremely rare. The excerpts given by Honjō indicate that it was a simplified version that attempted to recast Honda's crabbed style, sometimes to the detriment of the sense.

9. In the Introduction to *Honda Toshiaki-shū*, Honjō gives a list of articles about Honda and editions of his writings up to 1936.

10. Borton, p. 9. "Pawnshops, baths, and barber shops had all been established and were credited with bringing about the downfall of the country." See also Claudel for a discussion of similar criticisms leveled at the English farmers.

11. Quoted in Nomura, *Tokugawa Jidai no Shakai Keizai*, p. 97.

12. *Ibid.*, p. 130. The writer was an obscure *rōnin* named Yamashita Kōnai.

13. The *shingaku* school was founded by Ishida Baigan (1685–1744). Ishida's doctrines are discussed in Bellah, pp. 133–77.

14. Nomura, p. 214.

15. *Ibid.,* p. 194. An extended study of Tanuma and his regime may be found in Hall.

16. Nomura, p. 202.

17. Boxer, *Jan Compagnie,* p. 143.

18. Shiba, *Shumparō Hikki,* p. 471.

19. The "ever-normal granary," though discussed in China centuries before, was first put into practice in 54 B.C. For a history of the theory to modern times, see Bodde.

20. Nomura, p. 128.

21. *Ibid.,* p. 149.

22. Quoted in *ibid.,* p. 110.

23. Arai Hakuseki, *Hōka Jiryaku;* see also Murdoch, III, 266.

24. Quoted in Honjō, Introduction to *Honda Toshiaki-shū,* p. 38.

25. Kōno, "Aka-Ezo," p. 600. Kudō thought that open trade was far preferable to the smuggling then rampant between Japanese of the Matsumae clan and the Russians. Trade with the Russians might also force down the prices charged by the Chinese and Dutch for their wares. Kudō, p. 219.

26. *Keisei Hisaku* in *Honda Toshiaki-shū,* p. 58. During Tanuma's regime "domestic consumption of exportable sea products was strictly curtailed" in order to bring in foreign specie. See Hall, p. 86.

27. Shiba, *Tenchi Ridan,* p. 104.

28. Quoted in Johnson, p. 3. Tanuma actually succeeded in attracting gold and silver from abroad in payment for Japanese goods. See Hall, p. 86.

29. Malthus, *An Essay on the Principle of Population,* I, 12.

30. *Ibid.,* I, 8.

31. Malthus, *First Essay on Population,* p. 134.

32. Malthus, *An Essay,* I, 215.

33. Hung, *I-yen,* in Hung Liang-chi, p. 48.

34. *Ibid.,* p. 49.

35. Such remedies as Hung did suggest—the prohibition of extravagance, suppression of Buddhist and Taoist monks, development of new lands, etc.—do not appear to have been real solutions for him. See Lung.

36. Honda, *Seiiki Monogatari* in *Honda Toshiaki-shū,* pp. 183–84.

37. *Ibid.,* p. 170.

38. *Keisei Hisaku,* in *Honda Toshiaki-shū,* p. 40. Honda, in making this assertion, probably was influenced by reports of Russian successes in winning over the natives of the Kuriles. See Mogami, *Ezo Sōshi,* pp. 354, 382.

39. *Ibid.,* pp. 40–41.
40. Honda, *Seiiki Monogatari* in *Honda Toshiaki-shū,* p. 187.
41. Inobe, *Bakumatsu-shi no Kenkyū,* p. 462.
42. Honjō, *Kinsei no Keizai Shisō,* p. 56.
43. Honda, *Seiiki Monogatari* in *Honda Toshiaki-shū,* p. 170. Andō Shōeki, an earlier thinker, had declared that the Ezo natives ranged from six to eight feet in height! See Norman, *Andō Shōeki,* p. 237.
44. *Honda Toshiaki-shū,* p. 317.
45. Tsuji, pp. 310–12. See also Hall, p. 67.
46. Quoted in Honjō, Introduction to *Honda Toshiaki-shū,* p. 48.
47. *Honda Toshiaki-shū,* p. 323.
48. *Keizai Hōgen* in *Honda Toshiaki-shū,* p. 117.
49. Hayashi Junsai, quoted in Inobe, *Bakumatsu-shi no Kenkyū,* p. 391.
50. Krasheninnikov, p. 180. Sauer, p. 309, related, "Of their former customs there only exist their lascivious dances, and their impure language, with part of the dress."
51. Krusenstern, II, 69.

Chapter 6

1. I owe this observation to Professor Charles Issawi.
2. See Imaizumi, II, 124, for a reproduction of Katsuragawa's Dutch visiting card inscribed "Wilhelmus Botanicus. Keizerlyk-Doctoor van Japan." Katsuragawa (who sometimes called himself Kaneel-Rivier, a Dutch translation of his surname) was given the name Botanicus by Doeff, who noted (p. 147), "It was under this name that the pharmacologist exchanged letters in our language with the celebrated Professor Reinwardt during the latter's residence in the Indies, as I heard from the Professor himself." Katsuragawa's name figures in the membership list for 1848 of Het Bataviaasch Genootschap van Kunsten en Wetenschappen as a corresponding member. He is called "Botanicus W. eigenlijk Katsira Gawa Hoken." Presumably it was Professor Caspar Georg Carl Reinwardt (1773–1854) who recommended Katsuragawa as a member. See Imaizumi, II, 186–96.
3. Golownin, *Narrative,* I, 112.
4. Thunberg, *Travels,* III, 206.
5. This dictionary, the famous Doeff Halma, was based on a Dutch-French dictionary by François Halma. It was treasured by generations of *rangaku* scholars.

6. Watanabe, pp. 149–50.
7. Doeff, p. 106.
8. Numata, pp. 147–48.
9. Minakawa, p. 28.
10. *Ibid.,* pp. 16–17.
11. *Ibid.,* p. 65.

12. *Ibid.,* p. 47. The official report on the 1786 expedition credited Yamaguchi and Aoshima, Mogami's superiors, with these explorations, but bad weather in fact prevented them from reaching Etorofu.

13. *Ibid.,* p. 48.

14. The meager details of this revolt against a half-Japanese Russian named Petr may be found in Lensen, pp. 94–95.

15. The name is given phonetically in Japanese script as "Ishuyo" in many texts, but occasionally one finds "Ijuyosofu," which may represent a Russian name something like Izhuyosov. Nothing has been learned about this man apart from the descriptions given by Mogami and his superiors.

16. Minakawa, p. 61.

17. *Ibid.,* p. 62.

18. *Ibid.,* p. 63.

19. Remarks by Aida Yasuaki, quoted in *Ibid.,* p. 70.

20. *Ibid.,* p. 74.   21. *Ibid.,* pp. 80, 83.

22. *Ibid.,* p. 86.   23. *Ibid.,* pp. 87, 96.

24. *Ibid.,* p. 102.   25. *Ibid.,* p. 105.

26. *Ibid.,* p. 106.   27. *Ibid.,* pp. 149–50.

28. *Ibid.,* pp. 183–84.   29. *Ibid.,* p. 191.

30. *Ibid.,* pp. 227–28.

31. *Ibid.,* p. 232. See also above, p. 57.

32. *Ibid.,* p. 280.

33. So given in the manuscript of Siebold's diary, reproduced photographically in *ibid.,* p. 348; the word order is slightly different in Siebold, *Nippon,* I, 186.

34. Hora, p. 46.

35. Ōtani, p. 75.

36. Golownin, *Narrative,* I, 275.

37. Golownin, *Recollections,* pp. 20–21.

38. Hora, pp. 94–97.

39. These various quotations may be found in *ibid.,* pp. 111–13.

40. *Ibid.,* p. 119.

41. *Ibid.,* p. 102.

42. *Ibid.,* p. 128.

43. Shiba, *Shumparō Hikki,* p. 400.

44. Ōtani, p. 134.

45. Golownin, *Narrative,* I, 233–34.

46. *Ibid.,* p. 235.   47. *Ibid.,* p. 273.

48. *Ibid.,* p. 276.   49. *Ibid.,* II, 201.

50. Hora, p. 188.   51. Doeff, pp. 146–47.

52. Siebold, *Nippon,* p. 206. Siebold's text has "Jedo und Sachalin,"

but this is surely a mistake for "Jezo und Sachalin," a much more likely combination.

53. Ōtani, p. 149.

54. Hora, p. 248. I have translated *sarasa* as "batik" though it might be some other printed fabric from Indonesia. Japanese sources state that a length of this cloth was sent to Mamiya, but Siebold himself in his testimony declared that he had sent only a cotton towel (*tenugui*).

55. Siebold, *Nippon*, p. 261.

56. Itazawa, *Shiiboruto*, pp. 101–2. It is surprising that an illustrated edition of *Genji* (*eiri no Genji*) should have been forbidden; perhaps this description designated a vulgar or pornographic book which took its title, if not its story, from the famous classic.

57. Hora, pp. 254–55. The writer was Ozeki San'ei (1787–1839), a *rangaku* scholar who later committed suicide because of his involvement in a political group, the "Old Man's Society" (*Shōshikai*), which was accused of anti-shogunate activities.

58. A list of the confiscated materials is given in Itazawa, pp. 107–11.

59. Kure, I, 297.

60. *Ibid.*, p. 303.

61. Kawahara Keiga, the only artist allowed to visit Deshima freely, painted many pictures of the Dutch he encountered there. See Ono, pp. 109–13, for a description of his work.

62. Itazawa, pp. 136–37.

63. This and the following anecdote are found in Kure, pp. 356–58.

64. Hora, pp. 275, 287.

65. See Overmeer Fisscher, *Bijdrage tot de Kennis van het Japansche Rijk*, p. 42.

66. Hora, p. 313. Watanabe was writing here in the person of Mamiya's superior in the espionage service Nakagawa Chūgorō.

67. Siebold, *Reize van Maarten Gerritsz*, p. 339.

Chapter 7

1. For a brief discussion of the Chu Hsi school's interest in the "investigation of things," see Fung Yu-lan, *A Short History of Chinese Philosophy* (New York, 1948), pp. 305–6.

2. So stated by Hirata's nephew Ōwada Noritane in 1876. See Yamada, pp. 9–10. Biographical material on Hirata in Western languages may be found in Satow, "The Revival of Pure Shinto" in *TASJ*, III, Appendix (Yokohama, 1875); Hammitzsch, "Hirata Atsutane" in *Mitteilungen der Deutschen Gesellschaft für Natur- und Völkerkunde Ostasiens*, XXVIII,

part E (Tokyo, 1936); and Schiffer, "Hirata Atsutane: Taidō Wakumon" in *Monumenta Nipponica*, II, I (Tokyo, 1939).

3. Yamada, pp. 19–21.

4. *Kishin Shinron* in Muromatsu, III, 12–13. For drawings of a similar machine, see *Nihon Kagaku Koten Zensho*, VI, 540–47.

5. *Ibuki Oroshi* (1813) in Muromatsu, I, 4.

6. *Kodō Taii* (1811) in Muromatsu, I, 23.

7. *Ibid.*, pp. 6–7.

8. *Tensetsu Bemben* (1817) in Muromatsu, II, 58.

9. *Ibid.*, p. 60.

10. *Sandaikō Bemben* (1814) in Muromatsu, II, 17.

11. *Amenomihashira no Fumi* (1819) in Muromatsu, II, 13. See also *Tama no Mihashira* (1812) in Muromatsu, II, 70.

12. *Amenomihashira no Fumi* in Muromatsu, II, 14.

13. *Shizu no Iwaya* (1811) in Muromatsu, I, 22.

14. *Ibid.*, p. 76.

15. *Ibid.*, p. 60.

16. *Ibid.*, pp. 76–77.

17. *Ibid.*, pp. 22, 34. Hirata's description of the Golden Age in Japan was possibly influenced by the account of the Garden of Eden in Yamamura Saisuke, *kan* I, 2b.

18. *Seiseki Gairon* (1811) in Muromatsu, I, 96–97.

19. *Kabōsho* (1803) in Muromatsu, II, 26. This, Hirata's earliest published work, consisted of an attack on the writings of Dazai Jun. Many of its paragraphs begin with the words "Since the Chinese are basically like animals."

20. *Kodō Taii* in Muromatsu, I, 14.

21. *Tensetsu Bemben* in Muromatsu, II, 26.

22. *Tama no Mihashira* in Muromatsu, II, 65. See also *Indo Zōshi* (1840) in Muromatsu, XIII, 63–65. In this late work Hirata went so far as to credit India with being the source of "not only the astronomy, but the writing and medical arts" of the West. This view was not, however, typical of the opinions expressed in Hirata's major works. For the Copernican theory in Japan, see Szczesniak, pp. 52–61.

23. *Kodō Taii* in Muromatsu, I, 52.

24. *Ibid.*, p. 54.

25. *Amenomihashira no Fumi* in Muromatsu, II, 14; *Tama no Mihashira* in Muromatsu, II, 50. See also *Shimoto no Manimani* (c. 1813) in Muromatsu, II, 2. Hirata was even aware of the discovery in 1781 of the planet Uranus (*Amenomihashira no Fumi*, p. 10).

26. See Blacker.

27. *Senkyō Ibun* (1820) in Muromatsu, III, 56.

28. *Ibid.*, p. 171.

29. *Tama no Mihashira,* p. 15; *Tensetsu Bemben,* p. 26; *Amenomihashira no Fumi* in Muromatsu, II, p. 9. Hirata's belief that the moon had broken off from the earth may have been suggested by Buffon's theory of the origin of the solar system, reproduced in various Dutch works available in Japan at the time.

30. Letters of November 23, 1841, and June 12, 1842, to his adopted son Tetsutane. (In Watanabe Kinzō, pp. 604, 676.)

31. *Kodō Taii,* p. 43.

32. Material to this effect may be found in *ibid.,* pp. 43, 53–57; *Tama no Mihashira,* p. 20; *Ibuki Oroshi,* p. 22. In *Tamadasuki* (1825) in Muromatsu, IV, 138–39, Hirata shows that Japan is neither a cold country like Russia where the sun is so faint that the salt of the sea has no flavor, nor a hot country like India where the sun is so intense that the salt is too bitter to eat. (That was why, according to Hirata, the Russians attached to Rezanov's embassy of 1804 were so desperately anxious not to lose a grain of the Japanese salt given them.)

The ultimate source of Hirata's claims may have been the Japanese translation of *The History of Japan* by Kaempfer. Kaempfer wrote of Japan that "the Climate is exceedingly temperate, not exposed to the burning heat of the more Southern Sun, nor froze by the extream cold of the more Northern Countries. It is well known, that no Countries are so fruitful, none so pleasant and agreeable, as those which lie between thirty and forty Degrees of North Latitude." (Scheuchzer translation, reprinted Glasgow, 1906, III, 313.)

33. Kaempfer (III, 304) described "the Japanese, who confined within the limits of their Empire enjoy the blessings of peace and contentedness, and do not care for any commerce, or communication with foreign nations, because such is the happy state of their Country, that it can subsist without it."

34. This view is frequently stated in Hirata's writings, e.g. *Kodō Taii,* p. 42; *Tama no Mihashira,* p. 20; *Shizu no Iwaya,* p. 16; *Seiseki Gairon,* p. 17.

35. Hirata apparently learned of the Flood from the *Seiyō Zakki* by Yamamura (*kan* I, 4b, 7a). Hirata quotes part of an account of the Flood in *Wu-li Hsiao-shih* by Fang I-chih, a late Ming work (in *Seiseki Gairon,* p. 20), but it is apparent that he borrowed his quotation from Yamamura's work and not directly from Fang. Fang's information was presumably obtained from the Jesuits in Peking; Yamamura had had the benefit of Dutch books. (See *Tama no Mihashira,* pp. 62, 68–69.)

36. *Tama no Mihashira,* p. 69.

37. *Ibid.,* p. 96. See also *Kodō Taii,* p. 53.

38. *Tama no Mihashira,* p. 92. See also *Ibuki Oroshi,* p. 5.

39. *Kishin Shinron,* p. 30. The source of this error was probably the

Seiyō Zakki, kan II, 26a–27a, where Yamamura speaks of the worship of the sun, moon, and stars called "natuur dienaar god" by the Dutch. However, Hirata thought that the Dutch not only had a word for it but practiced it themselves.

40. These works are called in Chinese *Chi-jen Shih-p'ien, T'ien-chu Shih-i*, and *Ch'i-k'o*, respectively. For a discussion of the first-named work, see P. D'Elia, "Sunto Poetico-Ritmico di *I Dieci Paradossi* di Matteo Ricci" in *Rivista degli Studi Orientali*, XXVII, Fasc. i–iv, Rome, 1952.

41. This was Fujita Kenzō of Osaka. He was implicated in the trial of the medium Kirishitan-baba ("Old Lady Christian"), and the books were subsequently found in his possession. It is interesting to note that he was sentenced to be crucified by the famous Ōshio Heihachirō. (See Saegusa, *Nihon Kagaku Koten Zensho*, VI, 575–76.)

42. See above, Chapters 1 and 4.

43. *Honkyō Gaihen* in Muromatsu, II, 1.

44. *Chi-jen Shih-p'ien* (Ch'ing-chou, 1885), pp. 8a, 9b; *Honkyō Gaihen*, p. 20.

45. *Ch'i-k'o* (Hang-chou, 1614), p. 1a, and *Honkyō Gaihen*, p. 48.

46. It is to the late Professor Muraoka Tsunetsugu that we owe the discovery of the importance of the *Honkyō Gaihen* and the identifications of Hirata's Christian sources. (See his *Nihon Shisō-shi Kenkyū*, pp. 297–314.) Professor Muraoka was of the opinion that the Christian influence in Hirata's writings was very considerable, but did not take into account the possibility that Buddhism, Brahmanism, or another religion might have been responsible for some of the seemingly Christian doctrines in Hirata's works.

47. See *Tama no Mihashira*, pp. 20, 48; *Koshiden* (1812–25) in Muromatsu, VII, *kan* II, 62; *kan* III, 25. The source is again probably Yamamura, *kan* I, 2a–3b.

48. Muraoka, *Nihon Shisō-shi Kenkyū*, pp. 299–300.

49. *Ibid.*, p. 311.

50. *Tama no Mihashira*, pp. 92–93.

51. When Hirata openly discussed the *Kirishitan* religion, he was always at pains to revile it. This attitude probably reflects the official Japanese policy rather than Hirata's reaction to what he knew of Christianity.

52. *Honkyō Gaihen*, p. 30.

53. *Koshiden, kan* II, 47–48. See also *Kokon Yōmikō* (1828) in Muromatsu, III, 79.

54. So we may gather from the report in Yamada, p. 43, where Hirata's wife is quoted as saying that he only took off his clothes and lay down six times a month.

55. The two aspects were Takamimusubi and Kamumimusubi, identi-

fied by Hirata (*Tama no Mihashira,* p. 9) as male and female respectively. However, he generally wrote as if they formed one indivisible deity.

56. *Kodō Taii,* p. 27.

57. *Tama no Mihashira,* p. 62. In the *Indo Zōshi,* however, Hirata writes with greater respect of Brahma.

58. *Kodō Taii,* p. 28.

59. *Ibid.,* p. 29.

60. *Kokon Yōmikō,* p. 80.

61. *Kodō Taii,* pp. 53, 56. The same ideographs are used for God in Yamamura, *kan* I, 2a, which was probably Hirata's source.

62. An explanation of this curious statement may be found on p. 352 of Adachi, "Ueber den Penis der Japaner" in *Zeitschrift für Morphologie und Anthropologie* V, Stuttgart, 1903.

63. For Kōdayū see above, Chapter 3. This particular observation is not found in the usual reports of Kōdayū's journey.

64. *Ibuki Oroshi,* pp. 25–26.

65. "Nature" might be a better translation for the character Ōtsuki uses.

66. Ōtsuki, *Ransetsu Benwaku,* pp. 493–94.

67. *Tama no Mihashira,* p. 61.

68. *Shutsujō Shōgo* in Muromatsu, I, 18, 56.

69. For a similar attitude among Confucian scholars, see above, Chapter 2.

70. *Shutsujō Shōgo,* p. 5. See also *Kodō Taii,* p. 63.

71. *Ibuki Oroshi,* p. 9. Hirata's views on foreign languages were largely derived from Motoori's. For the latter, see J. R. McEwan, "Motoori's View of Phonetics and Linguistics" in *Asia Major* (News Series) I, 109–18.

72. *Ibuki Oroshi,* p. 41.

Bibliography

The following abbreviations are used in the bibliography:

AEL   *Annales de l'Ecole Libre des Sciences Politiques*, Paris.
IB   *Iwanami Bunko*, Tokyo.
JAOS   *Journal of the American Oriental Society*, New Haven.
KKS   *Kokusho Kankōkai Sōsho*, Tokyo.
NAW   *Nieuw Archief voor Wiskunde*, Amsterdam.
RC   *Rekishi Chiri*, Tokyo.
SZ   *Shigaku Zasshi*, Tokyo.
TASJ   *Transactions of the Asiatic Society of Japan*, Yokohama
    and Tokyo.
YB   *Yūhōdō Bunko*, Tokyo.

Amenomori Hōshū. *Tawaregusa*, in *Meika Zuihitsu-shū*, vol. 2, YB, 1926.
Anesaki Masaharu. "Kirishitan Kyōshi no Nihon Sennyū," SZ, vol. 40, 1929.
Arai Hakuseki. *Sairan Igen*, in *Arai Hakuseki Zenshū*, vol. 4, KKS, 1906.
Arisaka Takamichi. "Shiba Kōkan cho Dokushō Bōgen ni tsuite," in *Historia*, No. 10, Nov. 1954.
Ayusawa Shintarō. *Yamamura Saisuke*. Tokyo, 1960.
Ayusawa Shintarō and Ōkubo Toshikane. *Sakoku Jidai Nihonjin no Kaigai Chishiki*. Tokyo, 1953.
Barthold, V. V. *La Découverte de l'Asie*. Paris, 1947.
Bellah, Robert N. *Tokugawa Religion*. Glencoe, Illinois, 1957.
Benyowsky, M. A. von. *Memoirs and Travels*. London, 1790.

Blacker, Carmen. "Supernatural Abduction in Japanese Folklore," *Asian Folklore Studies*, XXVI, 2, 1967.

Bodde, Derk. "Henry A. Wallace and the Ever-Normal Granary," *Far Eastern Quarterly*, vol. 5, no. 4, New York, 1946.

Borton, Hugh. "Peasant Uprisings in Japan of the Tokugawa Period," TASJ, 2d Series, vol. 16, 1938.

Boxer, C. R. *Jan Compagnie in Japan 1600–1817*. The Hague, 1936.

———. *The Mandarin at Chinsura*. Amsterdam, 1949.

———. "Rin Shihei and His Picture of a Dutch East-India Ship," TASJ, 2d Series, vol. 9, 1932.

Broughton, W. R. *A Voyage of Discovery to the North Pacific Ocean*. London, 1804.

Ch'en Ch'ang-heng. *Chung-kuo Jen-k'ou Lun*. Shanghai, 1932.

Ch'en Fu-kuang. "Sino-Russian Diplomatic Relations since 1689," in *Chinese Soc. and Pol. Sc. Rev.*, vol. 10, Peking, 1926.

Chiba Sen'ichi. "Edo Jidai ni okeru Seiyōshi no Juyō Jōkyō," in *Kokugo Kokubun Kenkyū*, No. 34, June 1966.

Claudel, Paul. "L'Impôt sur le Thé en Angleterre," AEL, vol. 4, 1889.

Doeff, Hendrik. *Herinneringen uit Japan*. Haarlem, 1833.

Droppers, Garrett. "The Population of Japan in the Tokugawa Period," TASJ, vol. 22, 1894.

Du Perron, E. *De Muze van Jan Companjie*. Bandoeng, 1948.

Ebina Kazuo. "Honda Toshiaki no Tsūshō Kōeki-setsu," RC, vol. 17, 1911.

Feenstra Kuiper, J. *Japan en de Buitenwereld in de Achttiende Eeuw*. Gravenhage, 1921.

———. "Some Notes on the Foreign Relations of Japan," TASJ, 2d Series, vol. 1, 1924.

Golder, F. A. *Russian Expansion on the Pacific, 1641–1850*. Cleveland, 1914.

Golownin, W. M. *Narrative of my Captivity in Japan*. London, 1818.

———. *Recollections of Japan*. London, 1819.

Goodman, Grant Kohn. *The Dutch Impact on Japan (1650–1853)*. Leiden, 1967.

Gotō Rishun. *Oranda-banashi*, in *Bummei Genryū Sōsho*, vol. 1, KKS, 1913.

Hall, John Whitney. *Tanuma Okitsugu*. Cambridge, Mass., 1955.

Haren, O. Z. van. *Van Japan*. Zwolle, 1775.

Harima Narayoshi. "Rokoku ni okeru Nihongo Gakkō no Enkaku," SZ, vol. 33, 1922.

———. "Rokoku Saisho no Kennichi Shisetsu Adamu Rakusuman Nisshi," SZ, vol. 34, 1923.

Harrison, John A. *Japan's Northern Frontier*. Gainesville, Florida, 1953.

Hayashi Fukusai. *Tsūkō Ichiran,* KKS, 1913.

Hayashi Shihei. *Jōsho,* in *Sendai Sōsho,* vol. 2, Sendai, 1923.

———. *Kaikoku Heidan* (ed. Muraoka), IB, 1939.

Hayashi Tsuruichi. "A List of Some Dutch Astronomical Works Imported into Japan from Holland," NAW, 2d Series, vol. 7, 1907.

———. *Wasan Kenkyū Shūroku.* Tokyo, 1937.

Hirazawa Kyokuzan. *Keiho Gūhitsu,* in *Kaihyō Sōsho,* vol. 6, Kyoto, 1928.

History of the Internal Affairs of the United Provinces. London, 1787.

Hokkaidō-shi (New Edition). Tokyo, 1937.

Honda Toshiaki. *Honda Toshiaki-shū* (ed. Honjō Eijirō). Tokyo, 1935.

Honjō Eijirō, ed. *Honda Toshiaki-shū,* in *Kinsei Shakai Keizai Gakusetsu Taikei,* Tokyo, 1935.

———. *Kinsei no Keizai Shisō (Zokuhen).* Tokyo, 1937.

———. *The Social and Economic History of Japan.* Kyoto, 1935.

Hora Tomio. *Mamiya Rinzō.* Tokyo, 1960.

Hung Liang-chi. *Hung Pei-chiang Shih-wen Chi.* Shanghai, 1934.

Imaizumi Genkichi. *Katsuragawa no Hitobito.* Tokyo, vol. 1, 1965; vol. 2, 1968.

Imamura Ichibei and Namura Gohei. *Oranda Mondō,* in *Kaihyō Sōsho,* vol. 2, Kyoto, 1928.

Inobe Shigeo. *Bakumatsu-shi Gaisetsu.* Tokyo, 1930.

———. *Bakumatsu-shi no Kenkyū.* Tokyo, 1927.

———. "Matsudaira Sadanobu to Ezo-chi Kaikō," SZ, vol. 45, 1934.

Irita Seizō, ed. *Hiraga Gennai Zenshū.* Tokyo, 1935.

Ishii Hakutei. *Nihon ni okeru Yōfūga no Enkaku.* Tokyo, 1932.

Itazawa Takeo. *Rangaku no Hattatsu.* Tokyo, 1933.

———. "Rangaku no Igi to Rangaku Sōshi ni kansuru ni-san no Mondai," RC, vol. 59, 1932.

———. "Rangaku to Jugaku," in Fukushima, *Kinsei Nihon no Jugaku,* Tokyo, 1939.

———. *Shiiboruto.* Tokyo, 1960.

Itō Takeo. "Honda Toshiaki no Haka ni tsuite," RC, vol. 40, 1922.

Johnson, E. A. J. *Predecessors of Adam Smith.* London, 1937.

Kaempfer, Engelbert. *The History of Japan.* Glasgow, 1906.

Kamei Takayoshi. *Daikokuya Kōdayū.* Tokyo, 1964.

Katsuragawa Hoshū. *Hokusa Bunryaku* (ed. Kamei). Tokyo, 1937.

Keene, Donald. "Hirata Atsutane and Western Learning," in *T'oung Pao,* vol. 42, Leiden, 1954.

———. *The Japanese Discovery of Europe.* London, 1952.

Klaproth, J. *San Kokf Tsou Ran To Sets.* Paris, 1832.

Komiyama Fūken. *Fūken Gūki,* in *Hyakka Zuihitsu,* KKS, 1917.

Kondō Morishige. *Henyō Bunkai Zukō,* in *Kondō Seizai Zenshū,* vol. 1, KKS, 1905.

————. *Kōsho Koji,* in *Kondō Seizai Zenshū,* vol. 3, KKS, 1906.

Kōno Tsuneyoshi. "Aka-Ezo Fūsetsu-kō no Chosha Kudō Heisuke," SZ, vol. 26, 1915.

————. "Anei Izen Matsumae-han to Rojin to no Kankei," SZ, vol. 27, 1916.

Krasheninnikov, S. P. *The History of Kamschatka and the Kurilski Islands.* Glocester, 1764.

Kropf, L. K. "Benyowsky," in *Notes and Queries for 27 April 1895,* London, 1895.

Krusenstern, A. I. *Voyage Round the World.* London, 1813.

Kudō Heisuke. *Aka Ezo Fūsetsu Kō,* in Ōtomo, *Hokumon Sōsho,* I, Tokyo, 1943.

Kumazawa Banzan. "Daigaku Wakumon" (tr. Fisher), TASJ, 2d Series, vol. 16, 1938.

Kure Shūzō. *Shiiboruto Sensei.* Tōyō Bunko series, 1967.

Lagus, Wilhelm. *Erik Laxman.* Helsingfors, 1880.

Langsdorff, G. H. von. *Bemerkungen auf einer Reise um die Welt.* Frankfort, 1812.

Lefèvre-Pontalis, G. "Un Projet de Conquête du Japon par l'Angleterre et la Russie en 1776," AEL, vol. 4, 1889.

Lensen, George Alexander, "Early Russo-Japanese Relations," *Far Eastern Quarterly,* vol. 10, no. 1, Ithaca, 1950.

————. *The Russian Push Toward Japan.* Princeton, 1959.

Lesseps, J. J. B. de. *Travels in Kamtschatka.* London, 1790.

Lung, C. F. "A Note on Hung Liang-chi, the Chinese Malthus," *T'ien Hsia Monthly,* vol. 1, no. 3, Shanghai, 1935.

Maeno Ryōtaku. *Seiyō Gasan Yakubun-kō,* in *Kaihyō Sōsho,* Kyoto, 1928.

Malthus, T. R. *An Essay on the Principle of Population.* London, 1826, 6th ed.

————. *First Essay on Population, 1798* (ed. Bonar). London, 1926.

Matsudaira Sadanobu. *Uge no Hitogoto,* IB, 1942.

Matsukaze Yoshisada. *Zeniya Gohei Shinden.* Kyoto, 1930.

Matsumura Akira, ed. *Rantō Kotohajime,* in Nihon Koten Bungaku Taikei series, Tokyo, 1964.

Mikami Yoshio. "On Shizuki's Translation," NAW, 2d Series, vol. 11, 1915.

Minakawa Shinsaku. *Mogami Tokunai.* Tokyo, 1943.

Miura Baien. *Kisan-roku,* in *Baien Zenshū,* vol. 1, Tokyo, 1912.

Mogami Tokunai. *Ezo Sōshi,* in Ōtomo, *Hokumon Sōsho,* I, Tokyo, 1943.

Morishima Chūryō. *Kōmō Zatsuwa,* in *Bummei Genryū Sōsho,* vol. 1, KKS, 1913.

Muraoka Tsunetsugu. *Nihon Shishō-shi Kenkyū.* Tokyo, 1940, rev. ed.

————. "Shisei no Tetsujin Shiba Kōkan," in Shiba, *Tenchi Ridan.*

————. *Zoku Nihon Shisō-shi Kenkyū.* Tokyo, 1939.

Murdoch, James. *A History of Japan.* London, 1925–26.

Muromatsu Iwao, ed. *Hirata Atsutane Zenshū.* 15 vols. Tokyo, 1911–18.

Nakamura, Kiyozō. "Edo Bakufu no Kinsho Seisaku," *Shirin,* vol. 11, Kyoto, 1926.

Nishimura Tei. *Nihon Shoki Yōga no Kenkyū.* Kyoto, 1945.

Nomura Kanetarō. *Tokugawa Jidai no Keizai Shisō.* Tokyo, 1939.

————. *Tokugawa Jidai no Shakai Keizai Shisō Gairon.* Tokyo, 1934.

Norman, E. H. "Andō Shōeki and the Anatomy of Japanese Feudalism," TASJ, 3d Series, vol. 2, 1949.

————. *Japan's Emergence as a Modern State.* New York, 1940.

Numata Jirō. *Yōgaku Denrai no Rekishi.* Tokyo, 1960.

Ogawa Teizō. *Kaitai Shinsho.* Tokyo, 1968.

Okamura Chibiki. *Kōmō Bunka Shiwa.* Tokyo, 1953.

Ōnishi Iwao. "Shiba Kōkan no Sekai-kan," *Kokumin no Tomo,* no. 233, Tokyo, 1894.

Ono Tadashige. *Edo no Yōgaka.* Tokyo, 1968.

Ōta Nampo. *Oranda Engi-ki,* in *Kaihyō Sōsho,* I, Kyoto, 1928.

Ōtani, Ryōkichi. *Tadataka Inō, the Japanese Land-Surveyor.* Tokyo, 1932.

Ōtomo Kisaku. *Hokumon Sōsho.* 6 vols. Tokyo, 1943.

Ōtsuki Gentaku. *Rangaku Kaitei,* in *Bummei Genryū Sōsho,* vol. 1, KKS, 1913.

————. *Ransetsu Benwaku,* in *Bummei Genryū Sōsho,* vol. 1, KKS, 1913.

Ōtsuki Nyoden. *(Shinsen) Yōgaku Nempyō.* Tokyo, 1927.

Overmeer Fisscher, J. F. van. *Bijdrage tot de Kennis van het Japansche Rijk.* Amsterdam, 1833.

Pelliot, Paul. "Le Hôja et le Sayyid Husain de l'Histoire des Ming," *T'oung Pao,* vol. 38, Leiden, 1948.

Playfair, W. *Inquiry into the Permanent Causes of the Decline and Fall of Powerful and Wealthy Nations.* London, 1805.

Ramming, Martin. *Russland-Berichte schiffbrüchiger Japaner.* Berlin, 1930. (Later published as *Reisen schiffbrüchiger Japaner im XVIII Jahrhundert.* Berlin, 1931.)

Saegusa Hiroto. *Nihon Kagaku Koten Zensho,* 6 vols. Tokyo, 1942–48.

Sakanishi Shio. "Prohibition of Import of Certain Chinese Books," JAOS, vol. 57, 1937.

Sansom, G. B. *The Western World and Japan.* London, 1950.

Satō Genrokurō. *Ezo Shūi,* in Ōtomo, *Hokumon Sōsho,* vol. 1, Tokyo, 1943.

Sauer, Martin. *An Account of a Geographical and Astronomical Expedition.* London, 1802.

Semyonov, Yuri. *The Conquest of Siberia.* London, 1944.

Sheldon, Charles David. *The Rise of the Merchant Class in Tokugawa Japan.* Locust Valley, N.Y., 1958.

Shiba Kōkan. *Kōkan Saiyū Nikki,* in *Nihon Koten Zenshū,* Tokyo, 1927.

———. *Oranda Tensetsu.* Edo, 1796.

———. *Oranda Tsūhaku,* in *Zuihitsu Bungaku Senshū,* vol. 6, Tokyo, 1927.

———. *Seiyō Gadan,* in *Zuihitsu Bungaku Senshū,* vol. 2, Tokyo, 1927.

———. *Shumparō Hikki,* in *Meika Zuihitsu-shū,* vol. 2, YB, 1926.

———. *Tenchi Ridan* (ed. Muraoka). Tokyo, 1930.

Shimmura Izuru. *Shiden Sōkō.* Tokyo, 1934.

———. *Shimmura Izuru Senshū.* 4 vols. Kyoto, 1943.

———. *Zoku Namban Kōki.* Tokyo, 1925.

Siebold, P. F. von. *Nippon. Archiv zur Beschreibung von Japan.* Wurzburg, 1897.

———. *Reize van Maarten Gerritz. Vries.* Amsterdam, 1858.

Smith, D. E., and Y. Mikami. *A History of Japanese Mathematics.* Chicago, 1914.

Strahlenberg, P. J. von. *An Historico-Geographical Description of the North and Eastern Parts of Europe and Asia.* London, 1738.

Sugita Gempaku. *Rangaku Kotohajime* (ed. Nogami), IB, 1939.

Szczesniak, Boleslaw. "The Penetration of the Copernican Theory into Feudal Japan," *Journal of the Royal Asiatic Society,* 1944.

Tachihara Jingorō (Suiken). *Narabayashi Zatsuwa,* in *Kaihyō Sōsho,* II, Kyoto, 1928.

Thunberg, C. P. *Travels.* London, 1795.

Tokugawa Jikki (ed. Kuroita). Tokyo, 1934.

Tokugawa Kinrei-kō (ed. Kikuchi). Tokyo, 1932.

Tokutomi Iichirō. *Bakumatsu Bunkai Sekkin Jidai.* Tokyo, 1936.

Tōkyō Kagaku Hakubutsukan. *Edo Jidai no Kagaku.* Tokyo, 1938.

Tsuji Zennosuke. *Tanuma Jidai.* Tokyo, 1915.

Tsukahira, Toshio G. *Feudal Control in Tokugawa Japan: the Sankin Kōtai System.* Cambridge, 1966.

Vixseboxse, J. *Een Hollandsch Gezantschap naar China in de Zeventiende Eeuw (1685–1687).* Leiden, 1946.

Vondel, Joost van den. *Werken.* Amsterdam, 1929–37.

Waley, Arthur. "Shiba Kōkan," in *The Secret History of the Mongols.* London, 1963.

Watanabe Kinzō. *Hirata Atsutane Kenkyū.* Tokyo, 1942.

Watanabe Kurasuke. *Kiyō Ronkō.* Nagasaki (?), 1964.

Yamada Yoshio. *Hirata Atsutane.* Tokyo, 1943.

Yamamura Saisuke. *Seiyō Zakki.* Edo, 1848.

Index